RHETORIC

RHETORIC

THEORY AND PRACTICE
FOR COMPOSITION

WALTER S. MINOT
Gannon University

Winthrop Publishers, Inc.
Cambridge, Massachusetts

Library of Congress Cataloging in Publication Data

Minot, Walter S
    Rhetoric, theory and practice for composition.
    Includes index.
      1. English language—Rhetoric.   I. Title.
PE1408.M564   808'.042   80-15382
ISBN 0-87626-769-X

Cover and interior design by Mary Ann Aufmuth

© 1981 by Winthrop Publishers, Inc.
17 Dunster Street, Cambridge, Massachusetts 02138

Printed in the United States of America
10 9 8 7 6 5 4 3 2 1

CONTENTS

Chapter Eight
THE SENTENCE   *201*

Chapter Nine
THE WORD *259*

PREFACE

When I was young and easy and first began work on *Rhetoric: Theory and Practice for Composition* quite a few years ago, I intended to compose a freshman writing text that would save the world—or at least revolutionize the teaching of composition. Now that my book has undergone the scrutiny of several editors and many more reviewers, my hopes are a bit more modest. I have, however, retained my enthusiasm for my substantive goal. That goal was to publish a text that was both solidly grounded in rhetorical theory, yet clear and elementary enough for average freshmen at state universities, community colleges, and other colleges where the majority of students need the help of one or two semesters devoted to composition. I believe that this book comes as near its goal as I can make it.

The underlying assumptions of *Rhetoric: Theory and Practice for Composition* are these: (1) writing takes place when a writer faces a situation in which he or she has to or wants to communicate; (2) the form of the writing is determined by the rhetorical situation, not by external standards or models; and (3) classical rhetoric provides a simple yet useful framework for learning to write. Using these assumptions, I have tried to create a freshman writing text that is practical, realistic, and theoretically consistent.

This text is practical in that it deals with the kinds of writing that most students will use both inside and outside of class. The focus is on using persuasion and exposition in practical situations such as reports for teachers or employers, letters to editors on public issues, and other forms of public and private discourse. The emphasis is on communication as it occurs in the student's experience.

Because this text is meant to be practical, most of the illustrations and examples of both good and bad writing are drawn from non-literary sources. There are selections from textbooks, popular magazines, scholarly journals, newspaper articles, letters to editors, student themes, and advertisements. The analysis of these selections emphasizes clear, persuasive communication rather than literary merit or the following of pre-established patterns such as comparison and contrast or definition.

What will, I hope, set *Rhetoric: Theory and Practice for Composition* apart from other freshman texts that aim to be practical and realistic is its consistent adherence to a theory of rhetoric. The theory is ultimately Aristotelian, focusing on the three basic elements in the rhetorical situation: content, audience, and persona. But this text is not simply a summary or rehashing of Aristotle's *Rhetoric*. Rather it is an adaptation of the basic theory of Aristotle and uses content, audience, and persona as the touchstones for evaluating rhetorical effectiveness. I have followed the lead of such people as Walker Gibson, Donald C. Bryant, Harold C. Martin, and Richard M. Ohmann in attempting to present the essence of Aristotle's theory without being slavishly pedantic in following the *Rhetoric*. For example, I have said a great deal less about figures of speech and types of argument than Aristotle did, but I've said a great deal more about wording, sentences, and other matters.

The plan of the book is to move from the larger problems facing the student writer down to smaller, subtler problems. The first chapter deals with the nature of the rhetorical system. It tries to suggest the decisions involved and the resources available when a writer faces a writing situation. The next three chapters each deal with one of the elements in the rhetorical situation, as outlined by Aristotle: content, audience, and persona. My strategy in putting these chapters first is to encourage students to see that they have been communicating all their lives and that the processes are not mysterious. They should, meanwhile, be learning that writing is merely an extension, albeit more conscious, of their previous experiences in communicating.

The middle chapters of the book deal with two of the major departments of classical rhetoric: discovery (invention) and organization (arrangement). The chapter on invention does not treat the classical topics as rigidly and as meticulously as some textbooks have. Instead, it suggests some of the major strategies for discovering what to say. It also suggests some of the possible steps in the pre-writing stage of composition. The chapter on organization does deal with the pattern of the classical oration, but that is not its chief emphasis. Rather it suggests a variety of organizational patterns based on argumentative structure, the probable reaction of the audience, and the importance of the persona.

The last three chapters deal with style, moving from larger to smaller units. The seventh chapter, on the paragraph, is a bridge between organization and style. In it I have relied heavily on the theories of generative rhetoric as developed by Christensen. The eighth chapter deals with sentences, and the last with words. I have treated gobbledygook in both chapters, but mostly in the last chapter. A whole section of that chapter is devoted to the causes and cures of gobbledygook.

In acknowledging those who helped me with the text, I would like to begin with those to whom I owe an intellectual debt. These scholars and students of rhetoric and composition, most of whom I know only through the written word in publication, were really my mentors before this project began. Professor Edward P. J. Corbett introduced me to classical rhetoric, for I first taught composition from his text, *Classical Rhetoric for the Modern Student.* Professor Walker Gibson taught me the intricacies of persona. Professors Harold C. Martin and Richard M. Ohmann also helped me a great deal when I used their very fine text in the late 1960s. Two anthologists, Richard Larson and Dudley Bailey (my chairman at Nebraska), provided me and numerous other budding rhetoricians with fine anthologies back in the 1960s. The late Professor Francis Christensen influenced me tremendously by revealing the structure and logic of paragraphs, as my chapter on the paragraph clearly indicates. Over the last year, my final chapters have been influenced and, I believe, improved by using E. D. Hirsch's notion of relative readability.

If I have slighted anyone, it is unknowingly. Because composition is just emerging as a serious discipline, the standards for scholarly achievement and recognition are not as clear as in literary studies. Thus, we often borrow concepts, strategies, and teaching techniques without being aware of their sources. (If any of you recognize material that I have unwittingly taken from you, you should accept this highest form of flattery along with my sincere apology for not publicly recognizing you.) Finally, I would like to acknowledge my debt to Aristotle, though it seems foolish to try to pay homage to the thinker who almost single-handedly invented western civilization. Nevertheless, his *Rhetoric* is probably still the wisest and most useful source of knowledge about rhetoric.

I also owe an intellectual and practical debt to my students, who have through the years inspired and challenged me. I would like to thank especially those who allowed me to use their work in my textbook: Pamela Elles, Richard Huff, Starr Kearney, William Lyth, Daniel Monahan, Michael Ryba, John Ryan, Carol Smith, Kathleen Sweeney, and Ann Jean Urmacher.

For typing, I owe special thanks to numerous helpful, accurate, and cheerful ladies at Gannon University's Faculty Service office. They have, at one time or another, typed various stages and revisions of my manuscript. They include Lenore Mulcahy, Rosemary Stewart, Kay Medairy, Lois Speice, and Mildred Kujan, who typed most of the final manuscript. For the final two chapters, I thank Jan Gorka. For other tasks such as tracking down sources, reproducing materials, and proofreading, I thank the following English department student workers: Gail Berndt, Kathy Brewer, Betsy Collins, and Ellen Stephenson. I also thank Robert Hammer, Director of Operations at Gannon College, for his help in getting the final manuscipt reproduced.

I must acknowledge the kind permission of Philip Kelly, Director of the Open University at Gannon University, to use material that I developed for a course manual, *Liberal Studies 11: Communications,* which was copyrighted in 1976 and 1978 by Gannon College. And I thank all my colleagues for their encouragement on this project, but Dennis K. Renner deserves my special regard, for he has shared not only an office with me but also my joys and sorrows with the manuscript. He has been encouraging when I have needed encouragement and sensible when I have needed good sense in dealing with this task.

I must also thank Margery Williams, my production editor, whose careful editing showed me that even English professors can learn something more about style; and Paul O'Connell, chairman of Winthrop Publishers, who saw the possibilities in my manuscript, encouraged me to improve it, and then committed himself to publishing it because he felt it had merit. And I wish to thank the reviewers of the manuscript, many of whose valuable suggestions I have incorporated into the text. These reviewers include Professor Richard Beal, Professor Frank D'Angelo, Professor Sam Watson, Jr., and Professor S. Michael Halloran. Mary Ann Aufmuth also deserves credit for her design and illustration of the book. For any errors or shortcomings in the text, however, I alone am responsible.

Finally, I dedicate this book to Elaine and Leslie, who urged me to work on it, even though it meant that I had less time to spend with them. Thanks for the patient encouragement.

RHETORIC

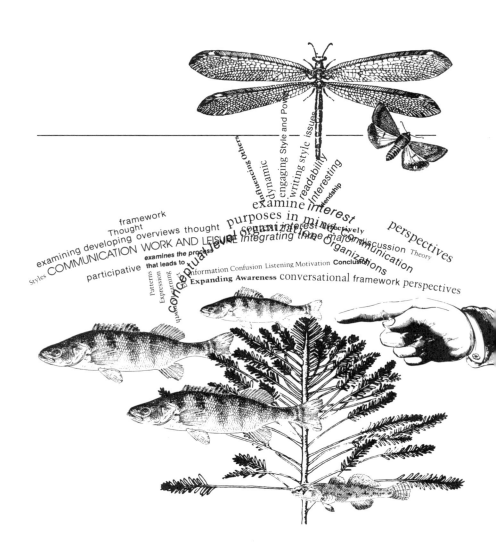

framework
Thought
examining developing overviews thought purposes in mind
Styles COMMUNICATION WORK AND LEISURE Integrating three majors
examines the process
participative that leads to
Patterns
Expression
Information Confusion Listening Motivation Conclusions
Expanding Awareness conversational framework perspectives

Chapter One

THE PROCESS OF RHETORIC

A Human Problem

"Your congressman is a public servant whose job it is to represent you in Washington." At least that's what your seventh-grade civics teacher, Miss Feeney, told you. Well, now it's time to exercise your rights and privileges as a voter and citizen. Now you will sit down and write a letter to the Honorable Wilbur D. Fairweather, congressman from the third congressional district. You'll tell him how you feel about a bill that will be coming up for a vote soon, the Honey Import Act. This bill would abolish all import quotas and import duties on honey.

After writing down the date and other niceties of the business letter that you learned in tenth-grade English classes, you get down to the serious task of telling your congressman what you think:

Dear Congressman Fairweather:

Vote against the Honey Import Act.

Sincerely,

John G. Andrews

Somehow that letter seems too short, too abrupt. Maybe you should try a gentler approach. Maybe you should say, "*Please* vote against . . . ." But that's not right either. You need to be forceful and say, "You'd better vote against . . . ." There, that's telling him. But what if he doesn't vote against the bill? Or suppose he gets a letter saying, "You'd better vote for the Honey Import Act"?

Although the Honey Import Act is a minor bill that probably doesn't affect or interest most of you, it does illustrate the basic problem of rhetoric: how can you get another person—in this case, the congressman—to do what you want him to? Or, in a more general sense, how can a speaker (or writer) get his audience (the person to whom he's speaking or writing) to react as the speaker wants him to?

One solution to the problem

One way to answer this question is to turn the problem around and look at it from the point of view of the audience. Why should the audience choose to do one thing rather than another?

Let's consider the possibilities of Congressman Fairweather's position. First of all, Fairweather may be so strongly in favor of the bill that nothing could dissuade him from voting for it. He might, for instance, be an advocate of free trade, a dogmatist who believes that all import quotas and tariffs are wrong. If that's the case, he probably can't be persuaded to vote against the bill. On the other hand, Fairweather may be unalterably opposed to the bill. He may believe that American producers should be protected and supported with protective tariffs, or he may believe that bees perform a valuable service to farmers by pollinating crops as they gather honey—a service that needs to be encouraged with economic incentives such as higher prices for honey. If that's the case, nothing that you can say is likely to change his opinion. Or Fairweather may be completely undecided. Perhaps he knows nothing about honey and its importance as a farm product. In this case, the congressman might be open to almost any suggestion from the people he represents. Finally, and most likely, Fairweather's position may be somewhere in the middle. He is slightly in favor of or opposed to the bill, but he would change his stand if public opinion were strongly against him.

We can represent Fairweather's possible opinions as a continuum from strong opposition (-5) to strong support ($+5$), as the figure below indicates:

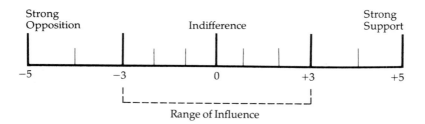

As rhetoricians, we will assume that if Fairweather's opinions are in the range from -3 to $+3$ he can be influenced by what we have to say. For example, if you want the congressman to vote against the bill and if his position is one of mild opposition, say -2 on the scale, your letter may encourage him to stand firm in his opposition. If, however, he slightly favors the bill, your letter could influence him to reconsider his position, especially if quite a few other people write him letters opposing the bill. These are the possibilities—unless, of course, you have more exact information about your congressman's position on the issue.

Let's assume that you don't know your congressman's position on the Honey Import Act and that you want to send him a letter stating your position. How will you go about influencing him to vote your way?

One possible approach

Instead of answering this question directly, we could again turn things around and look at them from Congressman Fairweather's perspective. Let's look at some of the letters he might receive from his constituents.

First, there are those letters that depend primarily on who the letter writer is. Here's one that the congressman might receive:

Dear Wilbur,

I think you should vote against the Honey Import Act. By the way, be sure to wear a hat and galoshes in this weather.

Love,

Mom

Or here's a more realistic one that uses the same basic approach:

Dear Wilbur,

Since we've known each other since we were kids, I'll get right to the point. I'd sure appreciate it if you'd vote against the Honey Import Act. After all, what are friends for if they can't help each other out a bit?
By the way, send my best to Effie and the kids.

Your friend,

Ed Brown

Both of these letters ask the congressman to vote against the bill solely on the basis of the writer's acquaintance with the congressman. Neither writer offers any inherent reasons why the congressman should vote against the bill.

Now let's look at another letter that uses the same approach.

Dear Congressman Fairweather:

As president of Thomas Valley Beekeepers' Association and on behalf of beekeepers throughout the state, I urge you to vote "no" to the Honey Import Act. We are counting on your vote.

Sincerely,

Erven J. O'Connor
President of T.V.B.A.

Or let's look at another letter:

Dear Congressman Fairweather:

As a longtime supporter of yours and as a precinct captain in eastside Grovetown, I know that you'll do the right thing when the Honey Import Act comes up for a vote. I look forward to seeing your name and those of your colleagues from the rest of the state in overwhelming support of the Honey Import Act. Be sure to vote "aye."

Sincerely,

Elsie Mae Pfieffer

Put yourself in the place of Wilbur D. Fairweather, congressman. What effect are these letters likely to have on you? Is there any reason why you should pay much attention to any one of these letters or to similar letters? What are the consequences of your vote?

As an experienced politician, Congressman Fairweather knows that his mom will still love him no matter which way he votes. He also knows that Ed Brown is an opportunist who likes to flaunt his friendship with the congressman but that his support may not be worth much. Thus, Fairweather probably won't be swayed by either letter. He can safely ignore both. "When the chips are down," he assures himself, "Mom will vote for me."

However, Erven J. O'Connor and Elsie Mae Pfieffer are different matters. O'Connor, though only one person, is writing as president of a large organization. He cannot be considered just one man, but he must be reckoned with as a political force who may be able to encourage substantial numbers to vote either for or against Congressman Fairweather. His plea will have to receive special attention. Mrs.

Pfieffer, too, is not merely one voter with one vote. She is a campaign worker who raises political funds, organizes political rallies, and gets sympathetic voters out to the polls on election day. Moreover, as Fairweather realizes, he owes Elsie a favor after all the work that she has done for him. Thus, she deserves special treatment, too.

Exercises

1. Consider the different ways in which you could use your own character and qualities in presenting yourself to Congressman Fairweather. What specific role would you choose?

2. Write a brief paragraph to Congressman Fairweather on the Honey Import Act. Present yourself as one of the following: an angry consumer, an angry beekeeper, a young beekeeper who raises bees as a hobby, or a devotee of natural foods who lives primarily on honey and wheat germ.

Another approach

There are other letters that depend primarily on the information they convey to persuade Congressman Fairweather how he should vote on the Honey Import Act. Such letters are often filled with statistics, "facts," and assertions about reality. These letters focus not on who is writing the letter but on what they have to say about reality. The writers are concerned with content—in this case, the effect that the Honey Import Act will have on the world (or their little portion of it).

Here is a sample of that approach:

Dear Congressman Fairweather:

The consumers of this country have been paying artificially high prices for honey far too long. By abolishing restrictions on the importation of honey, you will be putting honey within the budget of most families. As it is now, honey is too expensive for most families to use regularly. If you allow imports, the price will probably decline a good deal; at least that's what economists at the university have said.

I urge you to vote for the Honey Import Act.

Sincerely,

James Nevins

Or the letter might look like this:

Dear Congressman Fairweather:

According to government statistics, wholesale prices have increased by about twelve percent in the last few years. Also, the price of gasoline has increased by twenty cents a gallon, and the minimum wage has jumped almost a dollar an hour. Under these conditions, a lot of farmers in this district will go broke if the Honey Import Act passes.

Most of the farmers in this district had net incomes last year of only a few thousand dollars. Many stay in business because of their added income from keeping bees. But if the price of honey goes any lower, a lot of us farmers won't be able to make a living.

I ask you to support a decent standard of living for farmers by voting against the Honey Import Act.

Truly yours,

James K. Mullen

Both of these letters could help Congressman Fairweather make a decision, for both have laudable objectives—one to help consumers and one to help farmers—and both contain plenty of useful information. Indeed, both letters are reasonable and well documented. Although Congressman Fairweather cannot support both positions, he now has some sound evidence on which to base his judgement.

Exercises

1. Consider what other kinds of evidence—facts, statistics, arguments, or other material—a writer could use to persuade Congressman Fairweather how to vote. What kind of evidence would be most effective? How much evidence should he use, and how detailed should the presentation be?

2. List a few facts or bits of common information that you could use in writing a letter to Congressman Fairweather on this bill.

3. Using some of this material, compose a brief paragraph that you might include in a letter to Congressman Fairweather.

A third approach

There are letters which may rely on still another approach to persuading Congressman Fairweather. These letters may attempt to appeal to his emotions. They could be as varied as all the different human emotions and as strong or as weak as any of our responses to various human situations. Let's look at one such letter:

Dear Congressman Fairweather:

I am partially disabled, and I have been unable to hold a full-time job for many years. I am the sole support of my widowed mother and six of my little brothers and sisters who are still at home. My mother suffers from arthritis and cannot work, and my little sister Sue is confined to a wheelchair since the horrible accident that crippled her poor little legs. It was the same accident that killed my brother Jim.

I scratch out a bare and miserable living for my whole family by raising bees. If the Honey Import Act passes, I'll go broke and we'll starve. I beg and pray that you'll vote against that accursed bill.

Pleadingly yours,

Everett Perry

Mr. Perry's letter is designed to win sympathy through detailing his misfortunes. The writer hopes that Congressman Fairweather will feel sorry for him and seek to aid him by voting against the bill.

The following letter appeals to quite a different emotion:

Dear Fairweather:

If you want to get elected again, you'd better vote for the Honey Import Act. If you vote against it, you're through politically.

Yours sincerely,

Walter S. Brown

This letter appeals directly to one of our strongest emotions: fear. It threatens Congressman Fairweather by appealing to one of the strongest fears a politician can have—the fear of being out of office, out of work, out of power.

Here is another appeal to yet another emotion:

Dear Congressman Fairweather:

I know that you stand for America first and don't want to give everything away to foreigners and chiselers on welfare. Now it's time to stand up for America and the principles that made this country the greatest place on God's earth to live.

If you believe in America, vote against the Honey Import Act. We've got to watch out for Americans first.

Sincerely,

Sylvia Krown

This letter attempts to appeal to the congressman's sense of patriotism and, in the writer's eyes, to his sense of justice and fairness.

Another letter might make the same point quite differently:

Dear Congressman Fairweather:

Please vote against the Honey Import Act. That bill, if passed, would cost too many American beekeepers their livings and too many American farmers a decent margin of profit. We already have too many people without jobs and too many farmers going broke.
Protect Americans first.

Sincerely,

Eunice Bamberger

If Congressman Fairweather is an emotional man, some of these letters may touch him deeply. For example, he may feel very sorry for Everett Perry, who seems to have some very heavy burdens. However, he also realizes that one man's predicament cannot determine national policy, especially since he may receive in tomorrow's mail a letter from a crippled man who is supporting his widowed mother, ten brothers and sisters, twelve Korean orphans, and a cocker spaniel. Walter S. Brown's threatening letter, even though it appeals to the powerful emotion of fear, will probably be treated similarly. These emotional letters can be cancelled by similar appeals to opposite feelings. Thus, even though these letters may arouse the Congressman's emotions, they aren't likely to persuade him how to vote. They simply do not effectively relate the emotions they arouse to the issue at hand. (In fact, the threatening letter may backfire by arousing Congressman Fairweather's anger against the writer and his position.)

The letters from Sylvia Krown and Eunice Bamberger are more effective because they attempt to relate the emotions to the congressman's actions. The Bamberger letter, which is probably the more effective, is still emotional, but the emotion seems justified.

Exercises

1. Look at some ads in magazines for products like cigarettes, beer, liquor, automobiles, and cosmetics. Do they use emotional appeals? To what emotions do these ads appeal most frequently? Are these emotional appeals related to the natures of the products themselves, or are they simply directed at powerful human emotions?

2. What other emotional appeals besides those in the text might be effective with Congressman Fairweather? Is the congressman more likely to respond to positive appeals (praise, encouragement, and so forth) or negative emotions (fear, threats, blame, and so forth)?

3. Write a brief opening paragraph to Fairweather in which you seek to arouse his emotions.

The Three Appeals

If you were Congressman Fairweather and you had no prior commitment to vote either way on the Honey Import Act, how would you vote on the bill? Which letter or letters would be most convincing to you? Which rhetorical method was most effective—that based on the identity of the writer, that based on appeals to the evidence in the case, or that based on your emotional response to the situation?

There is, of course, no right answer. Some of you will respond one way, some another way, and others still a third way. Any one of these approaches can be effective, a truth that was recognized by the Greek philosopher Aristotle about twenty-five centuries ago. Aristotle analyzed the *rhetorical situation*—any situation in which one person communicates with another—as having three components: (1) a *speaker* (or writer), (2) an *audience* (or reader), and (3) a *message* (or content). Aristotle classified rhetorical means according to which element in the rhetorical situation was most prominent. Thus, if a speaker or writer emphasized his own character *(ethos)*, Aristotle called this appeal the *ethical* appeal; if the speaker emphasized the emotions of the audience, he called this the *emotional* appeal; if the speaker emphasized the content (the actual truth about the subject), he called this the *rational* appeal. Which is really the best to use? Interestingly enough, Aristotle said that the rational approach was the ideal method for rhetoric, but he said that the ethical (or personal) appeal was the most effective. However, he spent much more effort on analyzing emotional appeals than he did on analyzing the other two appeals. So Aristotle couldn't seem to actually decide on an answer, any more than we can.

An objection and a response

Now some of you will probably object to this inconclusiveness. You will argue that people are supposed to be rational, reasonable, and logical creatures. You may also think that appealing to someone's emotions is a way of deceiving him (as it often is in the real world). And you have probably been taught in your class (and in other books on writing) that logical writing is good and emotional writing is bad.

I will try to answer these objections as fairly and honestly as I can. First, rhetoric is the study of human communication as it *is,* not as it *ought to be.* Indeed, if people were computers or angels or just creatures of pure reason and logic, there would be no need for rhetoric. Pure logic would serve us all very well. But we all recognize that people have emotions as well as reason. Secondly, rhetoric does not exclude reason and logic. It merely recognizes that reason and logic are not always sufficient either to make a person respond as you wish him to or to get him to act as you wish him to. How many times have you argued about politics with your father and uncle? No matter how logical your arguments seem to be, they never change their opinions. (They, too, are probably amazed at your failure to respond to their logic.) Thirdly, rhetoric recognizes that emotional appeals have their validity too. No one can prove with facts or logic that it is absolutely better for an American to have a job than for a Saudi Arabian to have that job, but Americans are, in fact, more concerned about unemployment in America than in other countries. Such a bias is emotional, but quite natural and normal.

I should also point out that the ethical appeal, which is not strictly logical, is one that often works to our advantage. We trust the advice of parents, teachers, priests, ministers, lawyers, counselors, and friends—especially if we don't have any reasonable knowledge about the subject. For example, if a close friend says, "The movie at the Strand stinks," we will probably go to some other movie or to no movie at all. If a lawyer tells us, "Don't sign the contract; it's too full of loopholes," we probably won't sign. We trust the character of the speaker, even though we may not understand why. That's a normal part of living.

Rhetoric, then, is the study of how audiences are affected, whether by emotion, reason, or trust in the character of the speaker. Rhetoric (or a rhetorician, i.e., one skilled in rhetoric) evaluates a speech or a piece of writing according to how effectively a speaker or writer communicates certain opinions or information to an audience (either one person or a group) in a certain situation.

*Standards of rhetorical
effectiveness*

The explanation in the preceding paragraph seems clear enough, but it also seems pretty vague. How can we tell how anyone will respond to any appeals in any situation? Isn't that just a hit-or-miss procedure in which we're more likely to miss than to hit? Or, to put the question more generally and abstractly, can there be any system to rhetoric when rhetoric deals with the whims of human personality?

To answer that question, let's consider what may be a familiar situation for you and many other college students. Suppose you need fifty dollars for a weekend skiing or surfing or just having a blast. Don't you have a strategy for asking your parents for some money? Perhaps you write to your father at his office, or you may telephone your mother when you know your father won't be home. Or perhaps you write to tell how hard you've been studying—something that's shown by the A's on your last three exams—and explain how you really need some relaxation. In other words, you do have a rhetorical strategy—a plan for presenting your character and your case in the best possible light for your audience.

Now this example of asking a parent for money is a good rhetorical model in the sense that the effectiveness of the rhetoric is pretty easy to judge. If you get the money, your rhetoric has been effective; if you don't get the money, your rhetoric has been ineffective. That's a pretty easy situation to evaluate.

However, it is not always so easy to judge the effectiveness of our rhetoric because our rhetorical goal is not always an action or an objective result. Often our goal in writing is not to get somebody to do something. We may want merely to explain something to someone, or we may want someone to sympathize with us. Or we may want our audience to think more carefully about our subject.

A work of rhetoric must be judged in relation to its purpose. A textbook is rhetorically effective if students learn from it; the book must contain accurate information and must present that information clearly and in a well-organized pattern. A letter of condolence is effective if it represents your emotions about the deceased while offering comfort to the bereaved. A poem is effective if its readers, whoever they might happen to be, enjoy the poem.

The standards of rhetorical effectiveness for a personal letter intended for a friend may differ from those for a poem intended for the public, present and to come. And the standards will differ for an ad that is intended to sell a product and a letter that seeks to tell a close friend that you were thinking about him and that you care about him. However, the ultimate standard of rhetoric is still the same: you will want to know whether your message had the effect you wanted it to on your audience. That is the heart of rhetoric and the rhetorical method.

As a matter of fact, you and I and those around us have been practicing rhetoric for most of our lives. You've known for a long time that you don't talk to the family minister the same way you talk to your kid sister, and you know that you don't deal with a college English professor the same way you deal with your mother. (A lot of you have probably already discovered—perhaps to your dismay—that you can't deal with college professors in the same way that you dealt with high school teachers.) Because you've been practicing rhetoric all your life, the formal study of rhetoric won't be too difficult for you. The chief difference will be that your study of rhetoric will now be more systematic and rigid. You will be asked to think more carefully and analytically about your rhetorical decisions.

These few examples have probably been enough to show you that there is a method to rhetoric. Most of the rest of this book will deal with that method and how you can apply it to make your writing more effective. However, before doing anything else, let's get back to our original problem, Congressman Fairweather.

Deciding the Issue

How will Congressman Wilbur D. Fairweather vote on the Honey Import Act? How should he vote? What appeals will persuade him?

On most political issues we hope that right, truth, or justice will prevail. This normally means our own conceptions of right, truth, and justice, for all of us are aware that others do not always see things as we see them. Indeed, one of the premises behind our Constitutional guarantees of free speech and a free press is that men of good will often disagree sharply on many fundamental issues. Thus, when James Nevins wrote and asked Fairweather to vote for the Honey Import Act, he did so because he felt that the bill would lower the price of honey. James Mullen also felt that passage of the bill would lower the price of honey, but Mr. Mullen did not see this as a good thing. He asked Congressman Fairweather to vote against the bill so that farmers would not go broke.

Both men reasoned logically about the issue. Both agreed that passage of the act would lower the price of honey. But they did not agree on whether that result would be favorable or unfavorable. How would you decide?

One advantage of using the example of the Honey Import Act is that this is an issue on which few of us have any preconceived notions, feelings, or biases. If we talked about legalizing marijuana, granting federal funds for abortions, reinstituting the draft, increasing military spending, or deregulating petroleum prices, most of us might already have opinions on the subject that would interfere with our analysis of the rhetorical methods used in attempting to convince Congressman Fairweather. But in our hypothetical example there are few facts and no absolute truths. We have a case of what we might almost call "pure rhetoric." The basically opposite and equal rational arguments seem to nullify each other, unless we have strong biases towards either consumers as a group or farmers as a group. We're not sure which way of voting will ultimately help the district, the state, the country, and the world more.

The emotional appeals may rend our hearts, but these appeals are ineffective in themselves unless the writers can make valid connections between the emotions and the actions they desire. Thus, an ad on television that merely makes you feel sorry for a starving child in Bangladesh is only partly effective; unless the ad prompts you to send money, it has failed (at least with you). As for the ethical appeals, they partially cancel each other out, too. They seem a little too weak, a little too underdeveloped to persuade us. They seem to lack substance.

An ideal rhetorician

What, then, will influence us (or a congressman like Fairweather)? Let's try to compose a letter that combines all three appeals in a successful balance. Let's write a letter that is rational yet emotional, presented by a writer who is attractive and credible.

Dear Congressman Fairweather:

I have been pleased with your work for this district in Congress, especially your splendid efforts that resulted in the Spring Valley Flood Control Project. Because I know that you are anxious to make sound legislative decisions for your constituents, I thought I would pass along some information to you about the Honey Import Act. This information should help you to understand why I think you should vote for the bill.

First of all, passage of the bill will mean more honey for Americans, which will mean lower prices. Second, the lowering of trade barriers will allow the major honey exporting nations to increase their trade with the United States, thus allowing these nations to buy more American goods. This will help these nations as well as us. Buying honey from our neighbors in Mexico and Argentina will help these friends in Latin America.

I know that farmers will complain about the loss of revenue, but they can easily raise other crops, like wheat and soybeans, something that farmers in other nations cannot always do. The price of honey has been kept artificially high for too long, and the farmers have been the only group to benefit from this protective legislation. Besides, the fact that we are a honey exporting nation indicates that there is plenty of profit in honey, with or without artificial price supports. The interests of the general public should outweigh the loss of income to farmers, which will not be that great anyway.

Thus, I urge you to vote for the Honey Import Act. I am sure, however, that whatever decision you make will be in the best interests of the district, the nation, and the world.

Sincerely,

Shirley L. Greene

Shirley Greene's letter should be an effective one because she uses all three appeals effectively. She starts out by appealing to Congressman Fairweather's emotions. Specifically she praises him for his achievements and then appeals to his sense of duty and his sense of fairness. She characterizes him as a man trying to do his best, something that probably will make the congressman a receptive reader.

Not only are Miss Greene's emotional appeals sound, but her ethical appeal is excellent. Her praise of Congressman Fairweather indicates that she is knowledgeable about him and sympathetic toward him. Moreover, she appears helpful and reasonable. She is not simply telling the congressman how to vote, but she is giving him information on her position. As she puts it, she is trying to make him understand her position in a rational way. But she does make her stand clear.

Her second paragraph relies strongly on a rational appeal. It contains both facts and carefully reasoned arguments. Underlying the facts and arguments are basic assumptions about the welfare of the United States and its citizens. Ultimately—and the premise can neither be proved nor disproved—she implies that the congressman's chief concern should be for America. The argument is one of self-interest, one of the most emotionally compelling reasons for doing anything.

The third paragraph, which anticipates objections that some might have to the passage of the bill, is also largely rational. However, such a phrase as "artificially high for too long" has some strong emotional overtones.

The last paragraph again appeals to the congressman's emotions. It praises his judgment and indicates trust in him. In doing so, of course, Miss Greene's ethical appeal remains high. Moreover, she does manage to restate her position at the beginning of the paragraph.

All in all, it is impossible to say how Congressman Fairweather will vote. However, we do know that he is very likely to read this letter sympathetically. The letter does what it should. It presents the writer and her content to the audience in such a way that the audience will be sympathetic and able to understand what she is saying. What more can a letter do?

A review and a preview

As we have seen, "good writing" is not an absolute. A piece of writing is not good or bad in itself. Rather, its effectiveness is to be judged by how well it fits the rhetorical situation. The elements of this situation are the speaker, the reader, and the content. If the writer is aware of all three elements, then his writing will skillfully control all three appeals: the ethical, the emotional, and the rational. Throughout this book, we will use these rhetorical standards, not grammatical or literary standards, to judge how effectively a writer communicates.

Although the three appeals are normally intermixed and interrelated in any writing, the next three chapters will deal with the appeals separately so that you may develop both your skills in analysis and your skills in expression. Later, we will treat organization, sentences, words, and even grammar in a rhetorical perspective.

Things to Do

1. Write a letter to your congressman or senator on an issue that you feel strongly about. When you receive his reply to your letter, analyze the appeals that he uses in his letter.

2. Look at some ads on television or in magazines and newspapers and analyze which appeals they emphasize.

3. Read the "Letters to the Editor" column in a newspaper or magazine. Using your own intuitive responses as guides, evaluate the letters by putting them in numerical order, with 1 for the best, 2 for second best, and so forth. Then try to analyze the letters to see if you can discover the reasons for your responses.

Writing Assignments

In doing any writing assignment, it might be a useful rhetorical exercise to list the following information at the beginning of your paper:

  I. Subject
 II. Audience (characteristics)

III. Speaker (description)
IV. Rhetorical goal
 V. Rhetorical strategy

Here, for instance, is a simple plan for the first assignment below:

   I. Subject—increase in state income tax
  II. Audience—State Senator Jones, a conservative
 III. Speaker—a mildly angry but still reasonable citizen
 IV. Rhetorical goal—to get Senator Jones to vote against the bill
  V. Rhetorical strategy—to show that budget cuts could be made to avoid this increased tax

1. Write a substantial letter on some controversial issue as though you were going to send it to a public official, a newspaper, or a magazine.
2. Write a letter to your teacher persuading him that you shouldn't have to do one of these writing assignments.

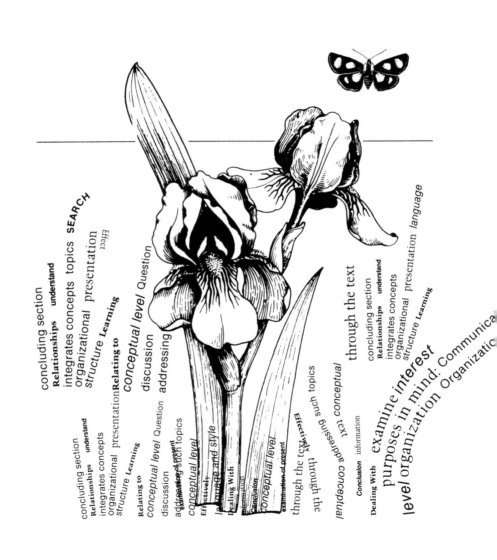

Chapter Two

CONTENT

Rhetorical Writing

The types of writing that this book will deal with will be the types that you, as an educated person, will be expected to use both in your classes and, more important, beyond the classroom. We will look at types of writing that you will use as employee, manager, college student, citizen in a democracy, and consumer. The major kinds of writing that you will probably be doing are *persuasion* and *exposition*. Persuasion is the attempt to change or strengthen an audience's opinion to agree with yours. For instance, you may want to persuade your boss that your plan for cutting costs in the shipping department is better than any of the other proposals that have been offered. Or you may want to persuade a politician, like Congressman Fairweather, to support your views. Exposition is explaining or clarifying what something means or how it works. You may have to explain to your psychology professor what a term like *defense mechanism* means, or you may have to explain to a group of employees whom you supervise just how the new grievance procedure will work.

For both practical and theoretical reasons, this book will not concentrate on writing either imaginative literature—poems, novels, short stories, and plays—nor on those purely personal forms of writing that all of us manage to write pretty adequately—personal letters, diaries, love letters, and so forth. Nor will the book deal extensively with descriptive writing (word pictures of persons, places, or things) or narrative writing (the telling of a series of events in story form). Although as rhetoricians we may use various techniques and devices from all of these forms of writing in support of our persuasion or exposition, the book will not emphasize them.

Rhetorical content

Because this book emphasizes exposition and persuasion, especially persuasion, you will see that certain kinds of content are more appropriate than others. Rhetoric has traditionally dealt with what Donald C. Bryant has called "the contingent"—those uncertainties in human affairs about which human beings disagree, debate, and argue.[1] For instance, the Honey Import Act is one of those uncertainties. Because the effects of passing the bill are so difficult to determine in any absolute and certain way, the subject is a proper one for rhetoric.

Among the proper subjects for rhetoric are matters of policy, matters of proposed future action like the Honey Import Act. When a writer urges a public official to vote for a bill, a citizen to vote for a candidate, or a consumer to buy a product, he is engaging in *deliberative* rhetoric, rhetoric about future action. A more extended form of deliberative rhetoric would be an extended essay in a magazine arguing that the United States should concentrate its resources on developing solar rather than nuclear energy. Or an editorial in a newspaper might argue that marijuana should be legalized or that the legal age for both drinking and voting should be raised to thirty-one.

The distinguishing marks of deliberative rhetoric are that it concerns the future and that it seeks actions from the audience rather than mere agreement. The language of

---

1. Donald C. Bryant, "Rhetoric: Its Function and Its Scope," *Quarterly Journal of Speech* 39 (December 1953), 406.

deliberative rhetoric often uses *should* or *ought* as key words.

Another proper subject for rhetoric is past action—what took place in the past. When jurors in a courtroom consider the evidence in a murder case, they are attempting to decide what took place in the past. As a matter of fact, the development of rhetoric in ancient Athens got great impetus from the need of citizens to defend themselves in court. Rhetoric that deals with judgements about the past is called *judicial* rhetoric or *forensic* rhetoric. Besides strictly legal matters, judicial rhetoric might consider whether Columbus was the first European to come to America, whether Lee Harvey Oswald acted alone in killing John F. Kennedy, or whether Shakespeare was a woman. Many historical and literary research articles and papers are examples of judicial rhetoric.

Unlike deliberative rhetoric, judicial rhetoric does not necessarily imply action. We can read a convincing argument that Leif Ericson came to America before Columbus, but we are content with merely knowing this information. We have no great desire to do anything with the information. We feel no need to go out and desecrate statues of Columbus. Of course, some judicial judgements may lead to action, but the action is really separate from the judgement itself.

Whether subjects that deal with the present are a whole new class of subjects for rhetoric, or whether they are merely forms of deliberative and judicial rhetoric, is perhaps unclear. Nevertheless, we do argue such issues as whether the incumbent president is an effective leader, whether mental telepathy is a reality, whether life exists elsewhere in our universe, and whether our national defense is sufficiently strong. The judgement about the president in our first example can only be made based on the past, so it might be considered judicial rhetoric. The judgement about the national defense probably points to policy decisions, so it might be considered deliberative. But questions about mental telepathy or life elsewhere in the universe are clearly about the present state of things and do not immediately imply any action. For want of a better term, we can call them subjects of *theoretical* rhetoric. The probabilities for or against the existence of life elsewhere in the universe can be argued intelligently until factual verification is possible.

You should not be too concerned about deciding whether something you are writing is an example of deliberative, judicial, or theoretical rhetoric. (I will say more about this in a later chapter.) What you should be sure of in a persuasive paper is that you are dealing with the contingent, with a subject on which there is disagreement and on which you can hope to persuade your audience. You would not argue an issue that is open to easy factual verification. For example, you would not set out to prove that the United States has fifty states, that World War II ended in 1945, or other such easily verifiable facts. Nor would you argue about scientific laws or other truths that are open to easy and accurate verification. Why argue about the velocity of falling objects or the number of legs a cat has when you can easily find the proper number?

Nor does rhetoric deal with matters of personal preference or taste. If you like vanilla milkshakes but don't like chocolate milkshakes, it is rhetorically impossible to prove to you that chocolate milkshakes taste better than vanilla shakes. Nor can rhetoric be used to prove that red is prettier than blue, that Paul Newman is handsomer than Steve McQueen, or that roses are prettier than carnations. Matters of taste may make pleasant conversation, but they are not fit subjects for rhetoric.

However, especially among experts, it may be profitable to debate whether the *Mona Lisa* is a greater painting than *The Last Supper,* whether T. S. Eliot is a greater poet than Walt Whitman, or whether *Hamlet* is Shakespeare's greatest play. Such arguments may be profitable if the participants agree on principles and criteria for judging works of art and literature. However, debate is futile if someone retreats into a subjective reaction: "I think Eliot's a greater poet because I like him better." A good book review will argue that a certain book is or is not worth reading, and it will give reasons. That's worthwhile rhetoric.

Of course, there are times when the truth is not in dispute, and you will have to write clear, precise, organized explanations of the material. That is good expository writing. Often, however, the line between exposition and persuasion is not altogether clear. In presenting an idea in a clear and organized fashion you are, in effect, often subtly arguing that the idea is a good one, one with which your audience should agree or which they should find useful. Whether or not that blurring of the distinction between the two is completely appropriate, it is true that good persuasion and good exposition share many characteristics in writing: clear expression, clear organization, and supporting details for main points. Good exposition is often as argumentative as persuasion in its structure and development.

Content
and Rationality

To say that the content of rhetoric is those subjects on which people disagree or on which they need to be enlightened does not really narrow the field a lot. It does exclude some subjects, but it also includes a great range of topics from mathematics to politics to buying an automobile. Moreover, it seems clear that a writer can't prove that legalizing marijuana will benefit society as clearly as he can prove that the sum of the angles of a triangle equals one hundred eighty degrees. Similarly, a writer will probably have a more difficult time convincing an audience that his particular interpretation of a poem is correct than he will in convincing an audience that reducing speed limits on the highway will help reduce automobile accidents.

One reason for this, though not the only one, is that different subject matters yield different degrees of certainty. Thus, in fields like mathematics and logic, one can construct an argument that follows so clearly step by step that one finds it impossible to disagree with. On the other hand, arguments about matters of politics, morals, and social values sometimes seem impossible to settle.

Nevertheless, almost any subject can be treated rationally. This means that a writer can choose to use material that is directly supportive of his content rather than relying on material that appeals to the emotions of the audience or on the strength of his personality. For example, let's consider these two automobile ads:

Playaround—the car for excitement, adventure, escape. Be free and wheel-loose in a sporty Playaround, the car that puts *you* where it's at. She'll love it as much as you do. So Playaround and live a lot.

In these days of fuel shortages and high gasoline prices, Stasha is the car that gets you there and back dependably and economically. Its four-cylinder, eighty-horsepower engine delivers about thirty miles per gallon of regular gas. Its twenty-gallon tank means six hundred miles of trouble-free driving. And Stasha is still priced under $4,000. Stasha—the sensible car for sensible people.

Even on a subject such as automobiles, which is likely to arouse many different responses from different people, we can see the basic difference between a rational appeal and a non-rational (though not necessarily irrational) appeal. The ad for Stasha is largely rational in that it makes specific claims about the automobile. The central claim is that Stasha is economical. As support for that claim, the ad describes the smallness of the engine, the expected fuel mileage, and the cost of the car. All of these supporting details are subject to verification. They can be checked and tested.

The ad for Playaround, on the other hand, is non-rational in that it makes no specific claims about the car itself. Rather it uses words like *excitement, adventure,* and so forth that appeal to the reader's desires and emotions. The Playaround, as its name suggests, is meant to appeal to a male reader's desire for adventure, especially sexual adventure. The next-to-last sentence even suggests that the car (and by implication the driver) will be attractive to some women. However, a reader is hard-pressed to find anything in this ad about the car itself. (If a reader bought a Stasha and its engine had two cylinders rather than the four that were advertised, she could probably sue the company and win her case; but a fellow would be laughed out of court if he tried to sue the makers of Playaround for a succession of dateless, dull Saturday nights.)

Claims and support

Making a specific claim and supporting that claim with material that is relevant to the claim is the heart of the rational appeal. The claim should be a proposition or assertion, or at least convertible to the form of a proposition. A proposition is a declarative sentence, and it should contain only one main clause. In the declarative sentence, the predicate (the verb and complement) says something about the subject. Claims must be declarative sentences, statements. They cannot be questions, commands, or exclamations. Consider the following sentences:

1. Brazil is in South America.

2. Fly to Brazil now!

3. Sunny Brazil!

4. Is Brazil a coffee-growing nation?

5. Brazil is becoming politically freer as its economy develops.

Only 1 and 5 are propositions. Both of them contain a subject and a predicate that makes a claim about the subject. Number 3 is not a proposition because it does not contain a verb. It could be converted to a proposition by adding a verb: "Brazil is sunny." Number 4 is a question, not a statement. Number 2 is a command, a set of directions, but it could be converted to a proposition: "You should fly to Brazil now." Of the two actual propositions, only 5 is the kind that is capable of rhetorical development. Number 1 is a bare fact, either true or false. But 5 makes a complex claim about the relationship between the economy and political freedom in Brazil. It is the kind of proposition that needs support for its claim.

In a later chapter you will learn specific ways and techniques for finding and developing supporting material for your claims. For now, though, it is enough that you know, in a general way, the difference between a rational and a non-rational appeal. You should be able to differentiate between rational and non-rational appeals in the writing of others, and you should be able to use rational appeals in your own writing.

Below are three samples of rhetoric. Read each carefully, and then see if you can determine which, if any, make rational appeals. Try to gather evidence from each to support your views. Here are the three samples:

A.

It is apparent from letters that newspapers are receiving throughout Pennsylvania that many gas customers do not have a clear understanding of the Fuel Cost Adjustment (FCA) as part of their gas bills. For example, some customers seem to think the FCA is an arbitrary charge in addition to the cost of their gas service.

We wish to make these points to your readers that may help to clarify the FCA:

1. The FCA is a procedure, authorized by the Pennsylvania Public Utility Commission (PUC), that enables gas utilities to recover the increased costs of the gas they have purchased from their suppliers. The increases or decreases in the costs are offset exactly by corresponding increases or decreases in the customer's gas bill.

2. The FCA has been part of the customer's gas bill since 1969. Recently the Legislature has requried that this element be listed separately. This has created confusion because many customers think this is a new, added-on charge.

3. The gas utilities make no profit from the FCA.

4. Viturally all of the gas costs that are recovered through the FCA are based on rates set by the Federal Energy Regulatory Commission (formerly the Federal Power Commission). These are beyond the control of the local gas utility companies or the PUC.

5. The FCA charges are not "authentic." They are based on data submitted to the Public Utility Commission which includes each supplier's name, the date, the amount, and the dollar impact of each supplier's increase.

6. The FCA is subject to a monthly review by the Audit Division of the PUC and to an extensive annual audit by the Commission.

7. The Fuel Cost Adjustment reflects the continuing increases in the cost of finding, producing and transporting gas. It now accounts for about 33 percent of the total revenue of the Pennsylvania gas companies. Without it, they would face financial disaster. Assuming they could stay in business, they would have to borrow enormous amounts of money at current interest rates—interest which eventually would be paid by the customers.

We hope that the above summation will explain that the FCA is not an arbitrary charge but is in fact a stringently regulated and necessary part of today's gas company revenues.

John H. Ware, III
President
Pennsylvania Gas Association[2]

B.

When there are so many things in this great country to be proud of, why do we have to be burdened with the awful shame of the consuming avarice of so many of our public servants?

In light of recent events which caused the loss of six or seven members of the Erie police force one would believe that this would create an additional burden on the remaining officers in their efforts to provide police protection for the citizens of Erie.

However, it appears that this cause for which we pay our taxes is forsaken for other devious pursuits such as hiding behind a fence at Bucyrus-Erie to entrap and harass the public in the guise of traffic safety enforcement.

It's not enough that I have to pay an unjust income tax to the city of Erie when I live outside the city limits and receive none of the services these taxes provide but I also have to be ripped off for $35 for going through the yellow at the traffic light. I vehemently protest these types of fines along with parking tickets that are deliberately perpetrated for the express purpose of filling the city treasury with funds to be used by thieving politicians to feather their own nests.

If the so called honorable mayor of Erie had an ounce of intelligence he'd realize that there are twenty-five traffic lights across 12th St. and that under the best conditions a driver will only catch five of these green. This simply means that thousands of drivers have to stop and start twenty times twice a day on their way to and from work resulting in the waste of hundreds of thousands of gallons of gasoline every year.

Our pompous leaders have no qualms about asking us to sacrifice during the energy crisis by turning our thermostats back, car pooling, busing, etc. But don't expect those dummies to have the simple foresight to synchronize the traffic lights with the speed limit to allow free-flowing traffic across town for the big savings in fuel consumption.

2. Letter, Erie *Times*, January 6, 1978, sec. A, pp. 6–7.

The next time you find yourself waiting in long lines for a few crummy gallons of gas don't ask Mayor Tullio to attempt to alleviate the problem because undoubtedly his only answer will be "It's not my job, man!" Plus he knows full well that to do such a thing would preclude one more means of his private gestapo to rip off the public.[3]

C.

There is a current tendency to call any field of study which deals with facts a science of one kind or other. Thus we speak loosely of the science of business, the science of politics, the science of psychology, and the science of law. Great strides are being made to systematize these subjects and to develop them as sciences. The stumbling block, of course, is that each one of these subjects is influenced by large measures of human actions. Happily or not, man has as yet been unable to observe in himself (or in his institutions) modes of behavior that are strictly reproducible.

Most of the phenomena and materials of nature appear to the human observer to be strictly reproducible. A 1-lb. weight delivers a given amount of energy if dropped from a height of 1 ft. Water freezes when its temperature drops to 32° F. Carbohydrates are oxidized in the tissues of animals to carbon dioxide and water. Because of such reproducibility, we speak of the study of nature as *natural science*.[4]

If you decided that A and C were examples of rational appeals and that B was not a rational appeal, you are correct. Let's look at them and see what the differences are.

Example A starts out to clear up a misunderstanding as the writer discusses his subject, the FCA, in a series of numbered, orderly paragraphs that stick right to the subject. The writer doesn't go off on tangents and doesn't get emotional. His main assertion or claim comes as part of the last paragraph: ". . . the FCA is not an arbitrary charge . . . ." Although it might appear that this letter is expository because the writer is merely clarifying what the FCA is, actually the writer seems to be trying to persuade

3. Letter, Erie *Times*, September 15, 1976, sec. B, p. 2.

4. Charles William Keenan and Jesse Herman Wood, *General College Chemistry*, 2nd ed. (New York: Harper & Brothers, 1961), p. 2.

people that the gas company's charges are both just and necessary. There is persuasion involved.

The writers of the paragraphs from a chemistry textbook (example C) are also doing two things: explaining what a natural science is and arguing that the word *science* truly belongs only to those studies which are reproducible. They offer specific examples, or facts, in their second paragraph to support their views. There is just a touch of emotion in some of the wording in the first paragraph, but the presentation is generally orderly and rational.

Example B is not a rational appeal. First, it is very difficult to determine what the writer's chief assertion is, though it seems to be something like this: "The traffic fine I received was unjust." The third and fourth paragraphs seem to indicate this, but the writing doesn't clearly state the point. Second, the writer spends a great deal of effort proving that numerous stoplights cause a waste of fuel. However, even if he is right, that doesn't prove that his fine was unjust. Third, the writer relies on emotional language and arguments to arouse the feelings of the audience. He argues that the real reason for traffic fines is not traffic safety but the greed of politicians, and he brings up the irrelevant issue of city income tax. The language he uses appeals to our unthinking emotional reactions to politicians: "consuming avarice," "entrap and harass," "thieving politicians," "dummies," and "gestapo." This letter to the editor is not a rational one.

Summary

In this chapter we have looked at the kinds of writing that normally involve rhetoric. We have seen that rhetoric deals with those subjects on which people disagree or on which they need clearer understanding. Such qualifications usually exclude factual material on which there is no disagreement and little to say, and matters of purely personal taste. Rhetoric is for those situations in which it is possible to persuade or enlighten an audience by supplying support. Rhetoric may deal with the past, the present, or the future.

Ideally, good rhetoric will consist of claims or propositions with support. If the support relates clearly and directly to the claim, we say that the appeal is the rational (or logical) appeal. If, however, the support doesn't relate to the claim or if the appeal relies chiefly on the persona, then the appeal is non-rational.

Since content is usually the chief reason for writing, we will discuss in greater detail how to develop your content in a later chapter.

Things to Do

1. Evaluate whether each of the following claims is an appropriate subject for rhetorical writing.
   a. Football is more fun to watch than basketball.
   b. The federal income tax should be abolished.
   c. Franklin Roosevelt was born in 1882.
   d. Laws against prostitution in the United States have done more harm than good.
   e. Violence on television helps people to get rid of aggression in a harmless way.
   f. The spirits of dead people can communicate with the living.
   g. This exercise is very enjoyable.

2. Read the letters to the editor column in your local newspaper or in your campus newspaper. Are the appeals chiefly rational or non-rational? Now read the letters to the editor in one of the following magazines: *Harper's, The Atlantic Monthly,* or *The Nation.* Are those letters chiefly rational or non-rational?

3. Analyze soft drink ads on television. What claims do they make about their products?

4. List three products that probably can be advertised well through rational appeals. List three that would be difficult to advertise through rational appeals.

Writing Assignments

Choose one of the writing assignments below. Be sure to include the kind of outline described in chapter one.

1. Write a letter in response to a letter to the editor or an editorial in your local newspaper. Be sure you use a rational appeal.

2. Write a letter to your campus newspaper suggesting an improvement or change that you would like to see on your campus.

3. Read the following hypothetical problem in rhetoric. It will be the basis for assignments in other chapters, too:

World War III has occurred. Nuclear warfare and radiation have destroyed virtually everything on earth. The following are the only survivors:
a. You, a college student working as a fallout shelter inspector during the summer.
b. Ten people of varied backgrounds in a fallout shelter on the east coast. Because of underground cables, you have been able to maintain teletype communication with the East Coast Ten. In fact, they have just notified you that their fallout shelter has enough food, water, and oxygen to sustain only *six* people for one year—the time needed for radiation to subside. Four of the ten people must leave the fallout shelter to face death from radiation. The six people that remain will be responsible for beginning a new society, a new world. The East Coast Ten have asked *you* to decide which six will remain and which four will die. The East Coast Ten will abide by your decision, but they have asked you to give them your reasons for deciding who lives and who dies.

Below is the list of people that make up the East Coast Ten. You must select *six* to live, and *four* to die.
1. Joan, a female science teacher, age 29, Oriental
2. Edward, male nurse, age 42, white
3. Pamela, female tennis player, age 19, white

4. Paul, male Lutheran minister, age 45, white
5. Harry, male agricultural professor, age 55, white
6. Ursula, female physician, age 60, white
7. Ronald, male mortician, age 39, white
8. Tish, female model, age 25, black
9. Willard, male lumberjack, age 30, white
10. Sue, female high school dropout, age 16, white, three months pregnant

You are to be yourself for this assignment. You are not allowed any special attributes or qualifications that you do not already possess. Similarly, you may not invent any information about these ten people. You must use only the information about them listed on this sheet. For example, you can rightly infer that the male nurse has gone to school for nursing and that at age 42 his good health could last for at least twenty years. But there is little else that you can rightly infer.

Now write a report for your own benefit and for the benefit of future generations explaining why you have chosen one particular person to die. Because you are seeking to clarify your own thinking and because future generations will probably be able to judge your decision in a detached manner, you are to use a purely rational appeal. Make your claim and support it with good reasons. Don't worry about your other appeals.

examine *interest*
purposes in mind: Communica
conceptual level organization Organizations

analytically objectives **Problems** observe
conclude questions decision **relationship**
discussions topic organizational
comprehensive text
techniques
introduction

Recognizing outlines questions
appropriate

Problems observe references examine *interest*
decision **relationship** purposes in mind: Communication
conceptual level organization Organizations

concluding section **understand**
Relationships integrates concepts
organizational presentation
Structure **Learning**

Relating to
Conceptual level Question
discussion
addressing such topics
conceptual level
Effectively
language and style
Dealing With
information **Others**
Concluding
conceptual level
dynamic
examining present Style and Power
engaging the text
through the text
writing style issues

readability
Interesting **communication**
friendship

Chapter Three

THE AUDIENCE

The Problem of Audience

When your six-year-old sister turns from the *CBS Evening News* to ask you a question, you may get upset or annoyed, especially if the question is, "What's an abortion?" In attempting to answer your sister's question, you have two problems to deal with—one intellectual and one emotional.

First, let's look at the intellectual problem. You could tell your sister that *abortion* means "the artificial expulsion of a fetus from the womb in the early stages of pregnancy" or some such definition from a dictionary. However, such an explanation is inappropriate to your audience, a six-year-old who probably doesn't know what *fetus, womb,* and *artificial* mean. Indeed, even if your sister is precocious and knows these words, she probably won't understand what the definition means. The concept of abortion is extremely difficult to explain to a child.

Your intellectual problem is, of course, compounded by your emotional problem. How can you explain the emotional significance of something like abortion to a six-year-old child without unduly upsetting, frightening, or worrying her? How should you discuss the matter with her—medically, morally, psychologically, sociologically? Or do you even want to discuss abortion with your six-year-old sister?

The problem that you have in explaining to your six-year-old sister what abortion means is a fine model of the basic problem of audience. *In dealing with an audience, you have to be aware of both the intellectual abilities and the emotional attitude of your audience.* Thus, the emotional appeal you use involves a lot more than just arousing the emotions of your audience. It means understanding your audience thoroughly and being sensitive to it in many ways. The golden rule of rhetoric is to be as careful of and as sensitive to your audience as you would like someone else to be toward you.

The Intellectual Problem

One of the basic problems of communicating with your audience is making your audience understand what you want it to. You know that different audiences require different sorts of explanations because their knowledge and experiences may differ quite a lot. Consider some of the people you ordinarily communicate with: your best friend, the person you date, your mother, your sister, your brother, your teachers, your boss. What diversity of experience and knowledge!

Suppose, for example, that you are taking an introductory course in sociology and that you happen to mention the course in a letter to your mother. When your mother, who never went to college, writes and asks you what sociology is, how are you going to explain it to her? You turn to your sociology textbook, and you see, once again, that sociology is "the synthesizing and generalizing science of man in all his social relationships."[1] That definition just won't do. Your mother wouldn't understand what it means. She probably isn't familiar with the words *synthesizing* and *generalizing*,

---

1. Arnold W. Green, *Sociology: An Analysis of Life in Modern Society*, 6th ed. (New York: McGraw-Hill, 1972), p. 2.

and she has only a foggy notion of *social relationships*. Thus, when you write and try to explain sociology to her you'll probably say something like this:

Dear Mom,

I don't know if I can really explain what sociology is because it's a very difficult idea. But I'll try.

Sociology is the study of how people act in groups and how groups act toward each other in a society. A society is a whole country or a large number of people who live together. Within a society, there are different groups—like different religions, different jobs, different social classes, and so many other groups. For example, we are middle-class, Baptists, and Democrats, and different people in our family belong to the Elks, Boy Scouts, PTA, AFL-CIO, Brownies, American Legion, and so on.

Sociology tries to explain how and why groups act the way they do and why people act differently in groups than they do alone. Remember how upset you were when you got home from the PTA meeting that passed the resolution to have Mr. Keefe remain as the principal of Elmwood School? You said that you didn't like him or his methods of education, but in the meeting you voted the way most other people did. You didn't want to go against the group. That's the kind of thing that sociology tries to explain.

Well, I hope you have some idea of what sociology is all about. By the way, I had to spend most of the ten dollars you sent me on books, so I'm broke. Could you send me a little more?

Your loving son,

George

That probably is a pretty good explanation of sociology for this audience. For one thing, it doesn't contain too many words that are difficult to understand. Your mother should comprehend the words. For another thing, it is full of familiar examples that are within your mother's range of experience. She knows what the PTA, the Brownies, and the American Legion are. Moreover, she knows about her actions at the PTA meeting. Thus, you have fitted the material to your audience so that your audience can understand what you're talking about.

However, when you sit down to take your exam in Sociology 1, you know you'll need something better, especially when you see this question: "Define *sociology*. Be sure your definition considers the problems of methodology, verifiability, and any other criteria that may be relevant (25 points)."

In order to do well on this question, you will also have to fit your answer to your audience. Thus, your answer will probably look like this:

> Sociology can be defined as the synthesizing and generalizing science of man in all his social relationships with others. It is synthesizing because unlike economics, political science, and other social sciences, sociology tries to view man's total life in society. It is generalizing because it seeks to study data on a wide scale and arrive at results that are objectively verifiable for all groups.
>
> Some people question whether sociology is really a science because its results cannot be verified in the way that results can be verified in the physical sciences like physics and chemistry. However, the results can be verified by statistical methods, and the goals and approaches of sociologists seek to attain objectivity. Thus, sociology tries to be scientific and objective.

Your explanation of sociology for your professor differs from the explanation for your mother in several ways. First, the definition for your sociology professor is full of technical words that only a well educated and knowledgeable person would understand. Such words as *synthesizing* and *generalizing* are those of well educated persons, and terms like *social sciences, data,* and *objectively verifiable* are technical terms that require special knowledge in specific areas of study. They are part of the jargon, the special private language, of scientists and social scientists. Second, the material in your examination answer is more general and abstract. You didn't use concrete examples such as the PTA or the American Legion. Even when you do use specific examples—economics and political science, or physics and chemistry—these examples are relatively abstract.

Third, your relationship with your audience isn't very personal. You don't use *you* or directly refer to your teacher. Rather, you seemingly ignore your professor and write about sociology itself, as you might write for sociology professors anywhere. Your actual audience seems to vanish—even though you are aware of its views on defining sociology—and is replaced by an audience that seems personally uninvolved in the subject.

Just as these two explanations differ as the audiences differ, so too would your explanations of the term *sociology* for your little sister, your older brother, or your boss. This is an elementary principle of rhetoric that you have been aware of all your life.

A more general problem

This elementary principle of rhetoric applies not only when you are writing to some one person that you know; it applies as well when any writer or speaker is confronted with a large and perhaps impersonal audience, either face to face or through the medium of writing. If you were asked to deliver a speech to or write an essay for the International Society of Graphologists about sociology, you probably wouldn't know where to begin because you wouldn't know your audience very well. Even if you looked in a dictionary to discover that graphologists study handwriting to determine a person's character, that probably wouldn't help a great deal. You still wouldn't have a very clear concept of who graphologists are and why they would be interested in sociology. You could probably do a bit better if you knew that your audience consisted of nurses, Republicans, elderly people, veterans, or some other group that you could define from your own experience. Then you would have some idea about their interests and abilities.

Let's take another example. One of the best known psalms from the Old Testament begins "The Lord is my shepherd." If you were a missionary visiting a particularly remote group of Eskimos, how would you explain this psalm to people who had never seen a sheep, much less a shepherd? Would you stick with a literal version of the psalm, or would you transform it into terms that they could understand? You could try something like this: "The Lord is the faithful keeper of His sled dogs."

Now not all audiences will be as tough as the Eskimos, but if you are going to communicate with an audience you must speak or write in language that it can understand, using materials that are within its range of experience. Indeed, among the greatest problems facing any teacher is how he can communicate material on which he is an expert to people who, almost by definition, know little or nothing about it. One of the chief complaints students have against many teachers is the classic remark, "He knows his material, but he sure doesn't know how to explain it to his students." That teacher's problem is a rhetorical one: he can't adjust his material to the abilities and knowledge of his students. He lacks the practical grasp of rhetoric that makes every good teacher realize that the proof of good teaching is good learning.

Exercises

1. Taking the example of the graphologists as your audience, try to think of how you might relate one of the following subjects to people who study character through handwriting: sociology, psychology, astrology, witchcraft, history, biology, criminology, or theology. Can you see some possible connections?

2. Compose a brief list of things that you would want to mention to graphologists about the subject that you've chosen.

3. What do you think of graphologists? Do you think they can really analyze a person's character from his writing, or do you consider them unscientific and unreliable? (You need not have any accurate information; merely trust your general impression.) Does this view of them affect your response to them as an audience?

An exception—maybe

There is one major exception to the rule that a good rhetorician fits his material to his audience's knowledge, and it actually confirms the rule. This exception occurs when a speaker or writer tries to impress (and probably to deceive) his audience by using fancy, impressive-sounding terms that the audience won't understand. For example, a teacher can frighten a student by telling her that her academic progress profile will be kept on file in the college's administrative offices. That sounds tremendously important until the student realizes that an *academic progress profile* means a *grade*.

Or take the graduate student who writes his doctoral dissertation to prove that external indicators of a superior level of academic performance in the classroom exhibit a tendency to have a high degree of desirability among the student population. What he wants to prove—as if it weren't already obvious—is that students like good grades.

The tactic is much the same in the ads that claim that Desert Lily Shampoo is fortified with TFX and makes hair manageable with the addition of H_2O. Such scientific-sounding jargon is meant to impress and deceive the unwary. Actually, it is suited to its audience in the sense that the writer is aiming at an audience that is unsophisticated and too easily impressed by pseudoscientific terminology. A well educated and alert audience would never be fooled by such meaningless terms.

Such a strategy takes advantage of the weakness and ignorance of the audience, especially when a writer is consciously trying to trick people. Thus, however rhetorically effective it may be in some cases, it is morally dishonest. However, it is rhetorically appropriate in the perverse sense that it is designed to deceive a particular audience.

Emotions and Communication

Unlike the Honey Import Act, the issue of abortion is likely to arouse very strong emotions. Thus it is an almost perfect example to use in discussing how people react emotionally on controversial subjects. (Some of you may even feel a bit uncomfortable about it being used in this text.) Abortion—like homosexuality, interracial marriage, school busing to achieve racial balance, pornography, and marijuana—is one of those subjects on which almost everybody is likely to have a deeply felt and strongly held position.

Suppose that a bill legalizing so-called "abortion on demand"—abortion available simply at the request of the pregnant woman—has gained enough support in your state to become an important political issue. Suppose, even further, that this is the year that you have decided to run for the state legislature. How are you going to go about persuading people to vote for you? What rhetorical strategies are open to you?

Let's assume, for the sake of the illustration, that you are generally opposed to abortion on moral grounds but that you recognize the political realities and moral differences within a pluralistic society like ours and might vote for a limited medical-need abortion bill. How are you going to present yourself and your views to the various audiences you might have to face in campaigning?

Let's consider some of the audiences you might have to face. For instance, you might have to speak to the Knights of Columbus, a Catholic fraternal organization that opposes abortion on religious and moral grounds. In presenting your views to them, you would probably want to emphasize your moral position, your personal opposition to abortion. In that way you would be fitting your message to your audience by telling them something that they would like to hear, something with which they could agree. However, if you wanted to be honest, you would also mention that you might *have to*—notice the sense of compulsion—vote for a limited abortion bill. You'd probably emphasize the limitations; and perhaps you'd also point out that your position is more morally correct than that of your opponent who favors abortion, and more politically realistic than that of your other opponent who is opposed to any sort of abortion bill.

In speaking to NOW (the National Organization for Women) you would probably try a slightly different approach. Because NOW is a feminist group, its members probably support the general position of abortion on demand, since they feel it gives women greater freedom of choice. In stating your position to NOW, you would probably emphasize practical political issues rather than your moral opposition to abortion. Again, you would emphasize the flexibility and political realism of your position as opposed to that of your opponents. You might say to them that for them, a limited bill would be better than no bill at all.

In speaking to a group of physicians—say the local medical association—you would probably win approval by emphasizing that they, as medical people, should have a strong voice in deciding the provisions of the bill. This appeals to their pride in their special knowledge and to their sense of medical and moral responsibility.

I could go on listing at great length groups to whom a politician might speak. There are the Ironworkers' Local 127, the Masons, the Junior Chamber of Commerce, the Ladies' Auxiliary of the Royal and Ancient Order of Hibernians, the NAACP, MLA, NCTE, AAA, YMCA, YWCA, and so on and on and on. Each organization is a different audience because each exists for a different purpose. Even if someone belongs to more than one of these organizations, as many of us do, he belongs to each one for a different reason.

Exercises

1. Consider some of the groups in which you might be classified, or the organizations of which you might be a member. List about ten of these groups.

2. Using this list, consider how each of these groups generally stands on some issue like abortion, legalizing marijuana, sex outside of marriage, interracial marriage, or homosexuality. Do all these groups agree on these issues?

3. Do you find yourself disagreeing with the general attitudes of any of the groups of which you are a part? Do you feel uncomfortable about these disagreements?

Rhetoric and morals

In reading some of these comments about adjusting your material to fit the emotions and views of your audiences, you may get the feeling that a speaker's rhetoric is just another name for hypocrisy or deceit. Doesn't "adjustable" rhetoric indicate lack of conviction? If a person thinks abortion is morally wrong, shouldn't he stand up and say so?

In answering these questions—which were asked, by the way, thousands of years ago in ancient Greece and which will probably still be asked thousands of years from now—let's clarify some things about rhetoric and the proper use of emotional appeals. First, this theory of rhetoric assumes that a speaker or writer has a position on the specific issue, even if the position is merely "I am uncertain at this time." If the speaker tells the Knights of Columbus that he strongly opposes abortion and, later that evening, tells NOW that he favors the most liberal abortion law possible, he has gone beyond the limits of adjusting his content to fit his audience: he's being dishonest. However, the dishonest speaker's rhetoric will be self-defeating, for people will quickly recognize that so many shifts of opinion indicate an untrustworthy speaker.

Second, in adjusting his material, a speaker is merely recognizing some important truths about human nature: people do not act on issues or problems unless the issues either interest them deeply or affect them in some direct way. Thus, birdwatchers get upset when a species of warbler approaches extinction; stamp collectors are thrilled by a new eight-cent stamp with a picture of Mickey Mouse on it; scholars of English literature are excited by the announcement of a previously undiscovered poem by Lord Byron; a certain group at your church may be interested in sending missionaries and financial aid to Ecuador. When the price of fuel rises drastically, people like truckers, who feel that their livelihood is threatened, are likely to take strong action. Or when people feel, justifiably or not, that school busing will endanger their children, they are likely to act, through legal or other means. Thus, a rhetorician must relate his interests and concerns to the views of his audience. Unless an audience knows how and why its concerns are related to the speaker's, it is unlikely to listen or to act.

Third, rhetoric is a practical art that aims at accomplishing things in the real world. A good rhetorician recognizes situations for what they are and attempts to gain the best results he can in any particular situation. If you wish to run for political office on a platform advocating the prohibition of alcoholic beverages, you are certainly free to do so; however, you are unlikely to have much national political influence, at least in the present political climate. Perhaps you'd accomplish more by working to limit the advertising of alcoholic beverages or by establishing educational programs for youngsters.

Fourth, rhetoric and rhetoricians concern themselves with issues on which it is difficult to attain certain and clear evidence. Rhetoricians do not debate the velocity of falling objects, the population of Los Angeles, or the date of Harry S. Truman's birth. They know there are better, more authoritative ways to answer these questions. Rather, rhetoricians deal with the contingent, with issues on which people disagree; and quite often they advocate a course of action to be taken. On such issues, the absolute truth is often difficult to determine. Thus, a good rhetorician is skeptical of inflexible moral positions.

Finally, a rhetorician, like any moral being, can and must decide when he wants to take a firm and unbending stand on an issue such as abortion. Rhetorically speaking, such a stand can be very effective. In the 1968 Democratic campaign, Eugene McCarthy was not nominated for the presidency, but he succeeded in making opposition to the war in Vietnam respectable by insisting on an inflexible plan for withdrawal from the war. Similarly, George Wallace gained a great deal of political support because, as an admirer commented, "He says the same thing in different parts of the country." And opponents of abortion have achieved considerable success politically in the last few years. However, even if your moral stand is less effective than these, it may be the one you have to take. The choice is still yours.

*Samples of rhetoric
for audience*

The audience is so important a component in the rhetorical situation that a writer may even say vastly different things to different audiences. For example, a brochure by a real estate firm might give this advice to a young married couple:

For a young couple, there is no finer investment than a home. A good home in a good neighborhood will keep pace with or even greatly exceed the rate of inflation. It will, moreover, allow the owners various tax shelters and benefits, which further reduce the actual costs of buying a home. Besides these financial benefits, a home gives the family security, comfort, and room to grow. Thus, the combination of personal and economic advantages makes home ownership an outstanding investment for a young couple.

To an older couple, however, that same writer might say something like this:

When the average couple reaches the age of retirement, they should probably consider selling their house. First, a whole house may be too large for just two people, and costs for heat and electricity are probably too high for those on diminished income. Second, routine maintenance tasks like trimming the lawn, repairing the plumbing, painting, and so forth are likely to be increasingly troublesome as the owners get older, which means they will have to be paying people to do things that they formerly did for themselves. Third, the money the couple could get from the sale of their house would provide a comfortable income if properly invested. Meanwhile, they would have a comfortable margin of cash and could enjoy the convenience of living in an apartment, free from all worries about repairs and maintenance. Finally, an older couple will probably enjoy living in an apartment complex with those who are their own age and have similar interests. In sum, for the older couple, cash and high-grade negotiable bonds are more secure and convenient than owning a house.

These two messages are quite different: one advises home ownership and one advises against it. However, the writer is not doing anything dishonest. He is merely recognizing that the interests, desires, and goals of one audience are not the same as those of the other. He recognizes that young people are different from older people. Thus, he tailors his arguments and appeals to fit each audience. For example, he not only emphasizes tax benefits to a young couple, but he also uses such emotionally favorable words as *security, comfort,* and *investment,* thereby appealing to the emotions of most young couples. However, he carefully avoids mentioning "routine maintenance tasks like trimming the lawn, repairing the plumbing, painting" because they might discourage younger couples. Those duties of home ownership are a cost, either in time or money, to young couples as well as to older couples. Nevertheless, both pieces of advice are legitimate adaptations of information for different audiences.

Many ads and other messages are like the two samples we just looked at; that is, they aim at or almost define the audience to which they are appealing. Here, for example, are the openings of two ads, one for investment seminars and one for an offer by a breakfast cereal company to get playground equipment in exchange for cereal box tops:

Our Bache seminars are designed for people who think an hour a week is not too much time to spend learning how to make the most of their money.[2]

Help your children! Help their school get the playground it needs. Free![3]

Both ads are designed to catch the attention of large audiences. The first is for those who want "to make the most of their money," which would probably attract the attention of most people. The second is again for a large audience: those who have children and would like to get something "free." Advertising copywriters consider *free* one of the most emotionally powerful words they can use.

2. Bache Halsey Stuart Shields Incorporated, ad, Erie *Times,* January 9, 1978, sec. B, p.4.

3. Post Cereals, ad, *Parade,* September 19, 1976, p. 10.

Most messages, however, are less direct in their appeals to audience. Either they are published in places where the audience is already largely defined for the writer, or they attempt to attract a certain segment of a larger audience. For example, consider the following editorial essay. Read it carefully and try to decide what kind of audience it was written for and what kind of magazine it appeared in.

Want to know the *real* reason for gun control laws and attempts to confiscate guns? It is basically very simple: we have gun control laws and we will have attempts to put more on the books because the politicians who administer our federal and state institutions are either too inept or too dishonest to face up to the basic truths of our society.

Americans as a whole today are not only cynical—following the political debacles of Vietnam and Watergate—they are downright disgusted at the mouthings of politicians who wish to cop out on the reasons for our social ills. One of these is the gun control issue. It is a handy cure-all for any politico who either doesn't understand what is going on or who hasn't the intestinal fortitude to run on a platform which tells it like it is. Because telling it like it is probably won't get him, or her, any votes. Neither will demanding that our dismal court system be revamped to impose stiff penalties on those committing a crime with a gun get many votes, though it needs to be done.

But even a stricter, more certain system of justice cannot answer the root problems of crime. The truth is that our unemployment rate is staggering for a country with the resources and technology we have. We have hunger and we have poverty and we have slums and ghettoes, and whenever a country has those it is going to have people committing crimes. They are going to commit crimes out of rage, frustration, hunger, and the need to feed those who depend upon them. They are going to commit crimes with guns, yes, but they are also going to commit crimes with switchblades, butcher knives, blackjacks, and pick handles.

The former mayor of the City of New York, John Lindsay, was an example of the typical politician who always turned to the gun issue whenever some poor wretch got drunk and battered somebody to death in a bar, or held up a delicatessen to get food, or tried to rob a bank and got into a shootout.

"More and stricter gun controls!" shouted the mayor—as have succeeding mayors, and governors and congressmen and senators across the nation—who know that it isn't guns but the *suffering of people* that causes crime.

But they also knew (and still know) something else: it is going to cost us *millions,* even *billions* of dollars to cure unemployment, create jobs, rebuild slums, educate minorities, stop the drug traffic, and any number of things that will make it unnecessary for people to have to steal and kill in this country. And they also know that talking about raising billions of dollars for vast social changes is going to be a highly unpopular issue with the voters because, like it or not, friend, *we* are going to have to pay for these social changes through taxation and bond issues, even though we are already having trouble making ends meet.

And so, rather than face up to honest issues, rather than risk losing voter support by calling for the real cures, the politicos will continue to clamber on the bandstand this bicentennial year and will harangue us with the same old tripe: Stop crime by banning the gun, registering the gun, forbidding assembly of the gun, or outlawing imported guns—as if the gun had a blasted thing to do with the despondent, disillusioned, sick, poor soul who looks at this great country from the stinking depths of his big city slum or southern shanty town and *knows* he is not going to get anything in the way of a fair shake from the politicians.

We need to educate his kids to give him some hope. We need to give him, or her, self-respect and pride and a decent job in a decent place so that he won't have to steal, mug, or kill—with a gun or any other weapon![4]

If you recognized that the audience is a group of people who oppose gun control laws, probably hunters or a sporting-gun group, you are becoming a good analyst of audience as a rhetorical component. And if you thought that the editorial would appear in a hunting or outdoors magazine, you are also correct. In fact the editorial by Jack Samson appeared in *Field & Stream,* a leading outdoors magazine.

Considering the place of publication, the editorial is well suited to its audience. First, the basic claim of the piece is that the demands for stricter gun control laws are the work of politicians who are either *inept* or *dishonest.* Probably the chief supporting argument is a claim that crime is caused by people rather than by any specific weapon such as a gun. A writer in such a magazine could not take a strong stand for gun control. He would be going too strongly against the

4. Jack Samson, editorial, *Field & Stream* (May 1976), p. 4.

basic beliefs and feelings of his audience. Second, the attack on politicians is a fairly easy and popular one, especially in an election year (1976). The author refers to Vietnam and Watergate, popular examples of political ineptitude or corruption. The audience is likely to agree with the writer. Third, because hunters are likely to be a broad group, a kind of cross-section of society, the writer uses a vocabulary that contains some sophisticated wording but that is chiefly simple and direct. The language is not for any one occupational group nor for either the very well educated or the very poorly educated.

The following sample of rhetoric appeared in the daily newspaper of Erie, Pennsylvania, an industrial city of about 150,000 people. To what audience is it directed? Will it be successful?

> Funny, but when a woman discovers she is pregnant and is glad, she says she is going to have a baby, but when she doesn't want it, she calls it a fetus and has it terminated by an abortion. That shows how a change in wording paints an entirely different picture of a situation.
>
> I guess that's why they say a picture is worth a thousand words. Anyone who has ever seen a picture of an aborted baby winces at the grotesquery of the dead child and wonders about the brutal procedure that destroyed that innocent child.
>
> If every day we put the picture of an aborted baby on the front page of this paper, what a fuss would be raised. All of our otherwise apathetic people would call or write deploring the paper for showing such a thing. They would term it "sensationalizing the press."
>
> They said the same thing about the pictures of the victims of the Vietnamese conflict and the starving peoples of Bangladesh.
>
> People, it's not sensationalism; it's the truth—and the truth sure hurts, doesn't it?[5]

The writer of the letter is, in a certain sense, writing to the readers of the newspaper. However, what specific segment of that audience is she appealing to? If she is writing for those who, like her, oppose abortion, she is likely to get some agreement. However, if she is writing to those who are in favor of abortion, her appeal isn't likely to get very far.

5. Letter, Erie *Times*, November 19, 1975, sec. A, p. 6.

She relies on emotional phrases like *grotesquery, brutal, procedure,* and *innocent child* which may arouse feelings of horror. But these feelings are not very likely to change the minds of those who favor abortion.

The problem with this letter, as with so many letters that appear in daily newspapers, is that the writer is appealing to the wrong audience. Her emotional appeals are probably effective with those who already agree with her, but they will do very little to change the minds of those who do not. This is often a shortcoming of people who use emotional appeals; they lose sight of who their real audience is. They forget that they are trying to change the minds of those who do not agree with them. Thus, such a letter is probably not very effective rhetoric.

Summary

In this chapter we have looked at audience as an element in the rhetorical situation. We have seen that a writer must be aware of both the intellectual abilities and the emotional attitudes of his audience. Although audience may at times be so important that it actually determines the writer's content, most of the time the writer has a content which he wishes to express. His goal as a rhetorician is to attract his audience and then convince it that his views are correct. To do this, a writer must often appeal to the interests and beliefs of his audience. If he merely expresses his own views but cannot persuade his audience, or at least get it to listen thoughtfully to his arguments, the writer is not being a very effective rhetorician.

As a rhetorician knows, communication involves both a sender of a message and a receiver, an audience. Because a rhetorician is aware of this, he never blames his audience by saying, "They don't understand me. They're too dumb." Instead, a good rhetorician makes sure that his audience can comprehend his message. He simplifies and clarifies as much as his audience needs simplification and clarification. He fits the material to its abilities. He also attempts to appeal to his audience's interests and needs. He shows his audience why it should care about what he has to say. He hopes to influence the audience for its benefit and his—a mutual benefit. In the succeeding chapters, we will be looking at audience again. We will learn specific ways, devices, and techniques for adapting our writing to an audience.

Things to Do

1. Read the following selection, the first half of a movie review from *Playboy*. Then answer the questions below.

The fuzzy line between all-permissive porno and so-called straight movies gets fuzzier every day. Witness *The Sailor Who Fell from Grace with the Sea*, co-starring England's vixenish Sarah Miles and Kris Kristofferson, who register as a white-hot romantic team even when they keep their clothes on. *The Sailor* has sex and nudity to spare . . . but displays flesh primarily to further the plot, not to detour it. The result is mature, sophisticated erotica, combining healthy heterosexual lust with undertones of psychological terror. Making his film debut as a director, screenwriter-adapter Lewis John Carlino chose a bizarre novel by Japan's late, great Yukio Mishima (who committed hara-kiri some five years ago), moved the action from a Japanese port to a harbor town in Devon and showed the good sense not to go berserk the first time he was let loose with a movie camera. In fact, a kind of Oriental simplicity shapes *The Sailor's* visual style (for which cinematographer Douglas Slocombe can claim substantial credit) and leaves the essence of the Mishima tale intact. It's a fiendishly cruel, hypnotic story about a frustrated young widow with a growing son who spies on her most private moments through a peephole between bedrooms—which makes him privy, on several occasions, to her intimacies with a rugged seaman (Kristofferson) from an American freighter that puts into port for repairs. The precocious little voyeur reports what he sees to the chief of a schoolboy gang that's into cigar smoking, dissecting household pets and generally defying parental authority. They begin to brood about the widow's lusty, roving sailorman as a good example of adult "betrayal" and convict him *in absentia*.[6]

6. Review of *The Sailor Who Fell from Grace with the Sea*, *Playboy* (June 1976), p. 36. Originally appeared in *Playboy* Magazine; copyright © 1976 by *Playboy*.

a. What is the audience for *Playboy?* Describe it.

b. Is this review appropriate for the audience?

c. Would a reviewer treat the movie the same way in *Seventeen, Ms., Parents' Magazine,* or *Time?*

d. What specific material in the movie does this review see as good which might be seen as bad in another magazine's review?

e. What specific words or phrases might not be used in another magazine—at least not with the same attitudes?

2. Go to the library and look up some reviews of *The Sailor Who Fell from Grace with the Sea.* Can you see how the differences in audience affect the reviews?

3. In looking through several different kinds of magazines, look carefully at their advertising content. Do the ads tell you anything about the probable audience for the magazine?

Writing Assignments

1. Write three movie reviews of a paragraph or two about a movie that you've seen recently. Your audiences for the reviews are to be (1) your mother or father, (2) a twelve-year-old girl or boy, and (3) a close friend. Be sure you use an outline for each.

2. Write a response to the letter about abortion in this chapter. Discuss the effect the letter had on you and then suggest to the writer specific ways to make her letter more effective. Use the kind of rhetorical outline found at the end of chapter one.

3. Go back to the survival problem at the end of chapter two. You are to write a letter to one of the persons you have chosen to die. Because you want that person to leave the shelter without causing trouble, you will have to work hard on a proper emotional appeal. Be sure you use the standard rhetorical outline found at the end of chapter one.

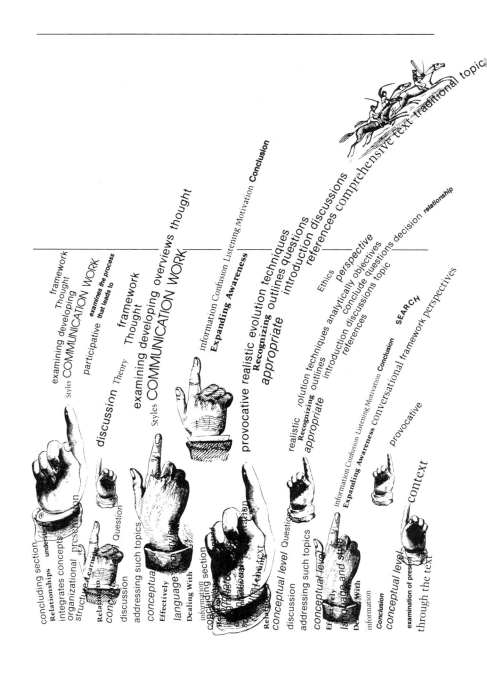

Chapter Four

PERSONA: THE CHARACTER OF THE WRITER

How Persona Works

The *persona,* or voice, is the character the writer presents in his writing. This is a fairly difficult concept to deal with, far more difficult than the notions of content and audience. In order to get a good grasp of the notion of persona, read the following letter to advice columnist Ann Landers.

Dear Ann Landers:

What has happened between parents and children in the last 15 years? The Bible says, "Raise up a child in the way he should go and he will not depart from it." Do you believe it? I don't.

Our own children are living proof. We have four. I stayed home and took care of them. We always went to church together. They had plenty of love, responsibility and discipline. Everything was fine until they started high school or went to college.

Within six months they fell in with friends who could twist and turn them any which way. "Peer pressure," they call it. Well, whatever it is I don't understand how it could have negated all the years of love and good training.

Our sons and daughters look like bums. They have no interest in decent clothes. They tell us they are agnostics. Three are college graduates, yet

61

they can't find jobs they like. They think it is hypocritical to do work that isn't "rewarding, exciting and stimulating." Don't they realize that life isn't all fun and pleasure?

Ann, you can do a lot of good by printing this letter and letting our children know that we, as parents, are fed up with their scraggly appearance, foul language, and total disrespect for authority.

My husband is in his early 50s and he is a broken man. We cry for each other, and for the thousands of other parents who feel they have failed. We did our best and can't figure out what went wrong.

Yes, we know many children go the right way, but this letter is for parents, like ourselves, who are sick at heart because we raised a generation of messed-up misfits. What can you say to us?

FAILURES[1]

Now that you've read the letter, answer the following questions: (1) Do you like or dislike the writer? (2) What is she like? (3) How do you know what she's like? (4) What are her children like? (5) Who is responsible for the rift between this woman and her children?

If you are like most of the students in my classes, you probably dislike the writer of this letter. My students generally agree that this woman is self-pitying, narrow-minded, intolerant, self-righteous, and rather unloving toward her children. The evidence for these judgments is in the letter—the attitudes, the emphasis, the wording, and other details. Most students believe that the woman's children are probably pretty normal, though some think they may be rebelling directly against an overly strict upbringing. Finally, most students agree that the woman is responsible for the rift between her and her children. A typical response is, "I couldn't put up with her picky nagging."

Are these assessments of the situation correct? Is the woman really to blame? How do we know that her children aren't really rotters?

Factually, of course, we don't really know very much about this woman and her children. The woman might be a

1. Letter to Ann Landers, Erie *Daily News*, August 26, 1974, sec. C, p. 12. Reprinted by permission of Ann Landers and Field Newspaper Syndicate.

living saint, and her children might be lazy and degenerate social parasites. However, that's not the impression that this letter creates. And, for all practical purposes, all we know about this woman and her children is what she tells us in this letter (and what we can infer from what she tells us). In rhetorical terms, she has a bad persona. Or, to use another technical phrase, her ethical appeal or personal appeal is very poor. (The term *ethical* comes from the Greek word *ethos,* meaning character, but the word *personal* seems like a better English word to use.)

If we look closely at the letter, we can see why this woman's personal appeal is so poor. First, her attitudes toward herself aren't very attractive. She seems self-pitying in the last two paragraphs when she writes of how she and her husband "cry for each other." That same note of self-pity occurs in her statement in paragraph two, "I stayed home and took care of them." In the same paragraph she appears self-righteous as she smugly lists the things she did for her children. Moreover, her blindness in thinking that the conflict between parents and children is something that started within "the last 15 years" and that "everything was fine" until her children got beyond her personal control is further evidence that she views herself rather self-righteously.

Second, the woman's attitudes towards her children probably strike us as harsh. She seems rather narrow-minded and intolerant. She seems overly concerned about their dress and appearance, which she doesn't approve of, and she is especially upset about their personal religious beliefs and their feelings about their jobs. In general she seems intolerant toward any beliefs and attitudes that are not the same as hers. She ultimately seems almost hateful, or at least uncaring, when she refers to her kids as part of "a generation of messed-up misfits."

Third, the very language that the woman uses weakens her persona. Phrases like "messed-up misfits," "look like bums," "scraggly appearance, foul language, and total disrespect for authority," and others are examples of the tired language of scolding parents. These phrases are clichés that readers have all heard before. They aren't likely to make much of an impression. The woman appears as a chronic complainer muttering the same old phrases over and over. Her language reveals that she hasn't looked at the problem very openly or freshly.

We could go on analyzing the letter in even greater detail, but most of our analysis would merely reinforce the initial impression. Whatever the exact reason for the persona, the result is that we, as readers, don't like it. In judging the persona we are judging the writer of the letter. If we don't like the persona, we aren't likely to agree with the letter.

The ubiquitous persona

Every piece of writing, from a personal letter to the directions for using a washing machine to an intense love poem, projects a persona, a character speaking. Even if the writer does not use the pronoun *I* and instead writes impersonally about his subject, there is still a persona present. Consider, for example, the following paragraphs from a chemistry textbook.

All matter exists in one of three states of aggregation, solid, liquid, or gaseous. A solid may be defined as a body possessing both definite volume and definite shape at a given temperature and pressure. A liquid in bulk, on the other hand, has a definite volume but no definite shape, while a gas has neither definite shape nor volume. Liquids and gases are both termed *fluids*. A liquid, insofar as it fills the container, will always adopt the shape of the container in which it is placed, but will retain its definite volume, while a gas will always fill completely any container in which it may be confined.

The distinctions among the three states of matter are not always as clear cut as the above definitions would imply. For example, a liquid at the critical point is indistinguishable from its vapor. Again, such substances as glass or asphalt, although exhibiting many of the properties of a solid, will, under certain conditions of temperature, become plastic and exhibit properties not ascribed to pure solids. For this reason such substances are usually considered to be supercooled liquids with very high viscosity.

The particular state of aggregation of a substance is determined by the temperature and pressure under which it exists. However, within certain limits of temperature and pressure a substance may exist in more than one state at the same time. In fact, under special conditions a substance may exist in all three states simultaneously. Thus at 4.57 mm Hg pressure and at 0.0099°C, ice, water, and water vapor may all be present simultaneously, and all be stable. This subject of simultaneous existence in more than one state will be discussed more completely in subsequent chapters.[2]

The persona here is not very emotional, not very personally involved with the subject. Rather he seems educated, knowledgeable, precise, and objective. This persona is the detached scientist.

The question for you as a writer, then, is not whether you will use a persona, but whether you will use your persona effectively. A good personal appeal can be a powerful means of persuasion for you, while a bad personal appeal, like that of the woman writing to Ann Landers, can weaken even sound arguments. You will have to learn to control your persona if you wish to write effectively.

Learning to control your persona should not be all that difficult, since you have been using personas for most of your life. You probably learned fairly early in life that you don't act toward your family's priest or minister the same way you act toward your kid sister or your best friend. In presenting yourself in different ways to different people, you are adjusting your speaking persona to fit your audience. You probably also adjust your persona to fit different situations and subjects. You don't act at a funeral the way you'd act at a party, nor do you treat a subject like choosing a mate with the same casualness that you would choosing a movie for a bit of diversion. Choosing the right personas for the ordinary situations of life is probably by now almost unconscious. You do it quite naturally.

But aren't you being a phony and hypocrite if you use different personas for different people? Shouldn't you just be sincere and be yourself?

Let's stop and consider a familiar situation—say a graduation party—at which many of your friends and relatives are all there together. You feel uncomfortable because

2. Samuel H. Maron and Carl F. Prutton, *Principles of Physical Chemistry*, 3rd ed. (New York: Macmillan, 1958), p. 6. © The Macmillan Company, 1958.

you almost instinctively recognize that the persona you use for your friends isn't quite appropriate in front of your parents and relatives. Moreover, the persona you display to your Aunt Susan, who is a justice of the Supreme Court in your state, seems a little bit stiff and a bit too serious for your friends. You have to shift too many voices too quickly to be comfortable.

In most social situations, however, you can and do find a persona that seems comfortable and appropriate. You are not being a phony as long as you don't do anything that betrays your inner character and as long as your persona fits the audience and situation. You need one persona in dealing with customers at the fast-food hamburger shop where you work, another for your history professor, and still another for your date. You shouldn't treat a date like either a history teacher or a customer.

Using a persona in writing is simply an extension of using one in speaking. But there are differences. In sitting down to write, you will be able to plan your persona more consciously and deliberately. You will not have to react instinctively and immediately, as you often have to in social situations. In other words, your audience will not catch you off guard. On the other hand, once you have chosen your persona in a piece of writing, you cannot immediately adjust it to your audience's reaction as you can in a social situation. Thus, there are both advantages and disadvantages to creating a persona on paper.

Exercises

1. List a dozen or so personas that you use during a normal day. Is there any conflict involved in playing all these different roles?

2. Can you think of any situations in which, because of the people present, you have difficulty finding a persona that suits everyone?

3. List the information you are likely to emphasize
   about your college life if you write to the following
   people:
   a. A brother or sister
   b. Your parents
   c. Your best friend
   d. A high school teacher
   Does the information you choose affect your persona?

Where voice exists

One important matter that we need to clarify is how and
where voice exists. Although voice may depend on the
actual character of the speaker as we know him, voice can
be created for an audience that doesn't have previous
knowledge of the speaker. For instance, we normally trust
our parents, our brothers and sisters, our friends, and our
teachers because of our previous experience with them.
Their voices are the result of a long series of actions.
However, a skillful rhetorician can create an appropriate
voice almost instantaneously. That's the kind of voice that
we will be concerned with here.

The rhetorical voice or persona exists on paper or in
speech. It grows out of the materials that the speaker uses.
This voice is an artificial character created by the writer to
gain the attention and trust of his audience. It may or may
not bear much relation to the actual character of the writer
or speaker. As a matter of fact, con men usually are quite
skillful in creating personas that people instantly trust. They
create characters who are so seemingly honest and helpful
that complete strangers often trust them with thousands of
dollars. So powerful is their rhetorical ability that they
almost always appear to be extremely sincere.

Teaching you to be a con man is not the goal of this
book. However, you can learn a lot about communicating
and you can have some fun by trying on different voices. As
long as you have some idea of who the real you is and as
long as you aren't planning to deceive anyone, it won't hurt

you to try on different voices, just as you try on different sizes and styles of clothes. Not all these voices will fit you, but you might be surprised to discover a new voice or two that fits pretty well. The ability to use a great many voices is a rhetorical skill that gives you more options, more flexibility, as a rhetorician.

Creating a Voice

Now that we've looked at the strategy behind voices and the social realities on which the theory of voices is based, let's turn to the actual process of creating voices. Let's examine some of the specific devices and techniques we can use to create the kinds of voices that will be most effective for us as rhetoricians.

In creating a voice or persona, you will have to be aware of your relationships to yourself, to your audience, and to your subject. Contributing to these effects will be the way you use words, sentences, and so forth. In investigating these devices, we will probably run into considerable overlap. Nevertheless, we'll try to separate and isolate different elements of the voice so that we can discuss them.

Here are two passages that have quite different personas. Read them, and then we'll see the ways in which the writers create these differences.

I'm 30 years old and I have these dreams.

I dream my knuckleball is jumping around like a Ping-Pong ball in the wind and I pitch a two-hit shutout against my old team, the New York Yankees, single home the winning run in the ninth inning and, when the game is over, take a big bow on the mound in Yankee Stadium with 60,000 people cheering wildly. After the game reporters crowd around my locker asking me to explain exactly how I did it. I don't mind telling them.

I dream I have pitched four consecutive shutouts for the Seattle Pilots and the Detroit Tigers decide to buy me in August for their stretch drive. It's a natural: the Tigers give away a couple of minor-league pheenoms, and the Pilots, looking to the future, discard an aging righthanded knuckleballer. I go over to Detroit and help them win the pennant with five saves and a couple of spot starts. I see myself in the back of a shiny new convertible riding down Woodward Avenue with ticker-tape and confetti covering me like snow. I see myself waving to the crowd and I can see the people waving back, smiling, shouting my name.

I dream my picture is on the cover of *Sports Illustrated* in October and they do a special "Comeback of the Year" feature on me, and all winter long I'm going to dinners and accepting trophies as the Comeback Player of the Year.

I dream all these things. I really do. So there's no use asking me why I'm here, why a reasonably intelligent thirty-year-old man who has lost his fastball is still struggling to play baseball, holding on—literally—with his fingertips. The dreams are the answer. They're why I wanted to be a big-league ballplayer and why I still want to get back on top again. I *enjoy* the fame of being a big-league ballplayer. I get a tremendous kick out of people wanting my autograph. In fact, I feel hurt if I go someplace where I think I should be recognized and no one asks me for it. I enjoy signing them and posing for pictures and answering reporters' questions and having people recognize me on the street. A lot of my friends are baseball fans, as well as my family and the kids I went to school with, and I get a kick out of knowing that they're enjoying having a connection with a guy in the big leagues. Maybe I shouldn't, but I do.[3]

If literary criticism may be said to flourish among us at all, it certainly flourishes immensely, for it flows through the periodical press like a river that has burst its dikes. The quantity of it is prodigious, and it is a commodity of which, however the demand may be estimated, the supply will be sure to be in any supposable extremity the last thing to fail us. What strikes the observer above all, in such an affluence, is the unexpected proportion the discourse uttered bears to the objects discoursed of—the paucity of examples, of illustrations and productions, and the deluge of doctrine suspended in the void; the profusion of talk and the contraction of experiment, of what one may call literary conduct. This, indeed, ceases to be an anomaly as soon as we look at the conditions of contemporary journalism. Then we see that these conditions have engendered the practice of "reviewing"—a practice that in general has nothing in common with the art of criticism. Periodical literature is a huge, open mouth which has to be fed—a vessel of immense capacity which has to be filled. It is like a

---

3. Jim Bouton, "Introduction: Fall, 1968," *Ball Four* (New York: Dell Publishing Co.). Originally published by World Publishing Company. Copyright © 1970 by Jim Bouton. Reprinted by permission of Harper & Row, Publishers, Inc.

regular train which starts at an advertised hour, but which is free to start only if every seat be occupied. The seats are many, the train is ponderously long, and hence the manufacture of dummies for the seasons when there are not passengers enough. A stuffed mannikin is thrust into the empty seat, where it makes a creditable figure till the end of the journey. It looks sufficiently like a passenger, and you know it is not one only when you perceive that it neither says anything nor gets out. The guard attends to it when the train is shunted, blows the cinders from its wooden face and gives a different crook to its elbow, so that it may serve for another run. In this way, in a well-conducted periodical, the blocks of *remplissage* are the dummies of criticism—the recurrent, regulated breakers in the tide of talk. They have a reason for being, and the situation is simpler when we perceive it. It helps to explain the disproportion I just mentioned, as well, in many a case, as the quality of the particular discourse. It helps us to understand that the "organs of public opinion" must be no less copious than punctual, that publicity must maintain its high standard, that ladies and gentlemen may turn an honest penny by the free expenditure of ink. It gives us a glimpse of the high figure presumably reached by all the honest pennies accumulated in the cause, and throws us quite into a glow over the march of civilization and the way we have organized our conveniences. From this point of view it might indeed go far towards making us enthusiastic about our age. What is more calculated to inspire us with a just complacency than the sight of a new and flourishing industry, a fine economy of production? The great business of reviewing has, in its roaring, many of the signs of blooming health, many of the features which beguile one into rendering an involuntary homage to successful enterprise.[4]

A good way to begin discussing the personas in these two passages is to use a rough distinction that critic Walker Gibson uses: the first voice is a talker, while the second is a writer.[5] The first writer, Jim Bouton, writes as though he were talking to us in a kind of monolog, while the second writer, Henry James, sounds like a writer. Nobody could or

4. Henry James, "Criticism," *Literary Opinion in America*, 3rd ed., rev., Morton Dauwen Zabel, ed. Harper Torchbooks (New York: Harper & Row, 1962), I, pp. 47–48.

5. Walker Gibson, *Persona* (New York: Random House, 1969), pp. 5–7.

would talk like that. The whole thing seems premeditated and probably carefully worked on and revised.

How did these two writers create such different personas? What specific techniques and devices did they use?

Stance, Attitude, Tone

Among the major differences between the two passages and the two personas that emerge from them are differences of stance, attitude, and tone.

Stance is the way the writer presents and views himself. Bouton uses the first person point of view or *I* very prominently. He is, of course, talking about his own personal experience, but even in that context, his use of *I* to begin almost every sentence conveys his sense of his own importance. James, on the other hand, generally uses the collective *we* or *us,* and even his occasional use of *I* ("the disproportion I just mentioned") is not very important. Indeed, he seems at times to be referring to himself in the third person as "the observer" whom he mentions in sentence three.

Related to stance, though slightly different, is *attitude.* The attitude is the writer's relationship to his subject matter. Bouton's subject is himself, more particularly his ambitions and feelings. And although he thinks favorably of himself and considers this material worth writing, there is also some irony in his public avowal of his dreams. The dreams are the kind that a twelve-year-old boy might have, but, as Bouton recognizes, they don't quite seem appropriate for a man of thirty. Nevertheless, Bouton claims his dreams, insisting on their authenticity. James's subject is literary criticism, more specifically the kind of reviewing that goes on in periodicals (magazines and newspapers). His attitude is that of a detached but interested observer. He does not look with favor on "reviewing." He carefully distinguishes it from more serious criticism, and uses some unflattering terms to describe it: "paucity of examples," "a huge, open mouth to be fed," "manufacture of dummies," and so forth. And there is a touch of sarcasm as he writes of reviewing as a "successful enterprise." If Bouton's attitude might be summed up as one of genial approval, James's is one of serious critical probing.

The *tone* of the two pieces is also different. Tone is the writer's relationship with his audience. Bouton's tone is open and friendly. He obviously considers himself close to his audience, for he immediately starts telling his readers about what are supposedly his intimate thoughts, his dreams of success and fame. Indeed, in the last paragraph of this passage, he seems to be answering an implied question that goes something like this: "Aren't those rather childish dreams for an adult?" And the seeming frankness of his confessions further assures the readers that Bouton is someone close to them, a talker confessing his innermost thoughts. James is not as close to his audience. Indeed, except for the use of *us* and *we*, James does not seem to address his audience directly. He seems more concerned with the subject itself, though he is probably appealing to an intellectual audience that shares his distrust of periodicals. Nevertheless, the relationship with the audience, the tone of superior knowledge that he shares with his readers, grows out of the treatment of the subject rather than out of any overt concern with audience.

We might conclude by noting that Bouton's persona is chiefly concerned with himself and his audience, while James's persona is chiefly concerned with the subject, the content. Bouton's persona is close to both his subject and his audience, while James's keeps some distance from his subject, at least emotionally, and probably even more distance from his audience.

The projection of these personas also grows out of specific devices of wording, sentence structure, and so forth that the writers use. We'll look at some of those differences.

Words

The words that a writer chooses are one of his chief means for establishing a persona. Often a writer's diction, his choice of words, will tell us about his intellectual abilities, his education, his feelings toward his subject and audience, and perhaps a good deal else. For instance, Bouton's use of baseball jargon—"saves," "spot starts," "stretch drive," and so forth—establishes him as an insider, someone who knows baseball. James's use of educated wording—"affluence," "engendered," "discourse," and "complacency"—indicates that he's probably well educated and certainly quite literate.

If we examine Bouton's passage, we'll find very few words, if any, that the average high school student wouldn't understand. Indeed, Bouton's words are generally colloquial, the kind that people normally use in ordinary conversation. He also uses some phrases—"I get a kick," "I feel hurt," and the emphatic "I really do"—that we are likely to hear in conversation but that we aren't likely to read or to write in situations that normally call for educated usage. This helps him to seem like a talker who is close to both his material and to us, his audience. Moreover, since most of his words are concrete, referring to things rather than ideas, he seems down-to-earth. Finally, Bouton's metaphorical language—"like a Ping-Pong ball in the wind" and "covering me like snow"—is infrequent and unoriginal, again reinforcing the persona as an "ordinary guy."

But if we examine James's passage, we see quite a difference. As we noted, he uses educated words, the kind of words that we might see in print or even write ourselves. They are, however, the kind of words most people, even Henry James, are not likely to use in ordinary conversation. Not that all of James's words are educated; he also uses simple words well and frequently. Nevertheless, his diction is different from Bouton's in this respect. His use of abstract words, words that refer to ideas rather than things, also marks a difference. Words like "criticism," "proportion," "doctrine," and so forth do not represent concrete realities. Moreover, James's use of metaphors, especially the extended metaphor of periodical literature as a train, are not likely to occur in conversation. Keeping the train metaphor in your head as you spoke would be a rare mental feat. All in all, James's use of words reinforces his persona as an educated, thoughtful persona who is more concerned with making his point precisely than he is with appealing to or being friendly with a large audience.

Sentences

The sentences that each writer uses are also effective in creating and maintaining his persona. Many of Bouton's sentences are loose, beginning with the subject (usually *I*) followed by the verb and then by other completing elements. Or else they are loosely joined compound sentences in which main ideas are stuck together by *and*. Very few of the sentences have subordinate clauses. Moreover, a great many of his sentences are extremely short, with fewer than ten words.

James's use of sentences is quite a contrast. His very first sentence begins with a subordinate clause, and the whole sentence is compound and rather long. The third sentence is also very complex. It begins with a relative pronoun in a subordinate clause, followed by a prepositional modifier set off in commas, and the subordinate clause is the subject of the main clause, which contains a further subordinate clause. The sentence then ends with a long complement made up of parallel constructions. The sentence is one that nobody could create and then speak in ordinary conversation. It is a writer's sentence, a carefully planned and artful sentence. And of course most of James's sentences are long and intricate. They too contribute to the persona that we described earlier.

Choosing a Persona

In choosing a persona for your writing, should you write like Jim Bouton or like Henry James? Which is better?

In an absolute sense, neither persona is better than the other. Each is appropriate for its situation, content, and audience. Each is effective. But if we try to make Jim Bouton sound more like a writer, more like Henry James, the results are disastrous. Look at these revisions of Bouton's last paragraph:

In truth I aspire to all these things. It would be useless to ask me why I, as a reasonably intelligent person of thirty who can no longer throw a baseball very swiftly, am struggling to maintain employment as a player, even if only in a marginal fashion. My aspirations are the reason for my having become a player in the major leagues and the reason for my still wanting to achieve success. I enjoy my athletic fame, and I receive great satisfaction from being asked to grant autographs.

The whole persona is changed, and Jim Bouton the writer lacks the appeal of Jim Bouton the talker.

In choosing and developing your own persona, you will probably not write like either Henry James or Jim Bouton. Those two are close to extremes of style. You will probably choose a persona somewhere in between. Indeed, you will probably use quite a few different personas, depending on the situation, the content, the audience, and your own feelings and attitudes about what you're doing. In creating your persona, you will have to control your stance, attitude, tone, wording, sentence structure, and other details.

An important thing for you to remember is that your persona should be a conscious choice, something that you decide upon, not just something that happens to you. Notice, for example, that one writer can use two different personas. Read the two letters and then answer the questions in the exercise that follows.

Dearest Ted,

I've just about had it with mice in the dorm. If they don't do something this week, I'm packing up and heading home.

It just made me and Lois sick to come back to our room and find packs of mice chewing away on my Milky Way. I screamed, and then when I thought of those crummy, icky rodents running all over my food and clothes and bed I just chucked up. I just can't stand this dump. I wish you could be here with me. Then it wouldn't be quite so bad.

Don't worry too much, honey, because really I'm OK and I can always find a place off campus until the end of the semester. I just can't stand ugly rats.

I'll write again tomorrow when I get hold of myself. Take care. I can't wait to see you next month.

Love and kisses,

Sue

Dear President Boone:

The women of Whalley Hall will not stand for mice in their dormitory. Lately there have been mice seen in almost every room in the dormitory. The Resident Advisors can confirm this.

Unless something is done immediately about this disturbing and unhealthful problem, many of us are planning to move out of Whalley for the rest of the semester. After that a good many of the women may leave this college.

I urge the college to take corrective measures immediately.

Respectfully,

Susan B. Yates
Resident of Whalley Hall

Exercises

1. How do Susan's stances differ in the two letters?

2. How do her attitudes differ?

3. How do her tones differ?

4. Are there significant differences in diction?

5. Are there significant differences in sentences?

6. Are there any other differences?

7. How would you describe the personas that emerge in these two letters?

Just as Susan (or Sue, as she calls herself in the first letter) uses two different personas, so, too, will you use or consider various personas in the writing you do for class assignments and for your writing outside of class. The range that's open to you is enormous, all the way from that of the talker, like Jim Bouton, to that of the well educated writer, like Henry James. Most of the time, though, your persona will not be at either extreme. For the kinds of situations and content that we called rhetorical in chapter two, you will probably want a persona somewhere in between. As a bit of practical advice, I'd suggest that you use standard grammar, mechanics, spelling, and other conventions of educated English. While such gifted writers as E.E. Cummings, William Faulkner, and James Joyce consistently violated the norms of standard written English in their writing, they were writing poems, novels, and other imaginative forms. Rhetorical writing is not normally the form for daring experimentation. However, you needn't be afraid to use *I* in your writing, nor should you be afraid to use contractions, colloquial English, and even a slang expression if it suits you. Good expression isn't a straitjacket of rules.

Here are some samples of personas that my own students have used fairly successfully. The following is an essay that one student wrote for a class at the high school from which she graduated. In this essay, she explains what a feminist is.

A feminist is a rebel. The feminist resists the established traditions and customs that society uses to define and control the status of women. The feminist advocates a new conception of women and contests the old. The feminist seeks to free women from the limiting effect of false definitions.

What established traditions and customs does the feminist resist? There are many; "a woman's place is in the home" is one prevalent attitude that feminists are working to change. At an even more basic level, feminists rebel at the definition of women that has made them unequal in status to men. The authority of tradition and custom dictates that certain qualities, called "feminine" characteristics, are requisite to being a woman. For example, to be feminine is to be gentle, weak, and delicate. These qualities, while having the appeal of desirable traits, are really severely limiting for a woman. The feminist feels this definition actually says that women are lacking in strength. The feminist feels that if to be a woman is to be feminine (weak), to be a woman is to be less than a man, for tradition also defines man as strong. The feminist wants to see a woman's abilities defined beyond this old notion.

The feminist supports a new and more realistic concept of women. The feminist defines the status of woman as such: to be a woman is first to be female, the sex that has the potential to produce ova and bear offspring, as opposed to male. Secondly, a woman is an adult female. Feminine qualities such as gentleness, weakness, and delicacy alone only serve to keep women at the level of a child. The feminist wants people to recognize women as capable adults and not as incompetent people just because the traits thought to be appropriate to a woman include weakness.

The feminist advocates expanding the range of a woman's abilities and resists the notion of a woman as "feminine" in this area also. When a woman goes beyond her biological role as a female, "feminine" qualities are even more inappropriate. Whereas gentle, weak, and delicate were perhaps acceptable traits in a mother, they are translated in a new way for a career woman. In the world outside the home, where strength and ability are necessary, "feminine" qualities translate into limiting factors, namely feebleness, frailty, and inferiority. Woman as feminine, therefore weak, cannot survive. The feminist rebels against this ideal that leaves women stuck.

The feminist believes that there are no real qualities of "femininity" determining the status and behavior of women, nor is strength a quality unique to men. The feminist believes that men and women are equally capable of strength and at the same time equally susceptible to weakness. The feminist pushes the idea that once the individual moves beyond that level of biological distinction, men and women are equal with respect to involvement in social relationships, economics, and politics. The feminist rebels at the attitudes that deny women as capable adults their rights and privileges in these areas. The feminist is simply a man or a woman who rebels against notions of women that restrict their lives. Armed with firm conviction, they fight to present a new image of woman to the world.

Even though the writer expresses some very strong opinions in the paper, she manages to keep a somewhat detached and impersonal persona. Among her chief means for attaining that detachment are her strict avoidance of *I,* her avoidance of emotional terms or emotional attacks on her audience, and her use of standard wording and sentence structure. Her use of the phrase *the feminist* rather than *I* is especially effective in making her opinions seem more objective. She seems to be merely explaining the subject rather than haranguing her audience.

This next passage is a brief explanation by a student who has studied journalism. He is explaining the term *mass media* for a friend of his who has not studied journalism:

You have asked me to describe the term *mass media*. Mass media are the network through which the public gets information. Included in this network are television, newspapers, magazines, and radio. It is through the mass media that people like you and me receive the information we need about what happened yesterday, what is happening today, and what might happen tomorrow.

In today's world, the mass media perform a critical task—that of providing information. Think for a moment what you would miss if you didn't have the six o'clock news, or the daily papers, or hourly radio newscasts. Without these services, which we often take for granted, what we know of the world around us would suffer greatly. The mass media are today a necessary part of everyday life, without which we would be lost.

The power of the mass media cannot be overlooked. The entire structure of our country, of the whole world actually, is influenced by it. Look at the Watergate scandal which rocked our nation's government several years ago. The media played a crucial part in uncovering the corruption in the Nixon administration and, some people believe, directly caused its downfall. When someone as powerful as the President of the United States can be affected, it is obvious that the media are a force to be reckoned with.

Mass media have become, in a relatively short period of time, a vast, influential, and highly effective part of our American life. They are often taken for granted, but are not to be underestimated. We may not always notice them, but what would we do without them?

The persona here is a bit more personal. He occasionally uses *I* and he refers to his audience directly by using *you*. His use of rather common examples and illustrations to explain his views shows a closeness to and concern for the audience. Nevertheless, he uses the standard wording and sentence structures of a writer rather than a talker. The persona is that of an informed and friendly conveyor of authoritative information.

The next passage is about the pleasures of chewing tobacco; it was written by a student as an assignment to write an informal essay for a men's magazine. Here are the three opening paragraphs of a substantially longer essay; they should be sufficient to establish the persona:

When it comes to vices, you can take your pick. You can smoke, and ruin your lungs. You can drink, and ruin your liver. You can gamble, and ruin your savings account. Or you can try chewing tobacco, and take a shot at ruining any number of things, not the least of which is your social acceptability.

I've been chewing tobacco for four or five years now. It has not turned my teeth brown, or made me deathly ill, or rotted my mouth away. It may not be the habit most conducive to elite social occasions, but it has its place. It may turn a stomach or two, but it will not cause cancer, or cirrhosis of the liver, or bankruptcy. It is enjoyable, it is relaxing, and it gives the chewer that "real tobacco flavor" that we are told about by television commercials.

Now when I talk about chewing tabacco, I'm talking about what is called scrap, or side chew, or shag tobacco. This is not to be confused with snuff, which is that grainy stuff that comes in cans. Shag tobacco comes in foil pouches, and is cut into leaves which you ball together and stuff into your mouth. It is not as strong as snuff, and also not as easily swallowed. Perhaps it should be pointed out here that swallowing a chew or its juice will lead to severe discomfort. Or, to put it another way, you'll probably lose your cookies. In the words of one veteran chewer, "Learn to spit. If you don't spit, you die." An exaggeration, no doubt, but anyone who has experienced such a gulp will attest to its basic accuracy.

The persona here is still a writer, but he comes very close to being a talker. He's very close to his audience, especially in the first paragraph. He uses *I* quite prominently, and he has a rather light attitude toward his subject. He generally uses a good many colloquial words and phrases—"take a shot at," "turn a stomach," "stuff," "lose your cookies," and "gulp." But he also uses such writer's words as "conducive," "discomfort," and "accuracy." The persona's tone, attitude, and stance all seem appropriate for his subject.

In general, all three personas, though different, are quite acceptable. Each fits the writer's general purpose in each case. It's also interesting to note that although there are three distinct personas here, there were only two writers. Two of the passages were written by the same student, who created both the second and third personas.

The important thing for you as a writer is that the choice of possible personas is quite large. You needn't restrict yourself to just one persona. You will, in fact, want to vary your persona to fit your subject, audience, and purpose. You'll hear even more about this in the next chapter.

The importance of persona

Aristotle considered the personal appeal, the appeal based on the persona or character of the speaker, the most powerful of all means of persuasion. He argued that if an audience trusts a speaker or writer, it will accept his advice and direction, especially on matters about which they have no first-hand knowledge. It is, therefore, very important to create an attractive and convincing persona. But what makes this ideal persona?

According to Aristotle, the ideal voice would be that of a moral, beneficent, and intelligent person. But that is a difficult voice to achieve. A more practical rule is to find the voice that fits the situation and audience. For example, read the following passage and then notice how the writer's personal weaknesses—his failures and his previous attitudes—make his persona more effective. Had a politician, an educator, or some other learned writer said the same thing, the argument would have been far less persuasive. The essay appeared in the New York *Daily News*, and was written by a young man who was then a copyboy but who hoped to become a professional writer. It is called "T-E-A-C-H All Mixed Up is C-H-E-A-T."

I was cheated. And I had to wait until I completed 12 years of elementary and secondary school and two years of college before I discovered it.

The decline of quality education and what to do about it has been a pretty popular topic around town these days, and it might make some sense to look at the problem from the perspective of a recent student, or victim, if you will.

You see, I graduated high school two years ago in the top third of my class, and went to college with dreams of becoming a journalist. It took exactly one year of college to show me that I couldn't write a well-formed composition, or even a grammatically correct sentence for that matter. A second year helped me realize my deficient literary background.

I wasn't alone. Professors had a number of us studying videotapes on grammar, spelling, composition and the like for our own survival. Literary works other profs would use to illustrate a point I never heard of—much less read.

What went wrong? Why wasn't I prepared? Well, in some ways I guess I typify the problem educators face today. I'm black, come from a broken home in a lower middle class neighborhood—and right from the start didn't exactly walk into the classroom each day from a background conducive to learning.

But it was more than that. I went to high school during the progressive era, when educational philosophers were talking about "joyous class-rooms," and we were all demanding courses that were "relevant" (whatever that meant).

The problem, as I look back now, was that the educators all gave in to us too easily. There we were, 15-year-olds, demanding courses that could be directly applied to jobs (practical use, we called it), and there were the teachers succumbing to the pressure.

Whenever a teacher did introduce us to quality work like Hawthorne and Hemingway, we would rebel, using the arguments of relevance and practicality—and they would usually give in. I can still remember beautiful "rap" sessions about Bob Dylan with a history teacher and courses like business math and retail work. Whatever we demanded, they gave us.

We simply had too much freedom. They should have fought us, at least tried to convince us of the benefits of true education. Looking back on an old high school composition, I see a paper filled with comma-splices and misspelling. The grade is 85%.

They tried to give us the "joy" and the "relevance" we were demanding and what we really needed was sentence structure and often a swift boot in the butt.

I got lucky. One day, simply out of boredom, I picked up a copy of *Grapes of Wrath* and was hooked. My mind exploded with interest, and suddenly I realized the world of experience in education I had missed. I have been reading frantically ever since.

I was already in college at the time. I've since quit. I have too much reading and learning to catch up on. Perhaps one day I'll go back.

Teaching is no picnic these days. We were wise-guys in school. Today, from what I read, many kids are plain violent.

But I see clearly now that students must be made to understand that a teacher is there for the purpose of teaching. Progressive education may have had some good influence, in that it led the way toward more open classroom discussions—give and take—in the learning process. But there must be a strict learning process.

Violent children must be separated from the regular classroom, both for their benefit and the benefit of the other students. But educators must realize that often a child acting out in violence is delivering a message about his or her background. And that background should never be used by a teacher as an excuse for a child's inability to learn.

Teachers, in fact, frequently don't realize the major role they play as parent substitutes. Male teachers were especially important to me, perhaps because I never had a real father.

But like parents, good teachers must know when to draw the line. Kids need direction more than relevance.

It looks now like they are beginning to wake up. There is a "back-to-basics" movement in education going on that is putting the emphasis on grammar, literature, history, math and other academic subjects.

For the 37,000 kids who have dropped out of the city high schools each year during the past several years, perhaps it is too late. Maybe a few will get lucky, as I did, and wake up. Society will pay for many others in welfare and even prison costs.

But I still have a younger brother just starting high school, and he already has some problems. I hope they can get to him; I hope they don't cheat him too.[6]

This passage is eloquent testimony to the power of an attractive persona. The young man seems so concerned and so sincere that his arguments take on a credibility that they might not have had if they had come from another persona. Here the persona becomes more important and effective than the content.

Things to Do

1. Read the editorial pages of a daily newspaper—the editorials, the signed columns, and the letters to the editor. Are these voices (personas) all the same, or do they differ? If your newspaper carries them, you

6. Roger House, "T-E-A-C-H All Mixed Up is C-H-E-A-T," New York *Daily News,* sec. C, p. 6. Copyright 1977 New York News Inc. Reprinted by permission.

might compare and contrast the personas of William Buckley, Carl Rowan, Jack Anderson, and other columnists.

2. If there is some newspaper column that you read regularly, analyze the persona that the writer normally uses. What specific techniques and devices does he or she use to create that persona?

3. Read the previous papers you have written in your class (and perhaps for other classes). Did you use the same persona in each paper? Were your personas effective? How could you improve your persona for your next paper?

Writing Assignments

1. Write a brief letter to your best friend explaining how things are going for you at college. Then write to your parents telling them how things are going.

2. Choose a subject about which you know a good deal—a hobby, a sports activity, an organization to which you belong—and explain to your audience how to begin getting involved with this activity, or else persuade it to become involved. You should use a persona that indicates that you have a lot of personal experience with and knowledge of that subject.

3. There is a babysitting service being established on your campus for the benefit of students with preschool children. The service is to be staffed by those who use it. The users will care for children when they are not in class. A question that has arisen is whether, in cases in which both parents are students, fathers as well as mothers should be required to babysit. You are to write three different paragraphs for the editorial page of the college newspaper. You are to use three different personas: a male chauvinist, a women's liberationist, and a persona that best represents your views (which could overlap one of the other two).

4. The following ad appeared in your student newspaper: "Earn $5,000 this summer. National firm needs hard-working, ambitious, aggressive, and intelligent students for summer work. Must be reliable, independent, and capable of making decisions. No experience necessary. Character is more important. Write to Box 407." You are to apply for this job.

5. Go back to the survival problem at the end of chapter two. You are to write to the whole group explaining why you feel you are capable of leading them. In other words, you need to develop your persona so that they will have enough confidence in you to accept your decisions promptly and confidently.

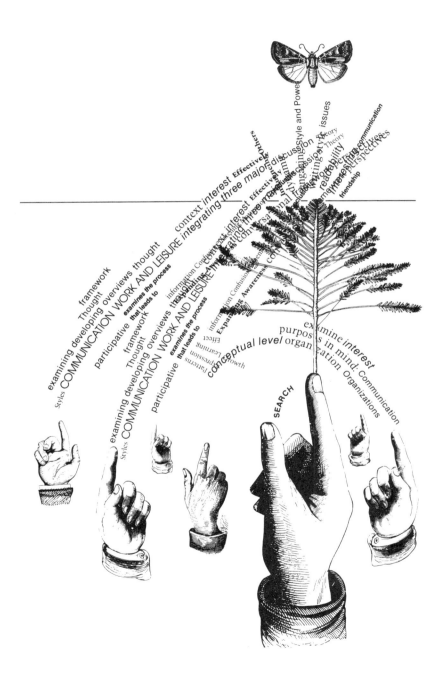

Chapter Five

DISCOVERING WHAT TO SAY

The Problem

In the previous chapters we have looked at the process of rhetoric and then at each of the main elements in the rhetorical situation (content, audience, and persona). Understanding all these things certainly helps us understand the rhetorical process. It helps us understand and evaluate our own rhetoric as well as the rhetoric of others. Moreover, it has given us some suggestions about our own writing. However, our central problem is still ahead of us: how do we know what to say and how to say it? How, in a given rhetorical situation, do we decide on the best strategy for achieving our rhetorical goals?

This problem is the problem of *discovery* or, as classical rhetoricians often called it, *invention*. This chapter and those that follow will attempt to provide a general method for composing and expressing. This chapter will specifically focus on how the major elements in the rhetorical situation—content, audience, persona—interact to produce effective rhetorical writing. You will learn how to consider each in producing a discourse.

Purpose

Before discussing the three major elements in the rhetorical situation, we should probably consider the hidden element in the rhetorical situation: *purpose*. The writer's purpose is a less objective element than the other three. It is often more difficult to identify than content, audience, or persona, for purpose does not exist on paper or in the social framework of the rhetorical situation. Rather it exists in the mind and the heart of the writer. Thus it may not be clear to the audience or even to the writer himself, though he certainly has some general sense of purpose.

Purpose can be considered as really two different purposes, an *external* purpose and an *internal* purpose. The external purpose is the rhetorical goal, what the writer hopes to accomplish in the external or real world. The internal purpose is the rhetorical strategy that the writer uses to achieve his goal. In deliberative rhetoric, of course, the external purpose is some action. For instance, a writer may want you to vote for Jones, buy a Hershey bar, stop littering, or stop smoking. Now if the writer is trying to get you to stop smoking, he has a wide choice of internal purposes or strategies open to him: he could present extensive evidence on how harmful smoking is to your health; he could attempt to scare you out of smoking by presenting a conversation between a widow and her young children, who are asking her when Daddy will be home again; or he could present the personal testimony of a smoker who is dying from lung cancer or some other dreadful disease that results from smoking.

In a judicial or theoretical situation, the external purpose is not so much an action as a judgement. The writer wants you to conclude that Ralph King did not kill Harriet Jonson, that Leif Ericson did land in North America before Columbus came to the New World, or that alien creatures are visiting earth. In such situations, the internal purpose may be quite close to the external purpose. For instance, if a historian is trying to convince other historians that Leif Ericson came to America before Columbus, his internal purpose will probably be to present evidence of Ericson's visits. Thus, the difference between the two purposes might seem small. In a courtroom, however, a lawyer might attempt to persuade his audience, the jury, that his client is not guilty by appealing to their emotions. As comedian Don Adams once asked an all-male jury about an attractive woman accused of killing her husband, "Is that the face of a murderess? Is that the figure of a murderess? Are those the legs of a murderess?"

The important thing for you as a writer is to be aware of just what your external purpose is and then to decide what general approach or strategy will help you achieve that purpose. Too often writers have only a vague sense of external purpose, and they choose the wrong strategy for achieving that goal. Especially on controversial issues, writers often offend or insult the very audience they are attempting to persuade. Let's look again at the letter about abortion, the letter that we looked at in chapter three.

Funny, but when a woman discovers she is pregnant and is glad, she says she is going to have a baby, but when she doesn't want it she calls it a fetus and has it terminated by an abortion. That shows how a change in wording paints an entirely different picture of a situation.

I guess that's why they say a picture is worth a thousand words. Anyone who has ever seen a picture of an aborted baby winces at the grotesquery of the dead child and wonders about the brutal procedure that destroyed that innocent child.

If every day we put the picture of an aborted baby on the front page of this paper, what a fuss would be raised. All of our otherwise apathetic people would call or write deploring the paper for showing such a thing. They would term it "sensationalizing the press."

They said the same thing about the pictures of the victims of the Vietnamese conflict and the starving peoples of Bangladesh.

People, it's not sensationalism; it's the truth—and the truth sure hurts, doesn't it?

Although we can't be sure of the writer's purpose, we can probably make a fairly good guess. Her external purpose may ultimately be to get abortion outlawed, but her more immediate external purpose is probably to get some members of the audience to rethink their moral views on abortion. Her internal purpose or strategy seems to be to get people to realize how advocates of abortion use a change of wording to hide the truth. However, her potentially good point gets lost in her second, third, and fourth paragraphs. In those paragraphs she attempts to support her claim by showing that abortion is physically ugly and repulsive. Such a strategy is not likely to get her audience to reconsider the moral issue. Rather, they are likely to dismiss the letter as mere emotionalism. Thus, the writer's internal purpose is not well suited to achieving her external purpose.

When most of us begin to write in a rhetorical situation, we start with a vague notion of a position or purpose. We are against abortion or pollution. We want fewer restrictions in the dormitories or higher salaries for the work we do. We want others to know that Martin Luther King, Jr., was a great man or that *The Gauntlet* was a bad movie. But unless we stop to think what our specific goal is and what strategy we can use to accomplish that goal, we are likely to write ineffectively. If we merely write the first thing that comes into our minds, our writing will probably satisfy us without persuading anyone else.

Exercises

1. Reread the editorial from *Field & Stream* (chapter three) and then answer the following questions.
   a. What seems to be the writer's external purpose?
   b. What seems to be his internal purpose?
   c. Is the internal purpose well suited to achieve the external purpose?

2. What are the external and internal purposes of the following works?
   a. The instruction booklet for a calculator
   b. A mathematics textbook
   c. A letter proposing marriage
   d. A recipe
   e. A job application

3. Watch some commercials for soda pop on television.
   a. What are the external and internal purposes of these ads?
   b. How are the two purposes related?

Achieving a purpose

The materials that a writer uses will grow out of his purposes. Often the initial purpose or impulse to write is very vague. As that general purpose becomes clearer and both an external and an internal purpose emerge, the need to decide upon a content and a means of developing the content becomes clearer. Sometimes the purpose becomes clear only as the other elements become clear.

Suppose in reading the editorial from *Field & Stream* you are generally dissatisfied with what the author has written. You disagree with him and you'd like to send a letter to him (for publication in the magazine). How are you going to go about it?

You know that your general purpose is to disagree with him, but that isn't sufficient. You have to decide what you are disagreeing with. Do you disagree that the real reason for gun control laws is that politicians are gutless? Or do you disagree that the real causes of crime are the social problems of suffering people? Or do you disagree with some other point? You almost have to decide what your content will be before you can clearly define your purposes in this situation.

The heart of your content will be a claim, an assertion. Whether you state it explicitly in your letter or leave the claim unstated, you should be able to state for yourself the point you want to make. You read over the editorial and you find the focus for your disagreement. You get especially upset with the last sentence in paragraph three and the last sentence in the whole piece. The writer seems to be expressing a version of the slogan, "Guns don't kill people. People do." That's something you can argue with because you know that somehow guns are different from other weapons. Thinking about that, you can now formulate your claim, your chief assertion: Guns make killing easier and less deliberate than other weapons.

You now have a main assertion, and that should help you decide on your purpose. Are you going to try to get all guns outlawed, or to get gun laws tightened? Or will you be content merely to clarify that one point and have your audience reconsider the matter? Your answer to these questions will also come out of your awareness of your audience. Because you know that the readers of *Field & Stream* are unlikely to respond favorably to a call for a complete ban on guns or even for more stringent controls on guns, you will probably be content to make your point about the gun as a matter of information to your audience. Perhaps a part of the audience will rethink the issue. That may be as much as you can hope to accomplish. Your external purpose, then, is to make readers realize that guns are different from other weapons, and your internal purpose is to offer some proof by showing the difference. With so limited a purpose, you can now decide on a persona—the detached, rational observer.

You now have a rhetorical plan for achieving your purposes. All you need is a little more work on developing your content, developing support for your assertion. Your original impulse to write came from the awareness that guns are somehow different from other weapons. You also know that murder rates are generally lower in countries where guns are not readily available. These two bits of material provide sufficient support for what you want to say. Now you write:

Dear Mr. Samson:

Although there is merit to your analysis of the reasons for the new gun control legislation, you may be misleading people when you argue that guns are merely scapegoats when murders are committed. Your argument overlooks the difference between guns and other weapons. Guns make murder easier and less deliberate than it is with other weapons. An enraged man who has a gun can very easily kill his neighbor by pulling the trigger once. If that same man had only his fist, a beer bottle, or even a knife, he might injure his neighbor, but he probably wouldn't kill him. Moreover, a person can better defend himself against other forms of assault, which require close physical proximity.

Proof of the argument is available in the murder statistics of such nations as Switzerland and England. Their murder rates are far lower than that of the United States. The reason is not that the Swiss or English are more moral than Americans or that they don't get enraged with wives, husbands, neighbors, and others. The reason is that they do not have firearms readily available. The results of their rages are more likely to be unpleasant but not fatal.

The very nature of guns ought to be considered in the legislative perspective.

Sincerely yours,

Alan M. Kingston

The analysis of the process of discovery from a vague purpose to a completed response sounded very mechanical. It may also have sounded artificial and unrealistic. And it could be. The process of discovery may begin without a clear purpose and then may grow out of the audience, the persona, or the content. Sometimes a writer may be struck by a single word or a conspicuous metaphor in somebody else's writing. That may become the basis for a whole essay. Thus, the process of discovery may be as unique and as individual as a person's mind and personality. There is no single acceptable method for discovering what to say, nor is there necessarily any fixed order in the process of discovery. Whatever works for you is acceptable.

Nevertheless, the material that follows will suggest a systematic method of discovery based first on content, then on audience, and then on persona. You will, of course, be aware of your purposes and how they affect these rhetorical elements. The suggestions for discovery suggest some specific probes or topics to use in trying to decide what to say and how to say it.

Finding the Issue

In finding and then expressing your content, the major problem is often that of deciding what the issue really is, what the specific point of your writing is. For example, in replying to the *Field & Stream* editorial, the writer did not raise moral issues about the use of guns; nor did he defend the integrity of politicians; nor did he argue that underlying social causes are not the ultimate causes of a lot of crime. He might have argued any one of these points or even all of them. But instead he chose a specific and narrow issue—the nature of guns compared to other weapons.

Another clear illustration of deciding on issues occurs in the courtroom when a lawyer defends a client accused of murder. A lawyer might argue that his client did not commit the act, that his client did not kill Sam Jones. But if there is clear evidence that his client did kill Jones, the lawyer might argue that his client acted in self-defense. That would mean that the killing was not a murder. If there is evidence that the client did not act in self-defense, then the lawyer might try to show that various circumstances should reduce his client's degree of guilt. Maybe the client will plead guilty to manslaughter rather than to murder. The lawyer must decide, based on the evidence available, what the real issues are. He must judge what is not being disputed and what is being disputed. Rhetorical writing normally deals with what is disputed, not with what is not under dispute.

In deciding upon the issue, you will then probably want to express your main point in a clear assertion, a single declarative sentence that states your point precisely. Even if you never use that exact sentence in your writing, it should help you clarify your thinking and decide which content to use. Often, however, you will want to clarify issues quite explicitly, as McGeorge Bundy does in the following paragraphs:

> I labor this point because both logic and sentiment suggest that it may be central to the thinking of a great many Americans, however little it may appear in records and arguments. *No one is arguing for the admission of the*

unqualified, and there is no finding in Bakke *that such admissions have occurred.* Indeed, there is not in *Bakke* any serious legal challenge to the generally accepted proposition that the elemental decision on whether a candidate is qualified for medical school must be left to the professional judgment of faculties and their agents.

So the issue actually presented to the Supreme Court is also the issue presented as a matter of real choice in our whole system of higher education. The question is not, as emotion so often suggests, whether we should push forward unqualified people. The question is much more subtle: Among the qualified, how shall we choose?[1]

After deciding upon the issue or issues that you wish to argue, you must then find support for the assertions you make. What follow are some of the main forms of support that you can use to bolster your claims about content.

Defining

Often the chief issue in a piece of writing or one of the chief forms of support for an assertion hinges on the meaning of a word. For instance, in an argument on abortion, someone might claim that abortions are unconstitutional because Article V of the Bill of Rights says that "No person . . . shall be . . . deprived of life . . . without due process of law." But if a writer is going to make that argument convincing, he will have to prove that an unborn baby, a fetus, is a *person*. Or to put the argument another way, he will have to prove that the word *person* refers to those not yet born as well as those already born.

At times, the definition itself may be the whole purpose of writing. A writer may want to explain to you what a certain term means. This is especially true in school and college, where a great deal of the learning you do is verbal, concerned mainly with words. Think, for example, of all the terms that you've learned for the first time or that you've

1. McGeorge Bundy, "The Issue Before the Court: Who Gets Ahead in America?" *The Atlantic Monthly* (November 1977), p. 47.

learned wholly new meanings for in this text alone. Terms like *persona* and *rhetorician* may be wholly new to you, while words like *rational* and *personal* have probably taken on new meanings that they didn't have for you before.

Before going any further, we will probably need a definition of just what *defining* is. Defining is a process of explaining what a word means. It deals with words and their uses. Now when we say that we want to know what a word means, what we are doing is placing it in its proper context (linguistically, culturally, historically, etc.). For example, when we pick up a dictionary and look up the word *moment,* we are trying to discover how speakers of English use that word most of the time; the phrase "a brief indefinite period of time" will satisfy us. But in a good dictionary we will also discover that a statistician in his work uses the term to mean "the expected value of a positive integral power of a random variable." Similarly, a good dictionary will also give nominalistic (historical) definitions such as the definition of *humour* in Elizabethan English.

Definitions that explain what words mean to the users of a language are *lexical* definitions, the kind of definitions that we find in dictionaries. Such definitions are useful in clarifying many arguments based on the ordinary uses of words.

Often, however, we will not be content with lexical definitions. In arguing a point to clarify an issue, we will not be content with a lexical definition. We may resort to a *stipulative* definition, a definition that we choose or that we create to suit our purposes. For example, if we say that "all men are created equal," we may want to stipulate that by *men* we mean *human beings,* not just *males.* Thus, we have chosen or stipulated one specific meaning from the acceptable ranges of lexical definitions. But in some situations we may want to go beyond the dictionary and actually construct our own definitions. For instance, if a sociologist is investigating the effects of poverty in a certain community, he may have to come up with a stipulative definition of poverty. He may say something like this: "For purposes of this study, a family unit will be considered *poor* if its total net income is less than $7,000 a year."

This stipulative definition is neither correct nor incorrect. Rather it is a convenient definition, one that allows the sociologist to say that a family either is or is not poor, at least by that definition. It is a special extension of what would otherwise be a vague term. Such definitions are especially helpful for specialized studies. We can more easily classify *gifted* students by defining them as "achieving a score of 140 on the Stanford-Binet test" than by defining them as "intellectually superior." Moreover, such definitions are extremely helpful as long as we recognize their limitations. First, we should remember that stipulative definitions are not lexical definitions. Second, we should recognize that while stipulative definitions are convenient, they may not always be doing the job that we expect them to. For example, a student might be intellectually superior but she might not be able to do well on a standard test because of a problem with her eyes. Third, we should be sure that our stipulative definition bears some relationship to the normal use of the term we are using (unless we are inventing a completely new term). For example, if we defined a poor family as "one having a net income of less than $50,000 a year" our definition would not be very helpful in studying poverty, at least according to the ordinary uses of the word.

As writers, we will often want to use *extended* definitions, definitions so thorough and full that the audience will have a deep and extensive knowledge of the term. Such a definition might use both lexical and stipulative definitions and might use many different approaches to defining. The normal pattern of defining is something like this:

term = class + difference:

Man is an *animal*.

Man, as distinct from other members of the class, is *rational*.

Man is a *rational animal*.

Basically we have a process of analysis; we put a word in a class and start describing it in such a way as to separate it from all other things in the class. Thus, by adding qualifications, we come up with a definition like this: "A woman is an adult, female human being." In actual practice, however, we will probably use a variety of strategies and devices for our extended definitions. No list of them could be complete, but what follows is a list that may help you; it is based on a list used by Harold C. Martin and Richard M. Ohmann in *The Logic and Rhetoric of Exposition.*[2]

1. *Synonym:*
   Charity is love.

2. *Analysis:*
   A *woman* is an adult, female human being.

3. *Synthetically* (in relationship to something else):
   Victorian poets are those English poets who wrote during the reign of Queen Victoria.
   Clergy means priests, ministers, rabbis, gurus and so forth.

4. *Negation:*
   The *whale* is not a fish.

5. *Likeness:*
   A *parasol* is like an umbrella.
   (or metaphorical):
   A *poet* is a man who stands out in storms all his life and once or twice is struck by lightning.
       —Randall Jarrell
   (or by comparison and contrast):
   A *strudel* is like a pie, but a lot smaller.

6. *Ostensive definition* (showing):
   This is a *fist*.

7. *Example:*
   An *epic* is a poem like *The Iliad* or *Paradise Lost* or *The Aeneid*.

8. *Functional:*
   A *wrench* is something that turns nuts.

---

2. Harold C. Martin and Richard M. Ohmann, *The Logic and Rhetoric of Exposition,* rev. ed. (New York: Holt, Rinehart and Winston, 1963), pp. 35–39.

(or operational):

work = force × distance

W(ft.–lb.) = F(lb.) × D(ft.)

$$Specific\ gravity = \frac{\text{weight of object}}{\text{weight of equal volume of water}}$$

9. *Etymology* (history):
Philosophy comes from the Greek words *phil* (love) and *soph* (wisdom).

Some good examples of extended definitions are the definitions of *feminist* and of *mass media,* both in chapter four. These aim at giving the reader insights into what the terms really mean.

Examples of how definitions are used to argue a point are found in several of the passages. The letter to the editor about abortion earlier in this chapter focuses on defining a term in its first paragraph and then concludes by arguing that the phrase "sensationalizing the press" actually means "the truth." Less vehemently, but still rather clearly, the definition of *natural science* in chapter two seems to argue that only those branches of knowledge that can obtain *reproducibility* deserve to be called *sciences.* That is a rather typical pattern for using definition: to establish a general definition or pattern of meaning and then to apply that pattern to a specific case or instance. For instance, we might argue that marijuana is a safer substance to use than ordinary cigarettes because it is not addictive. An addictive substance is one that causes physical changes in the user's body, thus making withdrawal from the substance physically uncomfortable. For instance, withdrawal from cigarettes, as any regular smoker knows, produces actual physiological symptoms, while withdrawal from marijuana does not.

Whether that argument about marijuana is convincing or not, it does show how definitions are used in arguments. Indeed definitions are widely used in all forms of rhetoric. They may be used merely to clarify terms or issues, they may be used to help a reader understand something more fully, or they may be used as standards by which to measure individual acts, situations, persons, institutions, and so forth. Much of what goes on in the courtroom deals with applying stipulative definitions (which laws are) to fit specific actions. The facts in a murder trial may be absolutely clear to everyone, but the jury or the judge may have to decide whether the defendant's actions are closer to the legal definition of first-degree murder, second-degree murder, or manslaughter. In an English class you may have to decide whether a book like Truman Capote's *In Cold Blood* is fiction or non-fiction, or whether Gerard Manley Hopkins is a Romantic poet.

Comparing

Another important means of developing or supporting an assertion is through *comparison*. If you claim that Babe Ruth is the greatest baseball player ever, you are implicitly comparing him to every other player who ever played baseball. You will need to present support that relates Babe Ruth and his achievements to other players and their achievements. In general you will probably have to use both *comparison* (likeness) and its opposite, *contrast* (unlikeness).

If we turn back to the letter in this chapter by Alan M. Kingston, we see that the main assertion is based on a comparison—the difference between a gun and other weapons. Moreover, one of his chief supports is based on the comparison of murder rates in the United States, England, and Switzerland. Had he wished to do so, Kingston might have gone into much greater detail to show how guns differ from blackjacks, pick handles, knives, and forks.

Sometimes the comparison itself is at the very heart of the argument. Notice how Rachel Carson uses comparison and contrast to open one section from *Silent Spring:*

We stand now where two roads diverge. But unlike the roads in Robert Frost's familiar poem, they are not equally fair. The road we have long been traveling is deceptively easy, a smooth superhighway on which we progress with great speed, but at its end lies disaster. The other fork of the road—the one "less traveled by"—offers our last, our only chance to reach a destination that assures the preservation of our earth.

The choice, after all, is ours to make. If, having endured much, we have at last asserted our "right to know," and if, knowing, we have concluded that we are being asked to take senseless and frightening risks, then we should no longer accept the counsel of those who tell us that we must fill our world with poisonous chemicals; we should look about and see what other course is open to us.

A truly extraordinary variety of alternatives to the chemical control of insects is available. Some are already in use and have achieved brilliant success. Others are in the stage of laboratory testing. Still others are little more than ideas in the minds of imaginative scientists, waiting for the opportunity to put them to the test. All have this in common: they are *biological* solutions, based on understanding of the living organisms they seek to control, and of the whole fabric of life to which these organisms belong. Specialists representing various areas of the vast field of biology are contributing—entomologists, pathologists, geneticists, physiologists, biochemists, ecologists—all pouring their knowledge and their creative inspirations into the formation of a new science of biotic controls.

"Any science may be likened to a river," says a Johns Hopkins biologist, Professor Carl P. Swanson. "It has its obscure and unpretentious beginning; its quiet stretches as well as its rapids; its periods of drought as well as of fullness. It gathers momentum with the work of many investigators and as it is fed by other streams of thought; it is deepened and broadened by the concepts and generalizations that are gradually evolved."

So it is with the science of biological control in its modern sense. In America it had its obscure beginnings a century ago with the first attempts to introduce natural enemies of insects that were proving troublesome to farmers, an effort that sometimes moved slowly or not at all, but now and again gathered speed and momentum under the impetus of an outstanding success. It had its period of drought when workers in applied entomology, dazzled by the spectacular new insecticides of the 1940s, turned their backs on all biological methods and set foot on "the treadmill of chemical control." But the goal of an insect-free world continued to recede. Now at last, as it has become apparent that the heedless and unrestrained use of chemicals is a greater menace to ourselves than to the targets, the river which is the science of biotic control flows again, fed by new streams of thought.[3]

3. Rachel Carson, *Silent Spring* (Boston: Houghton Mifflin, 1962), pp. 277–79. From *Silent Spring* by Rachel Carson. Copyright © 1962 by Rachel L. Carson. Reprinted by permission of Houghton Mifflin Company.

The whole argument about which path to follow is based on the contrast between filling "our world with poisonous chemicals" and managing the *"biological* solutions, based on understanding of the living organisms they seek to control. . . ."

In developing the argument, Rachel Carson relies not only on a direct comparison of two kinds of control of insects (chemical and biological), but she also relies on figurative comparisons, analogies or metaphors that compare things that literally are not the same. At the very beginning she compares the two choices to a fork in the road. She develops this comparison further by suggesting that one road is a "smooth superhighway." A bit further on, she uses a quote from Professor Swanson, which is mainly an analogy developing the likeness between science and a river. Now nobody would actually confuse science and a river by trying to wash himself with science, but a reader can understand the similarities between the two. This metaphor works to convince the reader that a brand new science, like a small stream, can easily grow larger, just as a river increases in its travels.

We use metaphors and analogies quite frequently. We use them both for purposes of clarifying and for purposes of persuasion. For instance, when we use a proverb like "People who live in glass houses shouldn't throw stones," we are trying to persuade someone to change his actions. We often clarify our points by relying on analogies. We might say, "Belonging to a fraternity is like being a member of a family," or "Doing math problems in your head builds your mind just as physical exercise builds and stretches muscle."

The use of comparison and contrast in writing is extremely common. It is used both to clarify and to persuade. Any time a writer makes a claim that compares two things, whether implicitly or explicitly, he will probably use comparison and contrast. If the main assertion contains phrases like "most important," "best," "better than," "superior to," and so forth there will be some comparing and contrasting. Moreover, claims in deliberative rhetoric are often supported by comparisons from the past. For instance, a writer might assert that any and all drugs ought to be made legally available to adults. To support this claim he might argue that such a change might greatly reduce crime. As support, he could show that the repeal of Prohibition (which had made alcoholic beverages illegal) greatly reduced the crimes associated with alcohol: the bootleggers were out of business. Such a strategy is extremely common, as are many other uses of comparison.

Cause and effect

Another focus for persuasion is the use of arguments about causes and effects. In deliberative rhetoric, we often argue that following a certain policy or course of action will lead to certain results. The person arguing for legalizing all drugs points to the beneficial effect of a reduction in crime. Someone who disagrees with him might argue that legalizing harmful drugs will lead to hordes of deranged addicts. In judicial or theoretical rhetoric, we often argue that certain effects, certain conditions existing now or occurring in the past, are the result of causes that occurred in the past. A politician or educator might argue that college students can't write well because they watched too much television or because they weren't taught grammar or because their parents didn't discipline them. Historians still write about the causes for the decline of Rome, the reasons for the rapid rise of Christianity, and the reasons for the decline of Spain as a world power after the sixteenth century.

The editorial from *Field & Stream* is a fine example of how cause and effect arguments are used to persuade. First, Jack Samson explains the causes of new gun control laws—politicians seeking to avoid the truth. Second, he argues that the real causes of crime are not guns but suffering people. Finally, he argues that the only cause that will reduce crime is massive social reform. In the first two cases Samson is arguing from present effects (gun control laws and crime) to their causes (politicians and suffering people), while in the third he is arguing from certain actions or causes (social reform) to an effect that he expects to occur (the reduction of crime).

The analysis of causes and effects is a complex process. A great deal of what you will learn in the sciences and the social sciences is the methodology for analyzing causes. You will also learn about causality in subjects like philosophy and history. Causality is a subject that has challenged great minds. Thus, to try to establish any few simple rules for you would be presumptuous. Perhaps, though, it would be worthwhile to suggest that you need to be cautious about analyzing causes in human affairs. Widespread occurrences or great historical changes do not occur for any one reason. The reasons for the fall of Rome, the decline of Spain, or the lack of reading and writing ability among college freshmen are not the result of single causes. These events result from whole groups and combinations of things. Similarly, being raised in a ghetto does not necessarily cause a person to become a murderer, yet it may contribute to that effect.

However cautiously, you *will* reason about causes and effects in human affairs. The process is so natural and so important that it is neither possible nor desirable to avoid it.

Evidence

Evidence refers to specific facts or truths that are readily verifiable and on which people are likely to agree. They are often supported by books, people, and ultimately things. They are a kind of check on the tendency of human beings to draw conclusions based on theory alone. For instance, if someone were to argue that women are biologically incapable of doing good scientific research, you could disprove that assertion by bringing up Marie Curie, who did a great deal of the first important research on radioactivity.

The kinds of evidence you may use can be found in standard reference sources like encyclopedias, almanacs, government studies, books, and magazines. Or you may use evidence based on your own personal experience or on the experience of others whom you know or trust. Ultimately you may even be able to use physical evidence itself: bone samples, chips of pottery, fingerprints, or other things that prove your assertions.

The value of printed evidence varies from source to source. Some sources are likely to be highly accurate and reliable, while others are quite unreliable. You can probably be sure that actor Robert Redford broke his arm in a fall if you read it in a reputable daily newspaper, but you can't be sure that his marriage is in trouble just because you read it is the gossip column of a movie magazine. You are probably already aware of those broad differences, and as you progress in your education you will become even more sophisticated and knowledgeable in judging sources of evidence. To attempt to solve the problem in so short a space is beyond the scope of this text.

The value of personal evidence can be quite high if you use it carefully and don't try to claim too much for what you actually know. For instance, if you have spent your whole life in a small town and have attended a public school system there since kindergarten, you probably have little valuable personal experience to justify the claim that American schools repress and discourage superior achievement. If, however, you have moved around a lot and have been in a dozen different school systems in various parts of the country, you might very well argue a strong case based on personal experience. And you can often rely on the experience of those who are knowledgeable about a subject. For instance, a medical doctor can often provide valuable testimony on the effect of certain drugs on the human body.

Physical evidence, if it is available, is often the most convincing and valuable form of evidence. For instance, when kidnappers are holding a victim, they often take photographs of the person holding that day's front page on a daily newspaper. That proves that the hostage is alive (or was alive at least until the time the newspaper was printed). In arguing that Leif Ericson came to America before Columbus, the most impressive evidence a historian can produce is physical evidence—artifacts like tools, personal effects, ships, and so forth that are found in North America and can be attributed to Vikings. In a courtroom, the value of fingerprints is almost certain to outweigh conflicting human testimony.

In general, evidence can be an important and valuable means of support. Especially on matters of judicial rhetoric or theoretical rhetoric, facts are extremely important. If you can assemble enough facts from reliable sources, you may be able to prove assertions about the past. But evidence is not likely to be crucial on matters of deliberative rhetoric. Evidence can show what things were or what they are now; it cannot prove what they will be. Consider the use of evidence about Helio-Thermics, a solar heating system:

More promising, though, is the design now being marketed by a little company in South Carolina called Helio-Thermics. Inspired by the hotness of attics in conventional houses, and working under a cooperative agreement with Helio-Thermics, an architect named Harold Zornig and an engineer named Luther Godbey, both employ-ees of the Department of Agriculture's Rural Housing Research Unit in South Carolina, designed this hot-air system. *Mother Earth News* has gushed over it. Indeed, it looks like one of the cheapest of all the heating systems available today. Sunshine gets into the Godbey-Zornig house through a double-glazed, translucent, fiber-glass roof, and strikes sheets of black-painted plywood located in the attic, heating up the air. Some heat moves into the living space by itself. There is also a one-half horsepower blower, hidden in a closet and activated by a device which Helio-Thermics likes to call "a computer" and which Godbey describes as "just a plain old solid-state control device." The blower drives air through the attic and down into the storage system, a bin containing forty tons of railroad ballast and located directly beneath the house's main floor. The system has worked well, delivering about 75 percent of the first Helio-Thermics house's necessary heat during an average 40° F winter in South Carolina. The "incremental" cost of this system in the little prototype house, which has 1000 square feet of floor space, was less than $3000. For a few hundred dollars more, the system can also provide 50 percent of the energy for a home's hot-water heating. These figures, which come from the USDA, probably make this system economical today. The trick to cutting incremental cost, Luther Godbey told me, is designing the system right into the house, using the solar collector to replace the roof, placing the store right in the foundation. He and Zornig also strove to minimize the use of expensive components such as ductwork.[4]

All the evidence, the factual details—seventy-five percent, forty-degree winter, $3,000, and so forth—support the assertion that "this system [is] economical today." They do not prove that the United States should begin converting to this solar heating system exclusively or immediately. The facts *do* show that a certain kind of heating system is practical in one area of the country.

Similarly, the evidence of personal experience or testimony can be very convincing. Here is part of the support one student used in explaining why she now thinks well of the mayor of her city.

My family and I live on a small street on the east side. The street hadn't been plowed in a few days and the snow was at car hood level. The lady next door called the city garages and complaint department at least a dozen times that day but to no avail. Finally at 8:00 P.M. she called the mayor's house. (Surprisingly enough, his number is listed in the phone book.) The mayor took the call and assured the woman that there would be a plow there in thirty minutes. He instructed her to tell the operator of the plow just how she wanted the street plowed and if she had any more complaints to call him back. The lady came over and told us what had just happened. I couldn't believe it! Sure enough, a plow was there in twenty minutes.

This personal testimony is excellent support for her assertion that the mayor is really concerned about the citizens of the community.

The methods of development—of finding and using materials—that we have looked at so far deal mainly with content. In the rest of the chapter, we will look at how audience and persona will affect the materials and methods we use in writing. Finally, at the end of the chapter, there

4. Tracy Kidder, "Tinkering with Sunshine," *The Atlantic Monthly* (October 1977), p. 78. Copyright © 1977 by the Atlantic Monthly Company, Boston, Mass. Reprinted with permission.

will be an outline suggesting how we may use all these separate devices in constructing our own writing.

Exercises

1. What kind of support will the following assertions probably need?
   a. The reason for the city's high crime rate is the great number of drug addicts.
   b. San Diego has the most healthful climate in the United States.
   c. The United States should solve its medical crisis through socialized medicine.
   d. Unless the federal government provides massive aid and supervision, the United States will not have a first-class educational system.
   e. The proportion of drug addicts among our young people is not surprising if one considers how older Americans use drugs, including alcohol.
   f. The spread of pornography in our society is like a cancer eating away at our morality.
2. Choose one of the assertions from the group above and indicate three specific pieces of evidence that you might use to support the assertion, either directly or indirectly.

Audience

The analysis of the kinds of things you might say about your subject, the kinds of support you might use, reveals the possibilities of the content. There are lots of different things you could say about almost any subject. But one of the limitations or constraints on what you actually say will be your audience. There will be some material that your audience cannot understand, and there will be arguments that it will not want to listen to. Some arguments will be especially appealing to your audience, while others are likely to offend it.

In deciding what you will say, you will have to analyze your audience carefully. You will have to decide who the audience actually is, what its intellectual abilities are, and what its attitudes and beliefs are.

Identifying the audience

One of your first jobs as a writer is to decide who your audience is. In some cases, your actual audience may be a single person whom you know quite well: a sister, a friend, a parent, a teacher, a boss, or an employee. In that case the question of audience is really quite simple.

In other cases, however, your audience may be a single person, but it may be someone whom you don't know personally or whom you scarcely know. For example, you may have to write to the president of your college, your senator, your state representative, the personnel manager of a company with which you are seeking a job, or a customer of the company for which you work. In a situation like this, part of your job is to decide just how you are going to treat that specific audience. Perhaps a good place to start is to consider that person's role in relation to you and what you have to say. Although the audience is a real person, you as a rhetorician will be creating an audience to fit your purposes and content. Thus, in writing to one of your company's dissatisfied customers, you might begin in this way:

Dear Ms. Cameron:

Because you are one of our oldest and most valuable customers, we at ASCO are concerned that you were dissatisfied with our last shipment to your firm. You have always treated us well, and we in turn have tried to serve your needs with high-quality products and service.

Such an opening to the letter is meant to placate the audience by assuring her that she is a valuable customer whom the company is anxious to serve. In effect, that opening defines the audience for the writer. His concern is with Elizabeth Cameron, customer, not Elizabeth Cameron, stamp collector, surfer, Unitarian, or anything else. Basically, the audience is a character whom the writer creates to fit the situation and content. Of course, the way the writer addresses the audience should also bear some relation to the facts in the situation and to the woman's personality.

In writing to a clearly identifiable group, you will probably have to define your audience by what it has in common with your content. In other words, you must evaluate its interest in or position on your subject. Thus, if you wanted the parents at your child's school to get angry about the poor quality of the math curriculum at the school, you, as president of the PTA, would probably identify your audience as "concerned parents." That audience identification would give you a focus for what you have to say about the curriculum.

In writing for publication, however, you seem to be writing for everybody. Your tendency is to think that your audience is whoever happens to read you. But to define your audience that way is a mistake. When you are faced with what seems like a vast audience, you must think about your audience more carefully. For instance, if you write to your college newspaper, you know that the audience will be mainly students, teachers, and other officials of the college. If you write to *Field & Stream,* you know that your readers will be hunters and fishermen. Even beyond analyzing readership, you may want to define your audience more narrowly by appealing to a more specific group. In writing to the college newspaper, your actual audience might be dormitory residents, basketball fans, women, foreign students, math majors, or some other specific group. At times the audience will be defined mainly by the writer's content and attitude toward it, as in this letter to a daily newspaper:

I sometimes wonder what our country is trying to do, especially to those on a fixed income and the poor and middle income bracket. Every time you pick up the paper prices are constantly going up.

The Erie County Energy Alternatives are trying in every way to prevent the P.U.C. [Pennsylvania Utility Commission] from adding more to our burdens. On September 21, 1976, at City Hall Chambers, from 10 A.M. to 4 P.M. there will be an open hearing on the new National Fuel Gas proposed increase. Please join us in this battle to keep warm this winter without the fear of having our gas shut off because we were not able to pay the high bills. We have a right to the necessities of life without having to fight the P.U.C. too.

I would hate to see some of their employees go through with the provocation we have to. So, again, I say to you be present September 21, 1976 and voice your objections.[5]

The letter partially defines the audience as "those on a fixed income and the poor and middle income bracket," but it then goes on to implicitly define the audience as those who oppose higher prices for natural gas. The writer invites those people to participate in a public hearing. Although this letter is aimed at a very large audience, it is not aimed at everybody. It probably will not appeal to the wealthy, to whom high gas bills are not a major burden, nor to officials of the gas company.

In sum, whether writing to an audience of one person or a potential audience of millions, you must have a clear idea of who your audience is or what potential audience you are aiming for. Just as you identify the issue in developing content, so must you identify and sometimes create the specific audience to whom you are writing.

The mind of the audience

After deciding who your actual audience is and how you are going to define it, you will then have to make some judgements about its intellectual level. You will want to know how knowledgeable your audience is about your subject, and you will want to judge its general intellectual level.

The knowledge that an audience has about a subject will affect both your content and your style. For instance, if you have discovered massive pollution in a nearby river, you might write two different articles about it for two different magazines. In a scientific journal written for other scientists, you might discuss algae counts, mercury index, and so

5. Letter, Erie *Times,* September 20, 1976, sec. A, p. 4.

forth. But in writing for the general public, you would probably use much less technical material. You might dwell on the dead fish, the stench of the water, the excessive weeds. Your content, your support, and your attitude toward your audience would probably be different in each article.

Generally speaking, you can be more detailed and technical if your audience is thoroughly familiar with your subject. If your audience consists of experts on the subject, you won't want to dwell on the basics, the commonplaces. But if you have a general or a novice audience, you will have to be much less technical. One of the real challenges any writer faces is trying to explain his hobby or special interest to somebody who knows little about the subject. Magazines are full of articles telling newcomers how to buy their first mopeds, CB radios, skis, or motorboats.

Judging the general intellectual level of your audience is a fairly complex task. It involves judging such things as the occupation, education, sophistication, experience, and general knowledge of your audience. If your audience is only one person, you may miss the mark badly. But if you are writing to an identifiable group or to the readers of a certain publication, you can probably make some fairly educated guesses about your audience. You have been making such judgements for a good part of your life, and as you grow in knowledge and sophistication, you will get better at it. You are aware, for instance, that people in the professions—doctors, lawyers, teachers, and the clergy—are usually more educated and more sophisticated than people in the crafts—plumbers, carpenters, bricklayers, and so forth. You know that people who work in the sciences— engineers, chemists, biologists—are better able to judge scientific evidence than those without familiarity with the sciences.

Having made a general assessment of your audience, you will then adjust your material to fit that audience. First, you will use a vocabulary that fits the educational level of your audience. You will not want to use a vocabulary so sophisticated that your audience won't be able to understand. Second, you will use supporting material that is within your audience's range of experience. Using quotations from Latin or Greek poets or references to ancient philosophers probably won't be very effective in communicating with the readers of *Popular Mechanics* or *Better Homes and Gardens*. Third, you will use evidence that your audience can understand. A group of citizens who are concerned about pollution in the local river need an explanation that they can understand. Presenting an explanation in scientific formulas would not be very effective.

Look at the two passages below. One is an explanation of a proverb for a student in the fifth grade. The other is the opening paragraph of the editor's column in *Harper's*, a magazine that has an audience of well educated readers who are interested in politics, literature, and the arts. The intellectual levels of the two passages are quite different.

"Don't count your chickens before they're hatched" means don't count on something to happen, because something might occur that will spoil it. Here is an example. Suppose you were going to a football game with your dad. Let's say your dad knew Joe Namath, who was going to be at the game, and he promised to introduce him to you. You bet money with your friends that you would be able to get Joe's autograph.

So now you're at the game and you're going to meet Joe after the game. But during the game one of Joe's legs gets broken again; he is taken to the hospital and you never get to see him. When you get home your friends are waiting, and you don't have his autograph. You end up having to pay your friends.

You see that you counted your chickens before they were hatched. You took it for granted that you would see Joe and didn't take into consideration that something could go wrong, which it did; and you had to pay for it.

Much of the pleasure associated with editing *Harper's* comes from reading the mail. The readers of the magazine show themselves to be a company of knowledgeable critics—sometimes discursive, often eloquent, always suspicious of the seasonable opinions put up for sale by the literary impresarios in New York City. They do not suffer peaceably the pronouncements of those whom they regard as fools, and they distrust the use of extravagant rhetoric. Toward the end of the summer I received a letter from a gentleman in Placerville, California, who said that he didn't want to read any more tendentious statements about Richard M. Nixon. He had met

Mr. Nixon several years ago, he said, and he didn't like the fellow, but he thought that anybody who wanted to denounce Mr. Nixon as the Antichrist ought to give specific reasons. Quite frequently the readers write at length, taking the trouble to set forth their views on the fall of Rome, the presence of parasites in the intestines of wolves, the failure of the Western ideal of citizenship, or the general lack of appreciation for the works of Louis-Ferdinand Céline. Sometimes they send suggestions for further reading, in the hope, usually forlorn, that the editor will "find his way back to the precincts of reason"; at other times they enclose passages from the anthologies of moral authority. Quotations from Plato usually appear in letters commending the magazine, those from Ezra Pound in letters that revile it.[6]

The adjustment of the material to the intellectual levels of the two audiences takes several forms. The vocabulary of each passage is different. Most of the words in the passage to the fifth grader are simple words that even a fifth grader could understand. But a fifth grader or even a college freshman may not know the meanings of such words in the *Harper's* piece as *discursive, tendentious,* and *forlorn.* Also, the range of materials used in each is quite dissimilar. The first writer's example is Joe Namath, a sports figure whom most Americans, especially young boys, will know. Lewis Lapham, the editor of *Harper's,* refers to one well-known American, Richard M. Nixon, but his other references are to Céline (a modern French novelist), Plato (an ancient Greek philosopher), and Ezra Pound (an influential but not a popular American poet). Finally, the explanation of the proverb is pretty direct. The hypothetical example does just what it's supposed to. However, the evidence that Lapham provides that those who write to him are "knowledgeable critics" is not all that clear and convincing. We, as readers, have greater room for judgement. All in all, then, the intellectual level of the audience has greatly affected the way the two pieces were written.

You should be careful to note that education and

---

6. Lewis H. Lapham, "The Easy Chair: Answering the Mail," *Harper's* (November 1976), p. 18. Copyright © 1976 by *Harper's* Magazine. All rights reserved. Reprinted from the November 1976 issue by special permission.

sophistication are not the same as intelligence. Many people, though they lack extensive formal education or wide experience from reading or travel, are quite intelligent, often far more intelligent than those with better educations. Therefore, you should not try to deceive an audience with shallow reasoning or poor evidence just because that audience is uneducated. You must fit your material to the audience's experience, but you mustn't assume that it is stupid.

The heart of the audience

Knowing your audience's intellectual level is only half of your job in writing to it. The other half of the job is to understand your audience's emotional position—its feelings, values, beliefs, and dispositions. Such knowledge will help you decide what material to use and what arguments will be effective.

Judging the emotional disposition of your audience may be a bit easier than judging the intellectual level. You have some knowledge of people's positions from your own experience. You know, for instance, that older people are likely to be more conservative and more resistant to change than younger people, especially in their moral, political, and social values. You know that Republicans are likely to be more conservative than Democrats, and that college professors are likely to be more liberal than businesspeople. These and hundreds of other commonplaces provide starting places for your knowledge of your audience, though you need to be cautious about relying too heavily on stereotypes of any social, racial, religious, professional, or cultural group. You must not rely so heavily on a stereotype that you reduce a whole group to one quality or trait. Nevertheless, you can guess that if the Chamber of Commerce strongly supports a piece of labor legislation, then most labor unions will probably oppose it.

When writing for specific publications, you can also make judgements about your audience by analyzing them as readers. You know, for instance, that *Playboy* and the *Ladies'*

Home Journal do not appeal to the same audiences or interests. You know that readers of the *Wall Street Journal* are likely to be businesspeople, while readers of *College English* are likely to be college English teachers. Readers of *Popular Mechanics* are interested in mechanics and other projects for the home handyman. Even a local newspaper defines its audience by geography and things associated with a specific area. Indeed, if you look carefully through an unfamiliar magazine, looking especially closely at the advertising, you should be able to tell a good deal about the audience.

Understanding your audience's emotional position should be a lot of help in deciding what to say. If you know your audience's feelings about a subject, you can decide how to approach it. Thus, if you and your audience agree on everything, the only thing you can write is support for the position, some friendly encouragement. But rhetorical writing is usually about disagreements. Therefore, your job is to decide where you agree with your audience and where you disagree. Points of disagreement will be your focus. If the disagreements are too great, you may have to choose a narrow area of disagreement. For example, when Alan M. Kingston wrote to the editor and readers of *Field & Stream,* he made a judgement about what to say based on what he knew about the audience. Because most of the readers of *Field & Stream* probably oppose any new gun control legislation, Kingston stayed away from any call for tougher gun control laws. Moreover, because an audience of hunters isn't likely to think killing animals with guns is immoral, Kingston didn't attack hunting as immoral. Rather, Kingston concentrated on one narrow issue, hoping to make headway there. Perhaps hunters could see that point without feeling threatened.

Knowing an audience's general feelings, beliefs, values, and dispositions will also help you decide what kinds of arguments and support you can use. Moreover, it may help you decide whether or not strong emotional appeals are likely to be effective.

Consider the following letter to the editor. Like the letter we analyzed earlier, it is about abortion, and it appeared in the same newspaper as the other letter. Thus, the audiences for the two letters were the same. The one major difference is that the following letter appeared in the fall of 1976, a presidential election year in which abortion was a serious political issue. Notice how the writer's sense of audience affects what he says:

> The most important issue of this and future elections is whether America will retain freedom of conscience and religion or will, by default, permit the dogmas and religious-ethical opinions of a minority group to become national law.
>
> Abortion is but one issue in this contest. But if, by our inertia, freedom of conscience is sacrificed on this issue, in the future our religious freedoms will be slowly eroded until all are lost and America is subjected to unqualified obedience to a clerical state.
>
> The price of freedom is indeed vigilance. It was from such religious domination that many of our founders fled.[7]

Although the writer of this letter is apparently opposed to the Catholic position on abortion, a position opposing all abortions on moral grounds, he does not specifically use the word *Catholic*, probably because he doesn't wish to offend Catholics in his audience. Moreover, he doesn't even argue the morality of abortion, probably because he knows that he's unlikely to change anyone's opinion. Rather he makes "freedom of conscience and religion" the chief issue. Such an appeal is a good one for the audience since most Americans, whatever their specific religious beliefs, do believe in freedom of religion. Toward the end of the letter he gets a bit emotional when he talks about the possibility of being "subjected to unqualified obedience to a clerical state" and cites the "religious domination that many of our founders fled"—an appeal to patriotic feelings.

Whether this letter ultimately had much effect on the 1976 election is impossible to determine. But the writer is a bit more cautious about his audience than the writer of the earlier letter. He does not attempt to change people's moral views nor to attack directly any segment of his audience. Moreover, his emotional appeals are related to the major issue he raises: religious freedom. Further, the language, though careful and educated, is not so complicated that the

7. Letter, Erie *Times*, September 17, 1976, sec. A, p. 9.

audience wouldn't understand it. The letter is likely to appeal to those who already agree with the writer, but it may also get some of the people who disagree with him to consider his position. The letter is more effective than a strong position in favor of abortion by choice or against anti-abortion forces. By not offending his audience, the writer stands a good chance of a fair hearing.

If you as a writer can evaluate your audience's position on an issue and then apply that knowledge effectively, you are more likely to write effectively. You need to recognize what deep beliefs and opinions in your audience you are unlikely to change. For instance, it is extremely difficult to change an audience's deep moral, religious, and social beliefs. So you should probably avoid head-on attacks on these beliefs. But you may be able to use an audience's beliefs as a basis for arguments. To use some specific examples, it probably would not be hard to persuade a Quaker, who by religious belief opposes war and killing, to favor stricter gun control legislation, but it would probably be impossible to convince him to support capital punishment. It's unlikely that you'll convince hunters to oppose hunting, but they might support stricter laws on handguns if you can show them that such laws may diminish attacks on hunting guns and on hunting itself. In other words, you must show them that a certain course of action is for their benefit. Ultimately the issue of interest is the chief rhetorical issue for the audience. The writer has to convince his audience that a subject is of interest and concern to the audience and that the audience's best interest lies in agreeing with the writer. If a writer can do this, he will win the heart and the emotions of his reader. Emotional interest is as important as intellectual interest in a subject.

Exercises

1. Briefly describe what you perceive as the intellectual and emotional qualities of the following groups.
   a. physicians
   b. auto mechanics

    c. American Legionnaires
    d. housewives
    e. nurses

2. Where are the following audiences likely to stand on this assertion: "The drinking age in Pennsylvania should be lowered to eighteen"?
    a. tavern owners
    b. college students
    c. the PTA
    d. the Methodist Church
    e. Parents Without Partners
    f. high school teachers
    g. the American Legion

3. How would the readers of the following magazines stand on premarital sex?
    a. *Cosmopolitan*
    b. *Seventeen*
    c. *Parents' Magazine*
    d. *Playboy*
    e. *Harper's*
    f. *Consumer Reports*
    g. *Reader's Digest*

Persona

In deciding what to say and how you will say it, you will also have to decide what kind of persona you will use. While content and audience may put constraints on your persona, there is still a variety of personas that you may use to write about any subject. Writers have used comic personas to write about death, God, and other subjects that are often considered somber, and they have written about what are considered trivial or humorous subjects in serious scholarly fashion. H.L. Mencken, the American critic and writer, used one of his most bitterly sarcastic personas in writing what was supposed to be a eulogy for William Jennings Bryan, an important senator and several times a presidential candidate. And in his great scholarly work, *The American Language,* Mencken apparently could not resist the temptation to depart from his erudite and serious persona. Buried among scholarly references in his footnotes, Mencken's mocking persona explains that the reason farmers don't invent much slang is that "farmers, as a class, are extremely stupid." Such a biased attack created a new dimension in the scholarly persona that Mencken was using.

Most writers, especially college students, lack the rhetorical skills to use such extreme personas. You will probably choose your personas from a far narrower range. Moreover, your personas will probably depend a bit more on purpose, subject, and audience. Most important, you want to make sure that your personas are the result of conscious choices, not just something that happens.

Persona and purpose

The persona that a writer uses should fit the rhetorical situation. It should fit his purposes, especially his internal purpose or strategy. And one of the basic decisions a writer has to make in relation to his strategy is whether or not the persona should be prominent or restrained. A persona is prominent when the reader is aware of the character of the writer; a persona is restrained when the reader is relatively unaware of the character of the writer and instead concentrates on the subject matter. The writers of the letter to Ann Landers and of "T-E-A-C-H All Mixed Up is C-H-E-A-T" in chapter four are examples of prominent personas, while the passages from the scientific texts earlier in this book exhibit restrained personas.

"T-E-A-C-H" is a good example of the effective use of a prominent persona. The force of the whole passage depends upon the personal experience of the writer. He is not a scholarly educator who has a great deal of evidence to back his assertions. Rather, he has his own experience. Since his personal experience is his main evidence, he has to make it prominent.

A prominent persona will often be necessary when your main strategy is to deal with personal experience. Discussing personal experience without using a prominent persona is likely to sound awkward and artificial. A prominent persona will most likely necessitate a first-person point of view or stance, too. You will probably use a prominent persona not only in supporting assertions with personal experience, but also in writing such autobiographical documents as applications for employment or college, or in offering personal advice as someone who is knowledgeable, perhaps even expert, on a subject.

A writer will normally use a restrained persona when his main purpose is to convey information objectively, as in science texts, scholarly studies, news stories in newspapers, reports in which personal opinion isn't supposed to be important, and reports of a group or committee rather than one person. Often a writer will avoid a prominent persona in a persuasive situation if he feels that his arguments, especially those depending on evidence, are strong enough to carry the case. A good example of such a restrained persona appears in the letter from the president of the gas association in chapter two.

A good many personas are somewhere between great prominence and great restraint. The prominence of your persona in rhetorical writing may depend on your attitude and tone, as well as on your purpose. A prominent persona, even in dealing with personal experience, can sometimes be ineffective. The persona in the letter to Ann Landers is one that offends the reader, turning him against the writer. The problems involved in creating a persona are too complex to depend on any single factor, as you will see near the end of this chapter.

Persona and subject

A writer's relation to his subject will also affect his persona. Part of the attitude you have toward your subject is determined by your main assertion, the specific claim you make about the subject. Either you view abortion favorably or unfavorably; you support restrictions on firearms or you oppose them; you believe guns are different from other weapons or you do not. But part of your relationship with your subject will depend on how close you are to the subject. Or, to put it in another way, your attitude may be involved or detached. That distance, which probably relates to purpose, will also affect the kind of persona you project. Consider the two letters in this chapter about abortion. In neither letter is the persona tremendously prominent, but the woman who discusses the physical details of abortion creates a different persona than the other writer does. Part of the difference comes from her direct emotional involvement with her subject. She seems to personally care about those babies, while the writer of the other letter, though slightly emotional, seems to have a merely intellectual rather than emotional interest in his subject. The woman is closer to her subject than the other writer. That affects her persona.

In deciding just how close you want to be to your subject, you will have to judge whether the subject needs a close persona and whether it will benefit from one. If an argument can stand on its own merits, a slightly distant attitude might be effective. But on moral and social issues, your emotional commitment may help to persuade your audience of the importance of the cause and of your essential concern for what is right. The great danger on important moral, political, and social issues is that in committing yourself to your position emotionally, you may seem biased, especially to an audience that may not agree with your position. This, of course, involves the relation of persona to audience.

Persona and audience

Just as you had to decide on the relationship of your persona to the subject, so too you must decide on the relationship of your persona to the audience. For instance, you must decide whether your persona will be close to or distant from the audience. You may want to be close and friendly, or distant and impersonal. Here there is a whole range possible, from the distance between the persona a writer would use in writing a compilation of data like a telephone book or set of mathematics tables to the personal relationship between close friends. In general, you should probably try to get as close to your audience as the actual social relationship allows. A warm, close persona can be persuasive as long as it is not presumptuous.

Besides distance or closeness, you should decide whether your persona is to be inferior to, equal to, or superior to the audience, to use three broad categories. The exact relationship you choose will probably depend in part on the social relationship with the audience. For example, in applying for a promotion, you wouldn't want to portray yourself as equal to your boss, nor would you establish a relationship of superiority in writing to a professor to request that she reconsider what you thought was an unfair low grade.

In some situations and organizations, the military for one, a writer may easily assume the persona of a superior without being rhetorically offensive. Similarly, a person who is an expert on a subject may rightfully and gracefully use the persona of a superior. And if a writer is writing to a superior, his persona may properly reflect that in the tone. However, in dealing with the kind of large audience whom you do not know personally, especially in a situation that calls for persuasion, you probably should adopt a position of rough equality with the audience. To treat such an audience as inferiors would be offensive, losing the case right there. To treat them as your superiors would detract from your position and authority as a writer.

The persona you choose may also depend on where your audience stands in relation to the position you are taking on the issue. It is probably easier to be close to an audience that agrees with your basic position than it is to be close to one that disagrees with you. Sharing a common belief is a bond that will allow you to get close to an audience. For an audience with whom you disagree, you will probably have to find some other means of establishing yourself. But one of the toughest jobs you'll face as a rhetorician is deciding which persona to use when you are not certain of your audience's position. You can better plan

a persona for a hostile audience than for an audience with
an unclear position.

The right persona

Although the relationships we've looked at in the last
few pages suggest approaches to persona, they don't fully
solve the problem. That's because creating the right persona
is a complex rhetorical task that depends on many things. It
requires well developed rhetorical and social skills, a sure
sense of self, and a sure sense of audience. Indeed, persona
is the least objective and most elusive of the basic elements
in the rhetorical situation. The writer is trying to appear to
be a certain kind of person, with certain definite virtues but
without any debilitating faults.

Quite often the right persona will be a very limited one,
a persona of one or two characteristics that fit the rhetorical
situation. The writer of a scientific paper should probably
appear as a detached, careful observer. The writer of a
letter of condolence should be sympathetic and kind. Someone offering his personal experience as evidence to support
an assertion needs to be honest and sincere. These and
many other limited personas may work very well. A person
need not have every virtue in order to project the right
persona. For example, the writer of a zoology textbook
probably won't and shouldn't show great concern for the
suffering of animals. That concern would detract from his
persona as a scientist.

Just how one persona and technique works well for one
writer but not for another is difficult to explain. The *Daily
News* copyboy who wrote "T-E-A-C-H" and the mother
writing to Ann Landers both use prominent personas to
write about personal experience. The technique should be
the right one for both of them. Yet when we read the two
passages, we like the copyboy but dislike the mother. Our
reasons for liking or disliking them are partly matters of
rhetorical techniques, yet the reasons are far deeper. The
reasons seem ultimately to reflect the whole moral characters of the writers. The copyboy is able to accept partial
blame for his own failures, and he seems concerned about

the welfare of others, those still in school. The mother is unable to accept any blame, and she seems more concerned about herself than about others.

What this analysis suggests is that persona is, at least in part, a reflection of the human personality. If that is so, your job as a rhetorician probably involves your finding a persona which fits you and with which you can be comfortable. You will have to be honest with yourself in judging which persona fits you and which doesn't. Simultaneously you will have to adjust your persona to your purpose, subject, audience, and situation. If you can do all those things well, your persona may be your most effective means of persuasion.

Exercises

1. If you had to write about each of the following subjects, what kind of persona would you probably use? Would your persona be prominent or restrained? How close would you be to your subject? How close would you be to your audience?
    a. potatoes
    b. premarital sex
    c. the mating habits of bats
    d. interracial marriage
    e. the Republican Party
    f. salted peanuts
    g. major league baseball

2. Briefly describe in a phrase or two the persona you would use to write about each of the subjects in 1.

3. Choosing one of those subjects, briefly describe the persona you would use in writing articles for the following publications:
    a. your college newspaper
    b. *Playboy*
    c. *Cosmopolitan*
    d. *Sports Illustrated*
    e. *Time* (or *Newsweek*)

Discovery:
An Overview

Because the process of discovering what to say and how to say it is so complex, you may find the following outline of the process helpful. You may use it at the beginning of the process, or you may use it as a review, either just before you begin writing or as a check on the first and subsequent drafts of the paper. It suggests some specific questions that you can ask yourself to help apply the material that you've looked at in this chapter, though not all of them will be applicable to every subject.

I. Purpose
   A. What specific result do you hope to get from writing?
      1. Will it be some action?
      2. Will it be some change in attitude, belief, or information?
   B. What strategy will you use to gain that purpose?
   C. How will the strategy lead to the specific result or goal you are seeking?
II. Content
   A. What specific issue or issues will you focus on?
      1. Does your main assertion express your view of the issue precisely?
      2. Have you adequate support to defend your view of the issue?
   B. Can you define the key term in your assertion?
      1. Will you use a lexical, a stipulative, or an extended definition?
      2. What class is the term in?
      3. How does it differ from the other members of the class?
      4. What specific strategy or approach to defining will best explain the term?
   C. How does your subject compare with other things?
      1. Is is like something else?
      2. Does it differ from similar things?
      3. Is the likeness literal or figurative (metaphorical)?

D. Does your subject belong in a causal relationship?
   1. Is it an effect of something else?
   2. If so, is it an effect of one cause or of many?
   3. Is the causal relationship with the supposed cause clear or questionable?
   4. Is it a cause of something else?
   5. Has it caused or will it cause something for certain or only probably?
   6. Were or are the effects beneficial or harmful?
   7. Has the cause created or will it create effects other than those desired or planned for?
E. Have you evidence to support your views?
   1. Is your evidence from printed or other published sources?
   2. If so, how reliable are the sources?
   3. Have you evidence from personal experience?
   4. Have you any physical or other primary evidence?
   5. Does your evidence prove your assertion absolutely, or does it merely support the assertion?

III. Audience
   A. Exactly who is your audience?
      1. Is it an individual, an identifiable group, or an implied group?
   B. What are the intellectual qualities of your audience?
      1. How well does your audience know the subject?
      2. Does the audience belong to any occupational group or social class?
      3. How well educated is the audience?
      4. How broad is its general knowledge?
   C. What are the emotional qualities of your audience?
      1. Does your audience have a specific position or stand on the issue?
      2. What basic moral, social, and other values does the audience hold?
      3. What common values do you share with your audience?
      4. Why should the audience be concerned about the subject?
      5. Does the place of publication help you to identify your audience?

IV. Persona
    A. How will your persona fit your purpose?
       1. Will your persona be prominent or restrained?
    B. How will your persona fit your subject?
       1. Does the persona view the subject favorably?
       2. How close to the subject is the persona?
    C. How will your persona fit the audience?
       1. What social relationships, if any, affect the relations of the persona and audience?
       2. How close is the persona to the audience?
       3. Should the persona be inferior to, equal to, or superior to the audience?
    D. Will a limited persona fit the rhetorical situation?

Writing Assignments

1. Go back to the survival problem at the end of chapter two. Assuming that you have already made your selections and four people have already left the shelter, write a letter to the survivors and to future generations explaining your choices. Because your leadership may be in question, you will have to maintain a credible persona.

2. Write an extended essay as a letter to the editor of your campus newspaper on a controversial or important subject on the campus.

3. Write an extended letter to the editor in response to an article in a magazine that deals with controversial issues and prints long letters. *The Atlantic Monthly, Harper's, Saturday Review,* and *Playboy* are especially good for this purpose.

4. Find an issue on which you have strong opinions, and then attempt to change the minds of a significant audience by choosing a place of publication for which to write.

5. Find an issue on which you have strong opinions, and then attempt to persuade your classmates to agree with you.

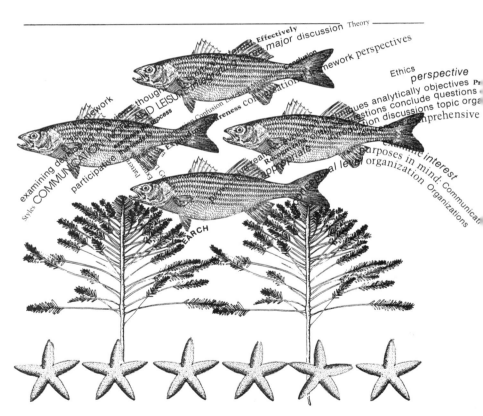

Chapter Six

ORGANIZATION

The Order of Things

Organization, which classical rhetoricians called *arrangement,* refers to the order or sequence of materials in a discourse. It is closely related to the process of discovery. After a writer discovers what he wants to say, he has to find an order in which to say it. The writer must decide what material to begin with, what material to end with, and how the various forms of support are to be placed in between. Finding the best order may be as important as using the right materials.

Order is important in rhetorical writing because rhetorical writing is always directed to an audience. If the writer offends, insults, or bores his audience at the beginning of the work, then the whole case may be lost right there. You've probably had the experience, perhaps in a doctor's office, of browsing through a magazine looking for an article to read. You probably rejected a good many articles because you didn't like the way they began. You passed them over and went on to something that had a better beginning. Similarly, if the writer's organization is unclear or confused, then the reader may stop in the middle or misinterpret what the writer is trying to say. Finally, if the writer says the wrong thing at the very end of the piece of writing, he may wipe out all the good effects he's created along the way. Some material that might not have been offensive to the reader if it had appeared early and been thoroughly explained by the writer may offend the reader if it's simply dropped in at the end of the work. Because of something at the very end of a work, you've probably turned against a speaker or writer who, up till then, had been very persuasive. The ending simply left you with a bad taste.

Because organization is related both to the discovery of what to say and to the effect on the audience, we will talk about two different kinds of organization or structure: argumentative structure and rhetorical structure. *Argumentative* structure has to do with the relationships within the content that we have discovered. It involves relationships among ideas, assertions, support, and so forth. *Rhetorical* structure has to do with the effects of order on the audience. It involves the audience's reaction to a message. The actual order or plan of organization that a writer uses in a piece of writing will probably be some combination of these two kinds of order.

Argumentative structure

Argumentative structure has to do with the relationships within the content. In persuasive and expository writing the writer usually has a main assertion or main point that he wants to make. In support of this main assertion, he probably makes a series of other assertions. The writer tries to get to a point at which he and his audience agree. In other words, if the audience agrees with the support that the writer offers, the audience should (the writer believes) come to agree with the main assertion or *conclusion* (as logicians would call it).

Argument, then, is a process of linking a main point or assertion to its support. That linkage may be direct or indirect. It may involve several direct links that independently support the main assertion, a continuous set of links that form one line of support for the main assertion, or some combination of the two methods. Such processes are easy to present in the form of diagrams or skeletons that are very much like standard outlines. We'll look at various forms of argumentative structure in some very simple examples.

Suppose, for instance, that you wished to write a letter to the editor of your local newspaper opposing increased limitations on the ownership of handguns. Your argumentative structure might take this form:

M.A. (Main Assertion): Except for specific and limited reasons, every adult citizen should be allowed to possess handguns.
  I. The Constitution guarantees a citizen's right to bear arms.
  II. Handguns give the citizen a means to protect himself and his property.
  III. People, not guns, cause crime.

The three assertions are three independent, direct supports for the main assertion. Their order could be rearranged without harming the strength of each. Thus, they are all on the same level and are numbered with Roman numerals. Even if someone were to disprove assertions I and II, they would not automatically have disproved assertion III. If you could prove assertion III, you would still have some support for your main assertion.

Instead of choosing three directly supporting assertions for your main assertion, you might choose to support your main assertions with one very strong line of reasoning. In that case, your argumentative structure would be something like a chain of reasoning in which each supporting assertion is linked to the one before it. The argumentative structure might look something like this:

M.A. Except for specific and limited reasons, every adult citizen should be allowed to possess handguns.
I. Handguns provide an ultimate protection for the citizen's person and property.
  A. They provide protection when the law is unable to protect the citizen from either common criminals or tyrannical government.

1. Taking away that ultimate protection by law is a denial of the very basis of and reason for government.
   a. Without the right to self-protection, the citizen has no way of guaranteeing any of his rights.
      i. The killing of so many European Jews by the Nazis would not have been so easy if handguns had been freely available.

The four supporting assertions in this example are linked in a specific relationship that depends on their order. Each assertion supports the one above it, and each is in turn supported by the one below it. Thus, each assertion is on a different level, as the numbering, lettering, and indentations indicate.

The order of these assertions might be changed somewhat. For instance, assertion *a* could possibly occur in support of *A,* in which case it might be re-identified as *1* and the original *1* might become a *2* or *a,* depending on the kind of underlying verbal links or support each had. But in general the order is relatively fixed and cannot be changed without changing the quality and strength of the whole series.

Yet another structure is possible by combining these two kinds of structure. For instance, you might wish to support the same main assertion by starting with assertions I and III from the first diagram and then putting assertion II third. In support of that assertion you would then use the materials from the second diagram. Thus, the argumentative structure would look like this:

M.A.
   I.
   II.
   III.
      A.
         1.
            a.
               i.

This structure combines the two orders, but its total force in persuading anyone will still probably depend on assertion III ("Handguns provide an ultimate protection . . ."). That assertion, by virtue of its extensive support, is the chief sub-assertion and the main focus of the discourse.

These diagrams, of course, represent only the skeletons of arguments. Most of these assertions will be supported by one or more other sentences and perhaps by whole paragraphs. The linking process continues all through the writing.

Except in textbooks on geometry, logic, and other technical subjects, very little actual writing is done in strictly argumentative structure. One brief sample that may come pretty close is the letter by Alan M. Kingston on page 92. Kingston's basic argument could be diagrammed something like this:

M.A. . . . guns are [not] merely scapegoats when murders are committed.
I. Guns make murder easier . . . .
    A. An enraged man . . . can very easily kill his neighbor. . . .
    B. Moreover, a person can better defend himself against other forms of assault . . . .
    C Proof . . . is available in the murder statistics . . . .

In most extended arguments, however, the order of the work is not strictly argumentative structure.

If, then, argumentative structure is not an order that most of us will use in writing, why spend so much time and effort discussing it? There are several answers to that question. First, being aware of argumentative order will help us, as rhetoricians, understand our material and arguments better. It will show us which arguments are internally strong and have support, which are weak, and how important any particular material is in the reasoning process. It will also prevent us from placing material in illogical structures. Second, knowledge of argumentative order will help us to better understand, analyze, and evaluate the rhetoric of others. We will be better readers, better consumers of messages. Finally, as writers we should know that argumentative structure is a good tool to help us move from one stage of the writing process to another. After we've listed some of the things that we can say and want to say, having some idea of how to arrange this material will help us determine which material to develop and how extensively to develop it. Thus, even if our writing never follows strictly argumentative structure, our awareness of argumentative structure should be in the background of our writing and thinking. Argumentative structure provides us with stability in the writing process.

Exercises

1. Choose one of the topics that follow and state your general position on it in the form of an assertion that you could support. The topics are abortion, capital punishment, sororities (or fraternities), homosexuality, legalizing marijuana, pornography, prostitution, civil disobedience, genetic manipulation of humans, and trial marriages.

2. List two words or short phrases that suggest information you could use to support your assertion.

3. Rearrange the material so that it seems to fit into some pattern of argumentative order. You may want to discard some of your items at this stage if they don't seem to fit in.

4. Using the words or phrases you have, number or letter them to indicate the pattern of argumentative order that you might use.

5. If necessary, revise or reword your assertion to better fit the materials you have to support it.

Rhetorical structure

We have seen how argumentative structure works. It is the order that we would probably use if human beings were always logical and if all subjects could be discussed in a purely logical fashion. It is an order that depends on the subject itself rather than on other elements in the rhetorical situation.

However, as we have seen in earlier chapters, most writing takes place within a rhetorical situation. Not only is there content, but there are such circumstances as audience, persona, purpose, social situation, and even what we might call a *climate of opinion* (a common set of positions and views on the subject). Because of all the circumstances in the rhetorical situation, a writer might have good reasons for not following a strictly argumentative structure. Instead, he might wish to follow a rhetorical order, an order that is more suitable for the rhetorical situation. This rhetorical order might depend on the audience's beliefs or ideals, the writer's need to establish a certain kind of persona, what a preceding writer or speaker may have said on the subject, or even how certain words or phrases help link ideas together. In sum, rhetorical order is the order that the writer thinks will be most persuasive and effective in a rhetorical situation. It may be close to argumentative structure, or it may be quite different. But it will be designed for persuasiveness.

A good example of rhetorical structure that is quite a bit different from argumentative structure is the editorial from *Field & Stream* in chapter three. Indeed, the important assertions that the writer is making have to be put in words somewhat different from the form they take in the editorial. Here is what I think the basic argumentative structure of the editorial is in its skeletal form (though some of you may get slightly different structures):

M.A. The real reason for gun control laws is that politicians are too inept or dishonest to face up to the basic truths of our society.
I. Politicians like to hide from the truth because it won't get them votes.
   A. The truth is that suffering people cause crime.
   B. The cure for suffering is politically unpopular.
II. Gun control is an easy scapegoat and a popular one.

If we go through the editorial looking at its rhetorical structure, we see quite a different structure, a structure that depends a good deal on the rhetorical situation. After asking a question that he hopes will attract his audience's attention—the italicized word *real* is especially attractive rhetorically—the writer does state his main assertion: that inept or dishonest politicians who won't face the truth are responsible for crime. That's argumentative structure.

But in the second paragraph the writer shifts his focus to the disgust of the American people. He mentions Vietnam and Watergate—two issues that have little to do with gun control—because these are emotional subjects that will arouse his audience's anger against politicians. He mentions gun control as a popular escape, but he doesn't dwell on it. Instead he continues his attack on politicians who lack "intestinal fortitude" because telling the truth "won't get many votes." He also tosses in but never develops the issue of the court system.

In the third paragraph, the writer begins to explain what he considers the real cause of crime. That seems pretty close to argumentative structure. However, he then interrupts the flow of the argument to attack John Lindsay, a prominent politician and gun control advocate, and then makes the attack general by attributing it to other politicians. This is where rhetorical structure interrupts argumentative structure.

The writer does finally shift back to what he considers the truth—that it is "the *suffering of people* that causes crime"—and he then talks about the cure. He emphasizes again the dishonesty of politicians by claiming that they "know" the truth but avoid it because they don't want to "risk losing voter support" on the issue.

In the next to last paragraph the writer restates his second important sub-assertion, that gun control is the scapegoat. But he doesn't prove or support it. Instead he dwells on the suffering of poor people and ends the paragraph with another attack on politicians, claiming that poor people won't get "a fair shake from the politicians."

Then the brief last paragraph, which seems like a conclusion, suggests that guns or other weapons are not the cause of crime. The writer probably ends on that point because his audience consists mainly of gun advocates,

sportsmen who are against gun control. Even if he has
made a good case about the dishonesty of politicians, that
doesn't prove that guns don't cause crime. But for this
audience, that's a good way to end.

In analyzing the structure of the whole editorial, a
couple of things should be clear. First, there is an underlying argumentative structure. Second, there is also a rhetorical structure that accounts for departures from argumentative order. Among the prominent departures are attacks on
politicians. The writer dwells on the faults of politicians,
hardly missing an opportunity to attack them, probably
because politicians are unpopular figures whose very mention will arouse the ire of the audience. The writer's beginning and ending, too, are more matters of rhetorical structure than argumentative structure. Opening with a question
is a good way to get the audience's interest, and closing with
an assertion about the cure for crime is a good way to end
for this audience, even though it is argumentatively out of
place.

As the example has shown, a writer may depart from
argumentative structure for rhetorical effect. But before we
go into any greater analysis of rhetorical structure, we'll
look at a few of its standard varieties. Then we'll go on to
suggest specific techniques and devices for achieving effective rhetorical order.

Classical structure

Organization or arrangement was an important concern
of the ancient rhetoricians of Greece and Rome. As the art
of rhetoric developed, the classical oration—for rhetoric
originally developed for oral situations—came to have a
fixed form. Most classical rhetoricians thought of the oration in five parts: (1) the *introduction,* (2) the *narration* or
statement of facts, (3) The *confirmation* or *proof,* (4) the *refutation* or *attack on opposing views,* and (5) the *conclusion.* Some
rhetoricians added a sixth part, a *division* or *clarification of
issues* that followed the narration.

Each of the parts of the oration served a specific function. The introduction or beginning was designed to pre-

pare the audience for what was to follow. It could be used either as a means of attracting the audience's attention to the subject or as a means of establishing the speaker's persona. The statement of facts (based on the judicial model) applied chiefly to *forensic* (or courtroom) rhetoric and attempted to state the events that had occurred. (If there were a separate division or clarification of issues, it would outline what the speaker planned to prove. But this could easily blend in as part of the statement of facts.)

The next two parts were the heart of the oration. In the confirmation or proof, the speaker would state his main assertions and develop support for them at some length. In the refutation, the speaker would attempt to refute or disprove the arguments that his opponent had used (or might use) against him. In a courtroom situation, the refutation might be extremely important. In our criminal law, a person accused of a crime need not prove himself innocent; if he can successfully refute the charges that the prosecutor brings against him, he will win his case. In both the confirmation and the refutation, the speaker sought to develop arguments that were clear, solid, and well supported.

Finally, of couse, came the conclusion. The conclusion was the place to end, and it could have a number of functions. It might serve as a summary, review, or place to draw an inference from the previous material. Or, if the orator felt he had been successful throughout his speech, he might appeal to the emotions of the audience, thus winning their favor as well as their intellectual assent.

Such an order seems fairly rigid, and it is. The rigidity grew out of the need for a standard order to aid the memory, since classical rhetoricians spoke without a written text and without notes. However, there was still room for flexibility. Among the things that classical rhetoricians still had to decide were whether the strongest arguments should come first or last, both in the confirmation and in the refutation. Also, some of the rhetoricians suggested that the refutation could be put ahead of the confirmation, especially if the opponent had made a very strong case. The advantage of beginning with the refutation may be especially important in the courtroom. The unknown writer of one ancient text on rhetoric, the *Rhetorica Ad Herennium,* went so far as to suggest that the standard order could be violated in many ways as long as the speaker had a good reason for each violation. Thus, a speaker might begin with his confirmation or refutation (skipping all introductory material) if he had especially strong evidence.

A writer can follow the form of the classical oration rather strictly and still seem neither stiff nor overly rigid. The following passage by Bayard Rustin follows the classical pattern rather closely:

The resort to stereotype is the first refuge and chief strategy of the bigot. Though this is a matter that ought to concern everyone, it should be of particular concern to Negroes. For their lives, as far back as we can remember, have been made nightmares by one kind of bigotry or another.

This urge to stereotype groups and deal with them accordingly is an evil urge. Its birthplace is in that sinister back room of the mind where plots and schemes are hatched for the persecution and oppression of other human beings.

It comes out of many things, but chiefly out of a failure or refusal to do the kind of tough, patient thinking that is required of difficult problems of relationship. It comes, as well, out of a desire to establish one's own sense of humanity and worth upon the ruins of someone else's. Nobody knows this, or should know it, better than Negroes and Jews.

Bigots have, for almost every day we have spent out of Africa or out of Palestine, invented a whole catalogue of Negro and Jewish characteristics, invested these characteristics with inferior or undesirable values, and, on the basis of these fantasies, have engaged in the most brutal and systematic persecution.

It seems to me, therefore, that it would be one of the great tragedies of Negro and Jewish experience in a hostile civilization if the time should come when either group begins using against the other the same weapon which the white majorities of the West used for centuries to crush and deny them their sense of humanity.

All of which is to say that we ought all to be disturbed by a climate of mutual hostility that is building up among certain segments of the Negro and Jewish communities in the ghettos.

Jewish leaders know this and are speaking to the Jewish conscience about it. So far as Negroes are concerned, let me say that one of the more unprofitable strategies we could ever adopt is now to join in history's oldest and most shameful witch hunt, anti-Semitism. This attitude, though not typical of most Negro communities, is gaining considerable strength in the ghetto. It sees the Jew as the chief and only exploiter of the ghetto, blames the ghetto on him, and seems to suggest that anything Jews do is inherent in the idea of their Jewishness.

I believe, though, that this attitude has two aspects—one entirely innocent of anti-Semitic animus. The first is that the Negro, in responding justifiably to bitterness and frustration, blames the plight of the ghetto on any visible reminder or representative of white America. . . .

Since in Harlem Jews happen to be the most immediate reminders of white American oppression, they naturally inherit the wrath of black frustration. And I don't believe that the Negroes who attack out of this attitude are interested in the subtleties of ethnic, cultural, and religious distinction, or that they would find any such distinction emotionally or intellectually useful.

It is the other aspect of the attitude that is more dangerous, that is consciously anti-Semitic, and that mischievously separates Jews from other white Americans and uses against them the old stereotypes of anti-Semitic slander and persecution. It is outrageous to blame Harlem on Jewishness. Harlem is no more the product of Jewishness than was American slavery and the subsequent century of Negro oppression in this country.

In the ghetto everybody gets a piece of the action: those who are Jews and those who are Christians; those who are white and those who are black; those who run the numbers and those who operate the churches; those— black and white—who own tenements and those—black and white—who own businesses.

Harlem is exploited by American greed. Even those who are now stirring up militant anti-Semitic resentments are exploiting the ghetto—the ghetto's mentality, its frustration, and its need to believe anything that brings it a degree of psychological comfort.

The Jews are no more angels than we are—there are some real grounds for conflict and contention between us as minority groups—but it is nonsense to divert attention from who it is that really oppresses Negroes in the ghetto. Ultimately the real oppressor is white American immorality and indifference, and we will be letting off the real oppressor too easily if we now concentrate our fulminations against a few Jews in the ghetto.

The premise of the stereotype is that everything that a man does defines his particular racial and ethnic morality. The people who say that about Jews are the same people who say it about Negroes. If we are now willing to believe what that doctrine says about Jews, then are we not obligated to endorse what it says about Jews, then are we not obligated to endorse what it says about us?

I agree with James Baldwin entirely. I agree with him that we should "do something unprecedented: to create ourselves without finding it necessary to create an enemy. . . ."

To engage in anti-Semitism is to engage in self-destruction—man's most tragic state.[1]

If we consider this piece as a classical oration, it divides along the following lines. The introduction occurs in the first paragraph. Rustin speaks of the bigot and emphasizes the "particular concern to Negroes"—an especially effective opening since the piece was first published in the New York *Amsterdam News,* a newspaper with a primarily black readership. The statement of facts occurs in the next five paragraphs as Rustin explains the basis of the urge to stereotype and then gradually focuses on the more immediate background: the growing hostility between Negroes and Jews in the nation's ghettos at that time (1967).

The confirmation or chief arguments occur in the next six paragraphs. Rustin claims that it would be a mistake for Negroes to blame Jews for their suffering, and he offers two arguments. He says, for one, that the rage against Jews occurs simply because Jews are white. But his most important argument is his second—that to blame Jews is to mistake the real causes of suffering, which are the history of slavery and the system of "American greed."

The refutation of possible objections occurs in the next two paragraphs. First, Rustin refutes the possible claim that he's idealizing Jews, making them all seem virtuous. Then he argues, emotionally, that the stereotypes of Jews cannot be right (whatever impressions his audience may have), for then the stereotypes of Negroes would also be correct.

---

1. Bayard Rustin, "The Premise of the Stereotype," *Down the Line* (Chicago: Quadrangle Books, 1971), pp. 171–73. Copyright © 1971 by Bayard Rustin from New York *Amsterdam News,* April 8, 1967. Reprinted by permission of Times Books, a division of Quadrangle/The New York Times Book Co., Inc. from *Down the Line:* The Premise of the Stereotype by Bayard Rustin.

The conclusion occurs in the last two paragraphs, and it is an emotional one. He quotes noted Negro writer James Baldwin and then ends with a ringing phrase that provides an emotional climax—"man's most tragic state."

Another piece of rhetorical writing that follows the same general pattern is Shirley L. Greene's letter in chapter one. Her introduction and brief clarification of issues come in paragraph one. Her confirmation comes in paragraph two, and her refutation in paragraph three. The conclusion comes in paragraph three. In both her letter and in Rustin's essay, the classical structure provides a solid framework for each work.

Although the form of the classical oration may seem a bit rigid, it is useful for discourse. A writer who wishes to follow this pattern will probably write a clearly organized work, even if the organization seems fairly rigid. Indeed, the form of the classical oration might provide real discipline for a writer who suffers from a lack of organization. It might help those who wander about hopelessly to put some order into their work. Our later discussion of structure will build upon some of the principles of the classical oration, though in simplified form.

Newspaper structure

The standard newspaper article follows the format of the *inverted pyramid*. In the inverted pyramid, the most important information is stated first. The information is added in an order of decreasing importance. By the time a reader reaches the end of a substantial news story, he is probably reading some rather unimportant details. The following story illustrates the inverted pyramid pretty well:

New car sales in the United States hit an all-time high of 1.15 million in May, rekindling industry predictions that 1978 will be a boom year for the automakers.

General Motors and Ford Motor Co. each posted their best sales month ever and led the domestic industry to cumulative sales of 962,985 units, up 11 percent over May 1977 figures.

Import car sales accounted for 194,000 of the industry total. Though down 15 percent from last year's record, it was the second best May ever for the imports.

"This performance gives added strength to our forecast of total U.S. industry sales of 15.5 million cars and trucks in the 1978 calendar year," GM Vice President Robert D. Burger said Monday.

Ford Vice President Gordon B. MacKenzie said with "leading economic indicators up slightly and a record number of people holding jobs, we would expect strong car and truck sales to continue through the summer months."

GM's May sales of 547,327 units set a new industry record for any month. It also amounted to a 9.7 percent increase over May 1977 sales. Ford's total of 269,382 was its best one-month performance, topping last year's figure by 19.3 percent.

Chrysler Corp. reported sales of 127,672 for the month, up 3.6 percent from a year ago. American Motors Corp. posted sales of 18,604 units, up less than 1 percent.

The combined industry total surpassed by 1.2 percent the previous record set in May 1973, prior to the Arab oil embargo and the onset of a two-year recession.

The foreign car makers, whose prices have risen steadily as a result of falling dollar values abroad, saw their share of the U.S. market fall to about 17 percent from the 20.8 percent share in May 1977 when they sold 219,000 units.[2]

The story states its main point—that sales "hit an all-time high of 1.15 million in May"—in the very first sentence. The specific details behind this information follow in succeeding paragraphs. By the time the reader reaches the last two paragraphs, he is reading some fairly minute details, especially those about foreign car sales.

The inverted pyramid, as a fixed rhetorical structure, has some definite advantages to it. It is a clear and convenient structure for presenting information quickly. A reader can begin reading and he will know exactly what the writer's main point is. He won't have to hunt around for a main assertion that is hidden in the work. Moreover, if he begins losing interest in the increasingly insignificant de-

2. Article, Erie *Times,* June 6, 1978, Sec. A, p. 2.

tails, he can stop reading with the assurance that he won't be missing anything important. That same fact also makes the inverted pyramid a convenient form for the editor of the newspaper. If there isn't room for the full story that the reporter wrote, the editor can cut paragraphs off the end of a story. He knows that he won't be leaving out any details that are essential to the story. As a matter of fact, I cut off the last four paragraphs of the story on auto sales as it appeared in my local newspaper, yet you were probably unaware that anything was missing. For all we know, the newspaper editor may have cut half a dozen paragraphs from the original wire service story.

Despite its advantages to both readers and editors, the inverted pyramid is not a very useful organization for rhetorical writing. It isn't flexible enough to present a clear argumentative order very well. Even newspaper writers don't use it when they write arguments. Their editorials will often follow something like argumentative structure or perhaps even a rhetorical structure. But if a writer's purpose is to convey a good deal of information, especially factual information, the inverted pyramid format is most useful. An approximation of the form, with the main assertion stated at the very beginning and supporting material following in decreasing order of importance, may be very useful in certain other kinds of writing. For instance, if you were to write a report for your company on where to locate a new production plant, you might state your conclusion immediately and then summarize the main reasons right after it. Then, even if the report were highly technical and filled with minute analysis, the reader would still understand your main thrust.

Simplified structure

To suggest any single organization for all rhetorical writing, whether persuasion or exposition, would be foolish. But it might be useful to suggest a very general pattern that can be modified in many ways. For purposes of our discussion, we can consider rhetorical writings as consisting of three parts: the *beginning,* the *body,* and the *ending.* This very rough pattern provides a convenient framework for almost all writing if we keep in the backs of our minds the classical oration, the inverted pyramid, and the relation between argumentative and rhetorical structures. What this means in practical terms is that the beginning of a work functions in any or all of the ways that the classical oration's introduction, statement of facts, and division functioned. The body is ultimately based on argumentative structure, but its arrangement can be modified to fit the rhetorical situation. It performs the functions of the confirmation and the refutation in a classical oration, and is the longest and most fully developed section of the work. The ending, quite clearly, does much the same as the conclusion of a classical oration.

This rough frame of organization is useful because it isn't so rigid that it will make writing mechanical. Yet, as good rhetoricians, we will have to pay close attention to our purpose, content, audience, and persona if we are to make any form of organization meaningful. Besides these major elements in the rhetorical situation, we'll also have to be aware of verbal links between arguments, standard positions and arguments on the subject, and many other things. If we relate organization to other rhetorical concerns, we will probably organize our material effectively.

Beginnings

What do we want a beginning to do? What do we expect it to accomplish? Basically, a good beginning can enhance all three rhetorical appeals. It can appeal to the audience's emotions, it can make the speaker's voice more attractive, and it can clarify the message or strengthen the argument. What the beginning will accomplish in any specific case will depend upon the actual situation.

Emotional appeals

One of the basic things that a beginning should do is make your audience want to read what you have to say. It should somehow persuade your audience that what you have to say is worth reading. That is why professional writers spend a lot of time planning how they will begin articles or stories. They are looking for *hookers*—devices to seduce potential readers. Often the title and first paragraph of a magazine article will determine whether a reader will stop his browsing and begin reading or will go on to something else. Notice how this writer attempts to attract and maintain the audience's interest in an article on jogging:

BULLETIN: Noted Physical Fitness Enthusiast Farrah Fawcett-Majors will appear in the tenth, 20th and 30th paragraphs of this article, jogging nude around the Central Park Reservoir, pausing every 50 yards to give a demonstration of rope-skipping. Aerobics points will be awarded to readers.[3]

Though the writer for *Time* was being humorous, he or she (the author's name isn't listed) knew that the promise of seeing or even reading about the noted pinup queen in the nude would probably arouse the interest of readers—especially males. Moreover, the writer mentioned three different appearances, which would help keep the reader's attention throughout the article.

Most attempts at emotional appeals will not be so blatant in their attempts to attract attention, just as most beginnings will have a closer relation to the subject of the article itself. One typical form of opening, especially in popular (non-technical) magazines, is the narrative opening:

Elaine and Jim Morse* smile and wave as their last guests drive off. Jim closes the door and turns, arms outspread, to Elaine. She snuggles against him, rubbing her cheek against his chest; he kisses the tip of her nose.

3. "Ready, Set . . . Sweat!" *Time* (June 6, 1977), p. 82.

"That was one terrific dinner party," Jim says, "even if I do say so myself. Everyone was having such a good time I was beginning to worry that they'd never go home."

"I know," Elaine murmurs, still enclosed in Jim's hug. "It's always that way. Sarah told me that she and Don would rather visit here than anywhere else. She said she figured our parties are always successful because our happiness spreads out in waves and washes over everyone in the room."[4]

*Names have been changed to protect the privacy of the individuals involved.

For some reason, the narrative opening appeals to our sense of humanity, our sympathy for or our curiosity about others. Even though we've never heard of Elaine and Jim Morse (and though we discover that the names have been changed), we are suddenly interested in them and what they will be doing. The narrative opening is effective insofar as it uses seemingly realistic details—specific "facts" like names and incidents. These somehow convince us of the reality of the situation. And if, as in this article, the opening illustrates a point the writer is trying to make, the emotional appeal will lead neatly into the rational content of the article.

Other devices to get the reader's attention right at the beginning of a piece are to ask a question or to state some startling, unusual, paradoxical, or other interesting bit of information or opinion. A good example of how a question can capture the reader's interest can be seen in the opening sentence of the *Field & Stream* editorial: "Want to know the *real* reason for gun control laws and attempts to confiscate guns?" A question, by its very nature, invites the audience's response, and thus involves the reader in the rhetorical process. That's why many ads open with questions, especially personal questions: "Would *you* like to increase your earning power substantially?" Such a question naturally invites the audience to read on, since most people are

4. Bernice Hunt, "What Your Sex Life Reveals about Your Marriage," *Woman's Day* (March 27, 1978), p. 60. Reprinted by permission of Robert Lescher Literary Agency and *Woman's Day* magazine. Copyright © 1978 by Bernice Hunt.

interested in making more money. An equally effective device for getting the reader's attention is the startling opening such as this:

> With all the concern about the soaring crime rate, it's hard to believe that any woman would actually help a criminal—especially one who hopes to make her his next victim. Yet every year thousands of normal, sensible women do just that. They unwittingly assist robbers, muggers and rapists to carry out their work with remarkable ease.[5]

A quotation can also provide an effective opening, especially if it expresses a paradoxical or startling belief, as this quotation does:

> "God looks after fools, drunkards, and the United States of America." This old saying was fulfilled again in the case of Watergate. For beyond its own sordid confines, Watergate has been redemptive—a disguised stroke of good fortune for the United States of America. That good fortune may yet turn to ashes, but I am one of those whom H.L. Mencken called the "optimists and chronic hopers of the world," and I see gain for this country in the reassertion of old ideals and the renewal of governmental processes.[6]

In general, then, we use emotional appeals at the beginnings of what we write in order to get our reader's attention and then to convince him that it will be worthwhile to continue reading, just as the classical rhetorician used the introduction to gain his audience's interest. We can and often will use the emotional appeal by itself at the beginning of a paper, but we may also use it along with one or both of the other appeals. The important thing to remember is that nobody, not even your English professor, enjoys reading what promises to be dull and commonplace.

5. Dwight Lane and Margaret Lane, "Criminal Attack: Are You a Likely Victim?" *Woman's Day* (March 1, 1978), p. 64.

6. Elliot Richardson, "The Saturday Night Massacre," *The Atlantic Monthly* (March 1976), p. 40.

Ethical appeals

The introduction of the classical oration was often used to establish the speaker's ethical appeal. Classical rhetoricians called this *ingratiation,* establishing oneself in the audience's favor. And the beginning is a good place to present a persona that the audience will respect, admire, like, trust, or whatever, depending on the situation. In short, the writer will try to establish a voice that is relevant to his total rhetorical purpose. He will try to find a persona that fits his subject, his audience, and his purpose. As we'll see, he can build up his ethical appeal either directly or indirectly.

At the beginning of certain kinds of writing, a writer or speaker may have to make direct and overt statements about himself that will support his persona. These direct statements are often in support of his qualifications or special abilities. Consider the following opening of an article by Elizabeth Canfield:

For the past twenty years I have been involved with family planning, abortion-law reform, pregnancy counseling, and education in human sexuality. For the past seven years I have been involved with student health services on the college level. I have had the opportunity to talk with thousands of girls and boys, and women and men, ranging in age from thirteen years to the seventies; they have responded to thousands of questions—both verbal and written—following lectures and discussions on sexual subjects. The similarity of concerns across national, racial, religious, and ethnic lines has been striking. The young woman from Ghana who sat in the office last week sounded amazingly like the one from Oklahoma who had been in earlier. The scholarly doctoral candidate from Pakistan would have been surprised if he could have met his counterpart from Idaho or California. It seems that what we all have in common is basic anxiety about human sexuality, from seeking birth control information to personal problems of an emotional nature.[7]

7. Elizabeth Canfield, "Am I Normal?" *The Humanist* (March-April 1978), p. 10.

The chief purpose of this opening paragraph is to establish the persona's qualifications to talk about human anxieties on sexual matters. She does this by listing the number of years she has worked in her field, the number of persons she has talked to, and the cultural breadth of her studies. In short, the author has done a pretty good job of convincing us that she is qualified to write about her subject.

Elizabeth Canfield's establishment of her qualifications is similar to what goes on in a courtroom. Expert witnesses—coroners, ballistics experts, fingerprint experts—normally begin by outlining their qualifications. But even in less formal situations, writers often begin by establishing their qualifications to write on the subject. Thus, if one of your professors writes a letter of recommendation for you, she may begin like this:

> I have known Suzanne Jacqueline for four years. She was my student in freshman composition and also in a senior seminar on Wordsworth. Moreover, I am advisor to the college's Writer's Club, of which Suzanne has been president for two years. Thus, I feel qualified to discuss both her academic abilities and her character.

Even students have the qualifications of experts on some subjects. Though you may not be experts in sociology, chemistry, or English, you probably know a lot more than your professors or your college administrators about the use of marijuana or liquor on campus, living conditions in the dormitories, the quality of food in the cafeteria, and so forth. Thus, you might begin a letter to the college paper by establishing your credentials:

> As an army brat who has attended eleven different schools and three different colleges in the last sixteen years, I have eaten food in many different cafeterias. I have some perspective on when food is merely bad and when it is downright disgustingly awful. With this much experience, I think I can comment fairly on the quality of the food in Grover Hall's cafeteria.

This writer is establishing her credentials as effectively as Elizabeth Canfield did. Because she has so much experience, we will take her comments more seriously than those of a freshman in his first week at college who says that the cafeteria meals are "the worst in the world."

Quite often, your direct ethical appeal will be less formal than the instances we've looked at, as in this example:

> Now all you folks know me pretty well and you know I don't drink or tell tall tales. That's why I know you'll believe me when I tell you that a giant space ship landed on my farm last night and . . . .

This beginning, too, is an example of direct ethical appeal in opening a discourse. It is one kind of beginning that you may want to use to establish your persona as worthy of belief and trust. It is one way of establishing ethical appeal quickly and forcefully.

Whether a speaker intends to or not, he will create a persona or voice—good or bad, favorable or unfavorable— just by the way he treats his audience and his subject. For example, the speaker who begins a speech by saying "Howdy, folks" has already begun to create a far different persona than the speaker who says, "Mr. Chairman, Members of the Council, and my fellow citizens . . . ." These and other differences in attitude toward your audience will help to determine whether your initial ethical appeal is favorable or unfavorable.

The speaker's attitude toward his subject at the beginning of his discourse may determine his persona for the entire discourse. Consider these two openings to editorials on the same political issue, and notice how the differences in openings create different personas in just a few lines:

> Governor George Forster's constant shifts of position on the issue of the state income tax seem so politically opportunistic that we must call into question his leadership ability and his political credibility. We urge the governor not to seek re-election next year.

Or:

> Governor Forster's stands on the income tax remind us of a boy trying to decide on which of the thirty-eight flavors of ice cream he'll eat. Like the

boy with too many choices, the governor can't seem to make up his mind. Such shenanigans are normal for politicians, but Governor Forster's on-again-off-again policies lead us to believe he doesn't know what he's doing. That's why we're sending him a Dear George letter advising him not to run again.

These two openings certainly create different appeals. The first writer is a serious, sober fellow that we'll listen to if we consider the governor's actions in a solemn and serious light. We respect this speaker as a man of judgement, seriousness, and forthrightness. The second persona is a much pleasanter fellow to read. He is casual, clever, and mildly cynical. However, he's not as forceful or as committed as the first persona, though he's certainly not afraid to take a stand. And whichever you prefer, you'll have to admit the differences in attitude toward the subject create different personas right away. Moreover, these personas will probably stick for the length of the editorials. The first speaker can hardly become jovial, and the second will have to stay casual, however serious his message actually is.

Rational appeals

Quite often a writer or speaker will pay little attention to ethical and emotional appeals at the beginning of a discourse. Instead he will concentrate on the subject itself. His beginning will be a preparation for the subject itself. It will focus on what is going to be discussed and how. Often this kind of beginning will also fulfill some of the functions of the statement of facts and the clarification of issues in the classical oration. It may outline the material that the work will cover. The persona will be unobtrusive and businesslike and will avoid appealing to the emotions. Here is a typical beginning that is rational in the sense that it focuses on the subject itself rather than on the speaker or on the emotions of the audience:

What I purpose to do in the following is not unique—it has been done before, although heretofore seldom in a way directly related to performance in the freshman writing course. I will give four case studies, each of a student whose attitude and peculiar combination of strengths and weaknesses typify that of a large group of students. The aim is to show the way several factors—psychological, sociological, even to a degree historical and religious—intersect to create the student as we encounter him in our writing courses. I wish to show how these factors are instrumental in causing him to write as he does and to offer, in a spontaneous if somewhat disorganized fashion, some of the insights I have derived from many such case studies I have made for my own benefit over the course of several years. These insights—I am calling them this for want of a more precise term—constitute, in the main, practical advice concerning ways in which to deal with students possessing the peculiar blend of traits which I will describe.[8]

Although the writer uses the first person pronoun, which is somewhat unusual in scholarly articles, his introduction is impersonal and rational. He indicates his subject, his method of proceeding and probably organizing his material ("four case studies"), the conclusions at which he'll arrive, and the value or purpose of the conclusions. This beginning is basically a lead into and a survey of the rest of the article. It seems more like a classical clarification of issues than an introduction as an attention-getting device. The writer seems to assume that his audience will be interested in the subject; thus, he does little to attract its attention with emotional appeals.

Another variation of this basic format is the introductory outline, the explanation of how all the material will fit together:

Ladies and gentlemen of the jury, I will show that my client, William Weber, is not guilty of the murder of Sharon Shaw. First, I will show that Mr. Weber loved Miss Shaw too much to have done her any harm. Second, I will prove that William Weber could not have been at the scene of the crime when the murder of Sharon Shaw is alleged to have occurred. Third, I will demonstrate that the witnesses testifying against my client are either unreliable or biased. Finally, I will refute the claims of the prosecutor, who

8. Bill Linn, "Psychological Variants of Success: Four In-Depth Case Studies of Freshmen in a Composition Class," *College English* 39 (April 1978), p. 903.

has attempted to present circumstantial evidence to convict my client. I will indicate how these claims are illogical or irrelevant. In sum, I will convince you that William Weber is not guilty beyond a reasonable shadow of doubt of the crime of murder.

This beginning certainly tells the audience what they can expect. It makes a claim and tells what evidence, what four points, will support that claim.

Sometimes the best beginning is no beginning at all. If you want to use a strictly rational appeal, you can often plunge directly into your subject. You might state your chief point or thesis and go on from there. This beginning is effective when you are sure that the audience is interested in the subject and is aware of your qualifications. Some good examples of such situations are the kinds of reports you'll write for employers and teachers, essay answers on examinations, and abstracts (or summaries), such as appear in scholarly or technical journals. (Nothing will make a teacher or boss more impatient than an irrelevant beginning that doesn't lead into the subject.) If your audience is interested in the subject, no beginning at all can be the best rational and the best emotional appeal.

Exercises

1. Examine how sections or chapters begin in various textbooks. Do most of them begin in the same way? Do they use rational appeals or do they begin with some other appeals? Do you find a pattern of differences according to which discipline the books belong to: sciences, social sciences, humanities, business?

2. Browse through a range of magazines—from movie fan magazines to scientific or scholarly journals, if possible—to see how articles typically begin. Do most begin with emotional, rational, or ethical appeals? Is there a consistent pattern within the different types of magazines?

3. Choose a subject in which you are interested and explain what kind of introduction you would write

for it in three different magazines with which you are familiar.

4. Compose *one* of these introductions.

The Body

The body of a discourse is its heart, its substance. It is the reason for the discourse and, as such, the only indispensable part of the work. We can get along without beginnings or ends, but we can't imagine a work without a body, a middle.

Rational order

The problem of organizing the body of a discourse may be simple or complex. After discovering what we want to say, what arguments we want to use, we can probably organize them in argumentative order, establishing a clear relationship among arguments, or at least showing no conflict among the arguments. Then we may still have to decide, based on such rhetorical concerns as persona, audience, content, and other matters, just what rhetorical order to choose. Sometimes, as in this student's paper, the order of arguments seems simple and almost natural:

Dear Ms. Doenone,

I am writing this letter in response to your letter "Obeying Laws." I feel your letter is based on a number of unwarranted assumptions.

In the first paragraph you state that it's about time everyone backed up the police and appreciated the fine job they do. This may be true most of the time, but there are exceptions. An example of this is pointed out in Mr. Brook's letter. The police at the Field House left while the parking lot was in turmoil, and they ejected people from the lobby.

In the next paragraph you state the assumption that if all of us back the police our children will respect them, and their job will be easier. Even if everyone backed them their job wouldn't be easier. They would still have the same job to do, but the people would have a different attitude toward them.

The last paragraph also contains unwarranted assumptions. You say we should get back to when kids knew that if the police got them, they would get it double when they got home. You are assuming parents today don't care if their kids are picked up by the police. This isn't usually the case; most parents care if their children get in trouble, and children of such parents are usually the ones that stay out of trouble. This statement also makes the assumption that kids would stay out of trouble because of fear of their parents. But such fear could cause the opposite results. Some kids would do the same thing again to get even with their parents.

The last sentence states, "If all parents obeyed the laws, the children would be more inclined to do so too." This isn't always true. Kids often break the law because of peer-group pressure. Their friends pressure them into doing things they wouldn't usually do.

Since your letter is based on these unwarranted assumptions, I think it is weak.

Sincerely,

John Wills

In replying to Ms. Doenone, John Wills made some rhetorical choices, yet he essentially followed a pattern of organization that was determined by his subject and rhetorical context. He used a very direct beginning, suggesting that he was going to talk about unwarranted assumptions. In making this choice, he also chose to state his main assertion at the end rather than the beginning. And, in terms of classical organization, he chose to use all refutation without confirmation. These were rhetorical choices. But in putting down actual arguments, the writer simply relied on the original letter to supply his organization. He replied to Ms. Doenone's letter paragraph by paragraph, with an extra whole paragraph devoted to Ms. Doenone's very last sentence. Thus, although the writer had to make some rhetorical choices, his major decision (about which he may not even have thought very much) was to follow the order that was already there—what seemed like "natural" order in this rhetorical situation.

Personal order

Sometimes the order that we choose depends on the persona or personal appeal. Such is the case in the following letter. The letter is a reply to a request from a friend about

whether he (the friend) should move into an apartment
with his girlfriend.

Dear Bill,

I have received your letter and have given this reply a great deal of thought.
You asked for my advice and you know I'm more than happy to give it to
you.

I don't believe you should live with a girl now or at any time during your
college career. The disadvantages far outweigh the advantages. I can speak
from experience as one who learned the hard way. You went to college to
get an education. You have to keep that first on your list of priorities. You
said you've met a girl and are contemplating living with her. Well, as you
know, I was eighteen years old and a student in college when I was
married. Also I was divorced when I was twenty. I started with the idea that
my ex-wife and I would simply live together. It seemed the "in" thing to do
at that time. It worked out fine for a while. Then there was a slip-up and
my ex-wife became pregnant. I got married because of that. It's pretty
unfortunate to get married because of a pregnancy instead of because of
love, but I couldn't have lived with myself if I had done it any other way. I
had to work full time plus go to school just to provide a place to live and
food to eat. After my ex-wife had the miscarriage, we found out we really
didn't care for each other, and we paid for our immature mistakes by still
living together because we each respected the marriage vows we had made
to each other. We finally decided there was no other way but to be
divorced. We wasted two years of our lives, we caused each other a great
deal of pain, and we hurt both our families. Sure, the parties were great,
the thought of having someone to sleep with every night was nice, but the
price we had to pay was far too high.

You're eighteen years old, Bill, and you're an intelligent person or else you
wouldn't be in college. Ask yourself if you're ready emotionally and
financially to support a wife and family. If your answer is no, then get to
work and do a good job on your courses. You will have four or more years
in college, and you will meet many girls and have many dates. Enjoy it
while you can. You have a whole lifetime to build a family. Lay the
groundwork now and you will be surprised how easy your desire to succeed
can be met.

I've spelled out my experiences to you hoping you can learn from them.
You'll have to make your own decisions then live with them. I hope I've
been of some help to you and have cleared up some of your confusion.

As always,
Jim

The writer's argumentative structure is very simple. It's something like this:

M.A. I don't believe you should live with a girl . . .
    I. I learned the hard way.
   II. You are probably not "ready emotionally and financially to support a wife and family."

But a good deal of the strength of the letter that Jim writes depends on the force of his personal experience. He ties his own personal experience to his main assertion. Then he follows a basically chronological order in tracing his relationship with his ex-wife. This simple story is the most convincing part of the letter. The paragraph in which Jim addresses Bill directly isn't very strong in itself, and it might not be effective if it came first. But following Jim's story, which takes up most of the letter, it's sufficient. Bill probably isn't too anxious to face the kind of experience that Jim has faced. Thus, the force of the letter depends on the writer discussing his personal experience first. In this letter, the order of arguments depends on the importance of the persona.

Emotional order

Quite often, however, the audience will be the most important factor in determining the order that a writer uses in the body of his work. In expository writing, for instance, we often explain an unfamiliar subject to an audience by beginning with something with which our audience is familiar. In persuasive writing, we often begin with those arguments with which our audience is most likely to agree, gradually working toward those on which there could be strong disagreement. Thus, if we were writing a piece opposing the use of government money for abortions and our audience was people who were undecided or mildly in favor of abortion, we probably would not begin with a strong moral argument. We might use other arguments first, hoping to gradually win our audience's assent. Eventually we might make some strong assertion like "Abortion is, in itself, an immoral act." But as good rhetoricians, we should recognize that starting with a moral position like that might immediately offend our audience.

The following piece from *Parade* (the Sunday newspaper magazine) is a good example of a discourse in which the structure is largely determined by the audience and the reaction that the writer expects it to have:

If you're just starting out in life, consider seriously the prospect of devoting your working years to a variety of jobs in government. These positions not only offer security and satisfaction but some of the most rewarding pension systems in existence.

Take the case of Evelle J. Younger, attorney general of California.

Younger, 59, is a double-dipper, who is any person drawing a tax-paid pension and a tax-paid salary at the same time.

Younger is paid $42,500 a year as attorney general of the state. Simultaneously he draws a pension of $530 a month from Los Angeles County, having previously served as district attorney of the county from 1964 to 1970.

Next June 19th he will draw a second pension as a retired major general in the Air Force Reserve. That pension will approximate $850 or more a month.

In January 1978, after he leaves his job as attorney general of California, he will collect a third pension of about $1450 a month for his eight years of state service.

Younger will receive a fourth pension in 1983 when he turns 65. For his past service as a superior court and municipal court judge, he will pull down another $1600 a month.

His four pensions, according to Dick Bergholz, veteran Los Angeles Times political reporter, will total $53,226 a year or $4435 a month.

Evelle Younger, however, intends to run for governor of California on the Republican slate. If he is elected or is appointed to a job in the federal government, each a reasonable possibility, he will become a quintuple-dipper, a man who receives four tax-paid pensions and a tax-paid salary.

There is nothing illegal about this pension setup. Younger has contributed to many of them, and it would be silly of him to turn down $53,226 a year or more in retirement pensions.

The point, however, is that we are approaching a crisis in government pensions in this country. They are rapidly developing into the taxpayers' nightmare.

Congress must pass adequate legislation to prevent this ever-growing monster of multi-dipping. Our children and grandchildren and our governments—municipal, state, and federal—will go bankrupt trying to pay them.

In the last 10 years, pensions of retired federal and military personnel, tied to the rate of inflation, have increased some 72%. And the end is nowhere in sight.[9]

The rhetorical structure of the whole piece, but especially the body, is quite different from its argumentative structure. At its barest, the argumentative structure is a chain of deliberative rhetoric that looks something like this:

M.A. "Congress must pass adequate legislation to prevent . . . multi-dipping."
I. ". . . our governments will go bankrupt . . . ."
  A. "In the last 10 years, pensions . . . have increased some 72%."
  B. The example of Evelle J. Younger supports this view.

The rhetorical structure, however, is quite different. After a beginning that seems like a bit of advice for young people planning careers, the body starts in paragraph two. The first seven paragraphs in the body discuss Younger's salary, his pensions, and the pensions he could receive—a total of $53,226 a year. The order here is roughly chronological, but it is likely to have a powerful emotional impact on the audience. Because the readers of *Parade* are newspaper readers, a very broad group that we could consider average citizens, they will be very upset at pensions that are worth two or three times what many of them make in a year. At this point, the writer has probably already convinced his audience of the main assertion, which comes in the eleventh paragraph. The first sub-assertion follows (it might be considered a rewording of paragraph ten), and the statistics on the last ten years add further support, perhaps showing that Evelle J. Younger isn't unusual. Nevertheless, the rhetorical

9. Lloyd Shearer, "Intelligence Report," *Parade* magazine, September 11, 1977, p. 16.

weight of the whole argumentative body is carried by the single example of one man, who may or may not be typical. In a time of disenchantment with politicians, Younger certainly makes a convenient rhetorical target.

The several examples that we have looked at suggest some of the possibilities of order in the body of a discourse. Some of the examples in earlier chapters suggest even more possibilities. We have open to us possibilities like the following: chronological order, from the known to the unknown, from cause to effect, from effect to cause, ascending order of importance, descending order of importance, point by point comparison (whether literal or metaphorical), from general to particular, from particular to general, and many other conventional forms of order. Whatever order we use, we should be aware of our argumentative structure and how our departures from it relate to the major elements in the rhetorical situation. Our awareness of such organizational patterns as the classical oration and the inverted pyramid should also help us make decisions about how to structure the body of a discourse.

Endings

What do we want an ending to do? What should it accomplish? Basically an ending is the writer's last contact with his audience, his last chance to influence that audience. It is the writer's or speaker's last chance to develop his three basic rhetorical appeals.

How can he best develop these appeals before leaving his audience? Which appeal should he concentrate on?

Emotional appeals

Most classical rhetoricians thought that the ending of a discourse was a place for emotional appeals, especially strong emotional appeals. This theory is probably a good one, particularly when the purpose of a speech or a piece of writing is to move the audience to action. In politics, for example, a candidate really must do two things. He must convince people that he is the better candidate, and he must further convince them that they should go to the polls to vote for him. That's why political speeches often end like this:

> As you've seen, my fellow Americans, the choice is clear. You can vote for my opponent and thus support a continuation of those policies that allow the rich and powerful to get richer and more powerful. Or you can vote for me and get policies that favor the little guy rather than privileged corporate interests. I want to return the government of this country to those who are the backbone of the country. I want to insure liberty and justice for all, not just for fat cats who now enjoy special favors and protection.
>
> But let me assure you that unless you get out to vote tomorrow, nothing will change in Washington. Unless you speak at the polls, you can expect more of the same treatment that you've suffered through for years. That's why I urge you to vote for me, Vincent Bookins. The fate of America is in your hands. God bless you and give you wisdom to choose wisely.

This ending, though a bit exaggerated, is fairly typical of the way political speeches end. It is full of vague wording that is highly emotional: *little guy, privileged corporate interests, liberty, justice, fate.* The ending is designed to get people to act by arousing their emotions, and is thus rhetorically appropriate in a speech asking for votes.

Often the same kind of emotional ending can be much briefer and more restrained, especially if the emotional appeals have been developed in the body of the work. Thus, an ad for a charity might end by saying, "And if you don't care, who will care for these helpless victims?" That direct appeal to the audience's emotions is legitimate in such situations.

Indeed, although many feel that appeals to the emotions, especially strong appeals, are undesirable or dishonest, they are ignoring some basic truths about human actions. People don't normally act on mere knowledge alone; they have to feel an emotional commitment to act. Thus, their emotions have to be aroused. The real issue is whether the emotions that a speaker or writer arouses are appropriate and justified in terms of moral and human values. If we are human, we should feel strong emotional revulsion toward murder, war, starvation, cancer, and other forms and causes of human misery. But we are probably too emotional if we are so concerned about the environment that we are willing to go to prison to protect a single tree in a park.

Finally, there are some purposes for which an emotional ending would be inappropriate. Suppose, for instance, you've just finished reading about and studying bisecting the angles of triangles. You'd hardly expect the chapter to end like this:

> Now that you've learned to bisect the angles of a triangle, it's your duty as an American citizen to show the Communists that Americans are the world's greatest angle bisectors. Go out and demonstrate the superiority of the free enterprise system of democracy by bisecting *one, two, three* big triangles every day.

The use of an emotional ending is clearly out of place here and wherever else your main goal is to convey information in a rational way.

Rational appeals

The end of a discourse is a good place for certain kinds of rational appeals. Among the chief rational functions of an ending are to review the content of a discourse, to summarize the material, and to draw conclusions from the material. These functions all involve clarifying and fortifying the material so that the audience ends up with a proper grasp of the material. All of these functions should flow out of the previous content in the discourse.

Let's look at the process of review, or *recapitulation,* at the end of a work:

> As we have seen, Romantic poetry has three dominant qualities. First of all, it is imaginative. That is, it stretches the limits of reality to include the marvelous, the miraculous, and the astonishing. Second, it is psychological or inner-oriented. Romantic poetry is to be judged by the power of its effects on the mind, heart, and emotions of the reader. Third, Romantic poetry values language for its own sake, glorying in the richness

of sounds, images, and structural patterns instead of literal content. These three qualities—imagination, psychological power, and verbal richness—are the most important characteristics of Romantic poetry.

This paragraph provides a good illustration of recapitulation. The speaker is not adding any new material; he is merely going over the material he previously covered. Recapitulation reminds the audience of what the speaker has said by going over each main point separately.

Similar in function to recapitulation is *summary*. When we summarize material, we condense it into a convenient form. Summary, like recapitulation, looks backward to material that we have previously covered. It does not introduce new material. And unlike recapitulation, summary involves unifying material rather than merely relisting items. Notice this ending:

Although "Politics and the English Language," *Animal Farm*, and *Nineteen Eighty-Four* use different literary techniques, they form a consistent argument concerning the English language. One finds pieces of this argument in his [Orwell's] essays and journalism. For example, in an editorial dated 1946, Orwell referred to the tendency of writers "friendly" to totalitarianism "to play tricks with syntax and produce unbuttoned-up or outright meaningless sentences." In the same piece, he comments negatively on one passage by a writer he considers totalitarian: "One non sequitur, one tautological phrase and two grammatical errors, all in sixty words" (*Essays*, IV, pp. 157–158).

It is important, I believe, to understand that Orwell's views on English were broadly and humanistically based. He was worried about the *individual*, and what the misuse of the language might do to him (and her). He was concerned about the total effect created by the misuse of words, grammar, syntax, metaphor, logic. The question he posed I infer to be something like this: How are honest rhetoric and linguistic competence related to the welfare of the free human individual? The answer is to be found in his work.[10]

---

10. A.M. Tibbetts, "What Did Orwell Think about the English Language?" *College Composition and Communication* 29 (May 1978), 166. Copyright © 1978 by the National Council of Teachers of English. Reprinted by permission of the publisher and the author.

This ending is a capsule, a miniature version of what the writer said in his paper. It is not, however, a point-by-point outline. It is rather an intellectual condensation of the substance of the paper, perhaps even in different words.

In drawing conclusions at the end of a work, a writer can add new material in the sense that he states explicitly what before was only implicit. Thus, having discussed how grocers gyp customers, the author draws these conclusions about Oswald Krell (the hypothetical manager of a small grocery store):

> Krell had accepted the outlook of big business; he shared the view that he was free to do anything the law did not expressly prohibit. If the law was silent with respect to the meaning of the word "special," then he was free to give the word his own meaning. His store, too, was laid out as a psychological trap for the customers to whom he otherwise provided courtesies and services—and he thought this was clever. He almost, but not quite, equated sharp practice with dishonesty. His view was rather like that of a great university that hires ringers for its football team and pretends that they are scholars, in that it is a view that lacks a moral base. It embraces the notions *If the other guys can get away with it, so can I* and *You're stupid if you don't do it.* Whatever is advantageous is seen as intelligent, and whatever is disadvantageous is seen as stupid, and advantage is measured in terms of dollars and cents.
>
> At bottom, if a moral swamp can be said to have a bottom, is the notion that business is a game, and that the point of playing a game is to win it. Since this is a prevalent American point of view, it is scarcely surprising that Krell should share it. Few, in any case, question who the losers are.[11]

Not only does the author draw together some conclusions from the work itself, but in the brief closing paragraph he is drawing a general conclusion about the meaning of dishonesty in business. The conclusion, though not an inescapable one, adds a new insight to the whole article.

In review, we can see that the three major forms of rational appeals in ending a discourse are review, summary,

11. John Keats, "Rip-Off at the Supermarket," *The Atlantic Monthly* (March 1976), p. 34.

and conclusion. They can also be combined with emotional appeals.

Ethical appeals

Trying to introduce direct ethical appeals into your ending probably won't be very effective. If you have not already established a trustworthy and sympathetic persona, it's probably too late to start. If you have established a solid persona, you may not want to call too much direct attention to it, because this may detract from your emotional and rational appeals. But you may want to use an indirect ethical appeal. This ending to a political speech delivered the night before the election is a good example of an indirect ethical appeal.

> Now, my fellow Americans, I hope that whoever is your choice, you will go to the polls tomorrow and vote for the candidate of your choice. Only by your participation in the electoral process can our democracy function smoothly and responsively to your will. Your vote is the voice that I seek to obey.

This candidate attempts to improve his ethical appeal by appearing impartial on a matter on which he is quite partial and by appearing wholly subservient to the will of the people. Our impression is supposed to be that this man is selfless and idealistic. This appeal is rather conventional, and it will only work if the rest of the speech supports the persona. In general, though, the end is not a good place for an ethical appeal, at least not a new ethical appeal.

Summary

Organizing a discourse is not merely a matter of following mechanical rules for arranging the material. Good organization involves the management of all three appeals—the rational, the emotional, and the ethical—at every stage of the discourse. As writers and speakers, we should be aware of exactly what we hope to accomplish in each section of our work.

At the beginning of our work, we want to gain our audience's attention and interest, establish our persona, and introduce our subject, or combine two or three of these appeals in the proper proportion. An ideal introduction can perhaps advance all three appeals. In our body, which is the heart of the work, we want to organize our material as forcefully as we can. The exact arrangement of our material will depend on the rhetorical situation. At the end of our work, we want to leave our audience with the right emotional attitude and the right grasp of the subject itself. Thus we can use emotional or rational appeals or both. We may, in some situations, use emotional appeals to arouse our audience to action. We may use various strategies of review, summary, and conclusion to reinforce the audience's awareness of the subject itself and to remind it of what it may have forgotten. As for ethical appeals, it is probably best not to stress them at the end of a discourse. If we have established a good persona throughout the work, it will carry through to the end. If we haven't, it's probably too late to start.

Things to Do

1. Analyze how commercials on television seek to get your attention in unusual, even bizarre ways. Identify three commercials and explain how they appeal to the audience.

2. Get either a weekly tabloid newspaper (like the *National Enquirer* or *Midnight*) or a movie magazine. What kinds of headlines or titles are on the cover? Does the content of the articles live up to the promise of the covers?

3. Analyze some famous speech or other historical document written for a specific historical purpose. How close does the body of the work come to ar-

gumentative structure? How do the beginning and the ending function? You might use Lincoln's Gettysburg Address, the Declaration of Independence, or any number of presidential speeches.

4. Analyze the structure of an editorial, an opinion column, or a letter to the editor in your newspaper. Identify the argumentative structure and the kind of beginning and ending the writer uses. Can you explain why the writer chose the specific structure he used? Could the writer have structured his material more effectively?

Writing Assignments

For each of the assignments listed below, include the standard outline as indicated in chapter one. However, you should add a sixth item to your outline: Rhetorical Structure. Under that item list the kind of beginning and ending you'll use and the main arguments. Here's what such an outline might look like for a paper advocating lower speed limits on highways:

VI. Rhetorical Structure
    A. Beginning: startling fact
    B. Arguments:
        1. Design of automobiles
        2. Power of lobbies
        3. Results of lower speeds
    C. Ending: emotional plea about saving lives.

1. Write a detailed reply to some editorial, opinion column, or letter to the editor with which you strongly disagree. Write the piece for your local newspaper or your campus newspaper.

2. Write a letter to the president of your college pointing out some situation, rule, or policy that needs to be changed. You may wish to suggest an alternative. (Relative to classical structure, you may want to think especially hard about a refutation—a set of argu-

ments that might refute the arguments that your audience would use in replying to you.)

3. Write a review of some movie you've seen recently and about which you felt strongly. Choose a place of publication for the review and argue strongly that the audience should or should not see the movie.

4. Use the form of a classical oration in writing to a public official (a senator, state legislator, school board member) urging that some action be taken on an issue of current concern.

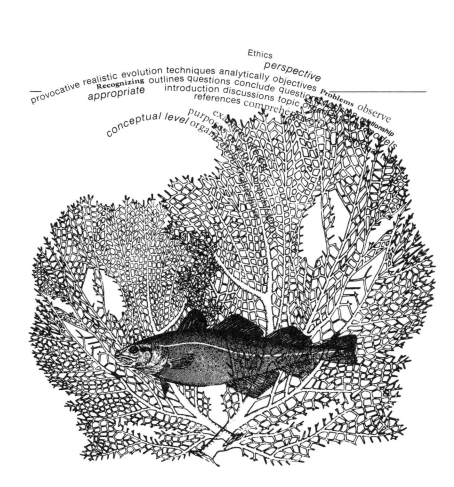

Chapter Seven

THE
PARAGRAPH

Paragraphs in Context

In the first four chapters we looked at the elements in the rhetorical situation as a whole and as separate components. In the next two chapters we looked at ways of finding material and then of organizing it. In this chapter and the next two (on sentences and words) we are going to be getting close to writing itself, that mysterious process by which ideas, perhaps only half-formed in our minds, begin to appear on paper. For this process the paragraph is perhaps the key unit, for it is the bridge between our larger rhetorical plan and the basic units of written English, sentences and words. In this chapter we will treat paragraphs as separate units, while remembering that they are parts of larger structures that flow out of a variety of rhetorical situations. We will isolate paragraphs and discuss how we can write individual paragraphs effectively. We will attempt to outline some general principles for writing good paragraphs.

What is a paragraph? One obvious answer is that a paragraph is a unit of writing that begins with a left-hand indentation and ends with a right-hand indentation (or with another paragraph's left-hand indentation). While this answer may seem too elementary, it does suggest some important truths about the paragraph. First, the paragraph is a *unit of writing*. It belongs to the written language. Paragraphs do not occur in the spoken language. Second, as a unit of the written language, the paragraph (unlike the sentence) is largely a unit of convenience for the reader. The purpose of the paragraph is to break up the monotony of the solid page of print. That is why the lengths of paragraphs vary in the handwritten page, the typed page, the narrow column of the newspaper, and the wide page of the normal book. Newspaper paragraphs, like those in the article about auto sales in chapter six, tend to consist of one or two sentences, while the paragraphs in a book may be as long as the paragraph by Henry James in chapter four.

As a unit of convenience, the paragraph can do more than simply break up the monotony of a page. It can divide the discourse into meaningful units. For the shorter kinds of rhetorical writing—essays, articles, reports, and serious letters—the paragraph is often the unit of argument. The typical pattern would be to have both an opening and a closing paragraph and then one sub-assertion and its support in each intervening paragraph. An example that comes very close to this pattern is the letter about natural gas prices in chapter two. Except for transitional paragraphs, which function to help shifts in thought and which are normally short, most paragraphs (what we'll call *substantive* paragraphs) indicate major ideas, units of argument, or other important divisions in a piece of rhetorical writing. That is how you should probably use paragraphs in your rhetorical writing, depending, of course, on other elements in the rhetorical situation.

Another way of looking at the paragraph is to use Robert M. Gorrell's suggestion that writing consists of a series of commitments and responses.[1] What this means is that many substantive paragraphs in rhetorical writing con-

---

1. Robert M. Gorrell, "The Writer's Commitment to His Reader," *Rhetoric*, Richard L. Larson, ed. (Indianapolis: Bobbs-Merrill Company, 1968), pp. 45–49. Originally published in "Very Like a Whale: A Report on Rhetoric" *College Composition and Communication* 16 (October 1965), 142–43 and "Not by Nature: Approaches to Rhetoric," *English Journal* 55 (April 1966), 10–13.

sist of an assertion or topic sentence that makes a commitment to the reader and of subsequent sentences that fulfill that commitment. Let's take, for example, this opening sentence to a paragraph: "There were three main causes for the defeat of Germany in World War II." A writer who begins his paragraph in this way has made a commitment to his material and his reader. He must talk about the defeat of Germany in World War II, and he cannot reasonably talk about World War I or about Germany's economic recovery after World War II. Moreover, he has committed himself to listing three causes rather than two, five, or some other number. This way of looking at a paragraph will be very helpful. We should avoid thinking of the topic sentence as the central idea or most general assertion in the paragraph (though it may be); we should think of it as the opening commitment. Such a notion of the paragraph will be the one we'll use in discussing how to write paragraphs.

A related notion of the paragraph is Francis Christensen's definition of the paragraph as "a sequence of structurally related sentences."[2] That definition is useful because it suggests that the sentences in a paragraph belong together, that they have some meaningful relation to each other. Christensen's theory of the paragraph will help us revise and improve paragraphs that we have written. It will suggest formal standards for testing and verifying how good a job we have done in writing our paragraphs.

Commitment and Response

The theory of the paragraph as commitment and response sees the paragraph as a dynamic unit, one which develops as a writer composes it. Rather than a single commitment and response, a complex paragraph is an inter-

---

2. Francis Christensen, "A Generative Rhetoric of the Paragraph," *Notes Toward a New Rhetoric*, 2nd ed., by Francis Christensen and Bonnijean Christensen (New York: Harper & Row, 1978), p. 79. Originally published in *College Composition and Communication* 16 (October 1965), 144–156.

locking series of commitments and responses. The opening sentence of a paragraph makes a commitment, and the next sentence responds to that commitment. But in responding to the first sentence, the second sentence is also creating a commitment that another sentence or set of sentences must fulfill. If a sentence makes commitments that are not fulfilled or responded to, then the writing process has gone awry, and the reader will be disappointed and confused.

In order to better understand this process of commitment and response, let's look again at the three paragraphs from the chemistry textbook on states of aggregation (pages 64–65).

In the first paragraph, the first sentence makes a commitment to talk about three states of aggregation, which it names. The next sentence begins to fulfill the commitment by responding to the first item in the series of commitments. In talking about a solid, it *specifies* or explains part of the first sentence. Likewise, the third sentence continues the response to the first sentence. It explains the second and third items in the series. The fourth sentence more or less *repeats* in summary the meaning of the preceding sentence by introducing the word *fluid*. The last sentence then further specifies or explains what fluid means.

In the second paragraph, the series is simpler. The first sentence makes a commitment or claim about difficulties in making distinctions. The next two sentences offer specific examples. The third sentence, with its complex detail, seems to need more explanation, a commitment which the last sentence fulfills with a more specific explanation or definition.

In the third paragraph, the commitment and response are somewhat different. The first sentence makes a straightforward commitment about the relation of the state of aggregation to temperature and pressure. But the next sentence *diverts* or *deviates* from that commitment (as signaled by the word *however*) and goes off in a new direction. This new direction is the real subject of the paragraph. Sentence three responds to sentence two by getting more specific; sentence four, in turn, specifies an instance of sentence three. Because the second, third, and fourth sentences seem so startling a contrast with the first sentence, the writers apparently felt that the whole paragraph created a commitment, a need for further explanation. Thus, they add a final sentence that committed them to talking about simultaneous existence later.

The three sample paragraphs are examples of good expository prose. They make commitments clearly and respond to them. Moreover, the passage illustrates what Robert M. Gorrell suggests are the three general types of responses to commitments: *specification, repetition* (or *restatement*), and *diversion* (or *deviation*).[3]

Specification

One of the most common patterns of response to commitments is to *specify*. This means to present examples, illustrations, or explanations that are more detailed than was the original sentence, the commitment. Indeed, this pattern of response is so basic and common that it often stands as the only pattern in many paragraphs, especially those which rely on evidence as a means of support. Consider the following example:

That Americans love to be scared half to death and that they are willing to pay good money for a scare is evident from the continued popularity of horror films. *Frankenstein* was so successful that it practically created a genre. *Psycho* and *The Exorcist* created psychological thrills. And *Jaws* was so successful that ambitious moviemakers could not resist making *Jaws II*, just as they made *The Bride of Frankenstein* to capitalize on the success of the original.

Quite often, the form that specification takes will be gradually more specific assertions following upon a very general assertion. Eventually such a series of commitments and responses may get to specific facts or instances. The paragraph from *Harper's* in chapter five offers one good

3. Robert M. Gorrell, "The Writer's Commitment to His Reader," p. 47.

example in a pattern resembling the inverted pyramid. Here is another example:

> Poets are too various to easily fit anyone's stereotype of them. Their life styles range from the most conventional to the most outlandish. Some have pursued ordinary business, professional, and social lives, while others have barely survived in bohemian worlds in which art rather than economics ruled. T. S. Eliot was a banker, John Donne a preacher, and Chaucer a courtier, while Whitman, Coleridge, and Poe led—with varying success—lives of uneasy poverty in devotion to their writing and to literature itself.

Repetition

Responding to a commitment by *repetition* or restatement is also quite common. In a certain sense, much of what we write amounts to repeating something we have already said in slightly different words. This is especially true when we use defining as a strategy for clarifying or arguing a point. This paragraph itself opens with a statement that is repeated in slightly different form in the second sentence. But repetition, with slight variations and movements forward, is also common in clarifying issues and making fine distinctions. An excellent example of this use of repetition can be found in both of McGeorge Bundy's paragraphs on the Bakke case in chapter five. Such use of restatement is also an excellent device to gain emphasis, too. When a writer repeats something, his audience will probably notice what he's saying.

The use of repetition or restatement is common, though it is not often that we will use it as extensively as Bundy does. More commonly, we will use it at the beginning of a paragraph for a few sentences to clarify ideas that we have introduced in the first sentence.

Diversion

Diversion or *deviation* is a contrast to repetition. Repetition means staying with the same material, while diversion means going off in a new direction. Diversion involves a shift in focus, direction, attitude, or idea. We saw such a shift in the third paragraph of the selection from the chemistry textbook. Another example is in the second sentence of the passage by Rachel Carson on page 100. In both examples, the paragraph seems to be committed to going in one direction, but the second sentence diverts it in a new direction.

Another pattern of diversion is also common, a pattern by which a paragraph shifts in the middle. The first paragraph in selection C in chapter two, for example, shifts in a new direction at the fourth sentence. Similarly, the following paragraph, which is the opening of a student paper, shifts in a whole new direction:

> On the outskirts of a small midwestern town lies one of our nation's most prestigious universities. This university is one which prides itself on its football tradition and academic excellence. It can be found in South Bend, Indiana, and it can be called Notre Dame. Until a few years ago you could always find the name "Notre Dame" right up there with terms like baseball, hotdogs, and apple pie. Today that name, along with all of that tradition, is in jeopardy. Unless Notre Dame fans, more specifically students and alumni of the university, start acting like educated beings, the university will lose a lot of its prestige. The reason behind all this is the hostile treatment which the fans have showered their head football coach with over the past few years. This involves the treatment of Dan Devine.

This paragraph starts in one direction, saying laudatory things about Notre Dame. But it begins to shift or deviate in the fourth sentence, and by the fifth sentence the paragraph has deviated in a whole new direction.

When deviation occurs in the middle of a paragraph, as it does in the last example, the writer has a choice. He can either keep the deviation within the paragraph or divide the paragraph in two, making the deviation a paragraph by itself. What the writer does will probably depend on just how long the paragraphs would be and on how closely the writer wants the ideas tied together. If two separate paragraphs would be too short or if the two segments seem to belong together, perhaps to emphasize a contrast, then the writer should probably use one paragraph.

It should be clear that these three patterns of response to commitments are very broad categories. We should not think of them as invariable rules that we have to follow. They merely suggest the ways in which many paragraphs are written, even though most writers move from one sentence to another without consciously fulfilling any abstract pattern of commitment. Moreover, as we have seen in looking at a number of paragraphs, most paragraphs are mixed. They contain at least two and perhaps even all three patterns of response within them, rather than a single kind of response (though a single kind of response is possible in some paragraphs).

Exercises

1. Read the following two paragraphs from a student paper and describe the pattern of commitment and response throughout each paragraph, sentence by sentence.

   Carter's reasoning, at best, is based on two premises. First, Carter wants to slow down the development of nuclear weapons in countries that don't yet have them. Second, he sees that these underdeveloped countries have neither the money nor the technology to build nuclear weapons. By not allowing the breeder reactor to be built here, Carter seeks to eliminate, or at least slow down, these developments.

   The plan would seem to be effective. If we stop developing nuclear technology here, it stands to reason that other countries will be set back decades in further technological advancements. However, a college student at Princeton, who described himself as one of the "poorer physics students on campus," developed a technique to make an A-bomb for about $2,000. If a college student can develop an A-bomb with only rudimentary knowledge of physics then a country could, also.

2. Choose one of the following sentences as the opening sentence of a paragraph. Then write three short

paragraphs, one each exemplifying the patterns of specification, repetition, and diversion.

a. Women generally mature earlier than men do.

b. Success in school does not necessarily result in success in life.

c. Love should be based on more than physical attraction.

d. College professors think they know everything.

e. Personal freedom should be the goal of a democratic society.

f. Women should be as free as men are in choosing careers.

3. Compose a single solid paragraph that uses all three forms of response. Start with the topic sentence you used for exercise 2, or choose another topic sentence from that exercise.

Coherence

A pattern of commitments and responses depends upon the exact words and phrases that a writer uses. When we sit down to write, we always write in words, and words themselves establish commitments and demand responses. So, too, do the sentence patterns that we compose. In short, when we sit down to write, we are establishing many subpatterns of commitment and response, both in the words themselves and in the sentences in which we place them. The general term that we use to describe the totality of commitments and responses is *coherence.* If a paragraph is *coherent,* it holds together well; its parts seem to belong together.

We will look carefully at many of the devices that we can use to gain coherence. Coherence is one of the basic qualities of a good paragraph, and we should be aware of it as we write. Most of the devices are so common that you are probably already using them. This discussion and explanation will merely serve to sharpen your awareness of them.

Devices of coherence

The following paragraph illustrates some of the common devices that writers use to gain coherence. You should notice especially the italicized words and phrases (that were not so marked in the original):

A good *chairman* is pro-*faculty* in his bias and in his relations with the administration, *but he* is also tough. *By this I mean* that *although he* is positively disposed toward *faculty* interests and supportive of the *faculty* of his department, *he* is also realistic about which of *their* requests it will be productive to grant, about what proposals will work out, about what recommendations to take and when to say "no." *Though he* will identify with the *faculty, he* may have to differ with *them* on important issues. *These* will not occur often, but *he* needs a veto and the strength not to be dependent on their liking *him. Above all, however, he* needs their *support,* for the *chairman* who gets into a struggle with his *faculty* and loses *their allegiance* cannot be sustained by the dean. *Faculty support* is the only true source of a *chairman's* power; a dean can augment or diminish that power by certain policies, but he cannot maintain for any prolonged time a *chairman* whom the *faculty* reject.[4]

Among the chief devices that hold this passage together are repeated words. The two key words in the passage are *chairman* and *faculty,* both of which occur in almost every sentence. If these specific words do not occur, then the pronouns that refer to them, *he* or *his* and *they* or *their,* act as links to tie the passage together. Other words that are repeated are *support* (or its synonym *allegiance*) in the last few sentences. Besides the pronouns that refer to key words, there are demonstrative pronouns that serve to strengthen the coherence between sentences. *This* in sentence two refers back to the whole first sentence, and *these* in sentence four refers to *issues* in the previous sentence, thus connecting the sentences. Another device of coherence and clarification is the use of phrases that both connect sentences and clarify the relationships between them. For instance, sentence two opens with the phrase, "By this I

4. Marilyn L. Williamson, *ADE Bulletin* (November 1976), p. 8.

mean," indicating that sentence two will restate sentence one. Similarly, "Above all, however," at the beginning of the fifth sentence indicates the importance of what follows in relation to what has gone before, but it also suggests a shift in direction, a deviation.

Although words are perhaps the chief means of coherence that any writer uses, sentence structure can also be important. It is in the example. Not only are *chairman* or *he* repeated often, but these words tend to be the grammatical subjects of most sentences and clauses, and they occur at the beginnings of the clauses, where subjects normally occur. Thus *chairman* is subject of the first, third, and fifth sentences and of important clauses in the second and fourth sentences. The use of identical grammatical forms and similar positions also serves as a device of coherence, keeping the reader's focus on the chairman as the subject of the passage, both conceptually and grammatically. Another way in which the sentence structures function in this paragraph is to divide sentences into two parts that suggest conflict. Thus, the first clause of the first sentence suggests one thing, but the word *but* suggests a deviation, a conflict between the two clauses. This two-part pattern continues in the next three sentences, partly marked by *although* and *though*. The repetition of these patterns of sentence structure and idea is a further aid to coherence.

As a close look at the sample paragraph indicates, most of the devices of coherence are part of any writer's standard repertoire. You all repeat words, use pronouns, use connective words or phrases, and try to structure sentences in a sensible way. In other words, you have been using devices of coherence all along, though you may not have been aware of it. Your job now is to continue writing paragraphs as you have been, moving from sentence to sentence and from idea to idea. As a help to you, we will be looking at the paragraph as "a sequence of structurally related sentences" —Christensen's notion. This will aid you in revising to improve the coherence and readability of your paragraphs.

Before we go on, it might be wise to talk about some of the devices of coherence in the sample in relation to what some of you have been taught previously. For instance, many of you have been taught not to repeat words, as the author of the paragraphs did. If you were writing the passage according to what you have learned, you would probably hunt around for synonyms for *chairman: director, supervisor, departmental leader,* and so forth. For another instance, many of you have been taught not to repeat sentence patterns, especially by putting subjects at or near the beginnings of sentences, as the author did. If you were writing the paragraph, you probably would want to revise the sentences drastically. You were taught to seek sentence variety. Why have the rules of writing suddenly changed?

There are several possible ways to answer this question. First of all, you were probably taught to use variety in both wording and sentence structure because, at your former stage of education, your teachers wanted you to develop flexibility with language. They wanted you to develop your vocabulary and your command of sentences. These goals, admirable in themselves, somehow became hard and fast rules that may be preventing you from communicating effectively in your writing. Second, as a practical matter, your use of variety may confuse your reader. If you use half a dozen synonyms for *chairman,* your reader may think you are writing about several different people. The theory behind variety is that it is more interesting than sameness; it avoids monotony. Even if that be true, your first goal is to write clearly so that your audience will understand you. For many of you, writing itself is difficult. Thus, if you want to interest your readers, do it with your content, not your style. Very few writers, even among professionals, are good enough to impress readers with their style. Third, the truth about good professional writers is that most of them don't use variety for its own sake. In fact, a study has shown that good prose stylists usually begin about three-quarters of their sentences with the subject.[5] Thus, if you want to use models of excellence for your standard, do as the pro-

5. Francis Christensen, "Notes Toward a New Rhetoric: I. Sentence Openers," *Classical Rhetoric for the Modern Student,* 2nd ed., Edward P. J. Corbett (New York: Oxford University Press, 1971), p. 442. Originally published in *College English* 25 (October 1963).

fessionals do: stick with basic patterns and basic words unless you have a darn good reason for your variations. In sum, variety is not a virtue in itself, and it may be a detriment to coherence and readability.

Exercises

1. Read the following paragraph and answer the questions about it:

> The wishful thinking in these newspaper stories is remarkable. In a *Times* book review of the same vintage, summer 1976, Anatole Broyard referred to "the feminist insistence on the power of positive thinking." But positive thinking has always been the mental process behind antifeminism, with its eternal dodges and reassurances: the status of women is natural, and women need only learn to enjoy it; the status of women is improving, and women need only cease from fuss. Positive thinking is wheeled out, not in the worst of times, when inequitable relations between the sexes go unquestioned, but in times when something better can be imagined. It was ancient Rome, where women had considerable but by no means complete freedom, that made a heroine of Arria. This positive-thinking woman beckoned her husband to a gentlemanly way out of his troubles with the authorities by stabbing herself, and saying, "It does not hurt." It was Rome, as well, that heard Cato's fatuous claim "We who govern all men are ourselves governed by our women." Arria was a fanatical sister of the women who sweat around in pantyhose, swearing they feel great. And Cato would be at home on the *New York Times*, where he could write stories that lie about the "liberation" of women today.[6]

> a. Are repeated words or phrases used for coherence? Point out specific examples.
> b. Are pronouns used? If so, how are they used? Point out examples.

---

6. Veronica Geng, "Requiem for the Women's Movement," *Harper's* (November 1976), p. 51.

    c. Are there words or phrases that clarify and con-
       nect sentences? If so, identify them.
    d. Does sentence structure act as a device of coher-
       ence? If so, explain how.
2. Read the following paragraph that an angry English
   professor wrote and handed out to the students in his
   class:

> From now on you students are going to live by strict rules in my
> class. First of all, you will attend every class, without exception,
> unless you have a medical excuse. That means a note from the college
> doctor or your own doctor. And too many of you have been wandering
> into class late every day. That's got to stop. So has all the talking and
> mumbling in class. It's so noisy in here I can't hear myself think.
> There have been too many late papers. I am not going to tolerate any
> more late papers. If papers are not in on time, I'll give them F's.
> Finally, I won't give you any more breaks; the rules are the rules.

    a. Is this paragraph an easy one to read?
    b. Is it coherent?
    c. What problems do you find in the paragraph?
       Explain in terms of what you've learned about
       coherence.
    d. Revise this paragraph using the various devices
       you've learned in order to make it more coherent.

Revising paragraphs

Writing paragraphs, word by word and sentence by
sentence, is a personal act that each writer probably does a
little differently. Nobody really knows just how things get
from inside the writer onto the paper. The process of
revising, however, can be much more conscious and subject
to rules. In fact, we can lay out some fairly rigid rules for
the paragraph as a sequence of structurally related sentences.

Just what do we mean when we define a paragraph in
this way? We mean that a paragraph not only conveys

content or information to a reader but that it simultaneously organizes the material so that the reader reads and interprets the material in the way the writer wants him to. To put it another way, a paragraph not only tells the audience *what* it should know but *how* it should know it. Let's look at an analogy. Reading a complex paragraph is like traveling along a treacherous road. Just as the highway department puts plenty of cautionary signs along a dangerous road—"Bad Curve Ahead," "Steep Hill," "One-Lane Bridge," and so forth—so too should a good writer signal to his reader where the reader is going and how he's getting there. A good writer puts plenty of signs out for his reader to follow. He is giving his audience directions on how to read the paragraph.

The directions that a writer gives his audience are generally of two kinds: *content* signals and *structural* signals. Content signals are words and phrases that define the relationships within a paragraph. Here are some content signals: *first of all, however, finally, most important, consequently, and also, because of this, as a result, in other words, similarly,* and so on. Structural signals are ways of structuring material in sentences. For instance, similar ideas should be stated in similar sentence patterns, with similar wording. In that way the reader can clearly see the relationship between the ideas, examples, incidents, and so forth.

If we apply these principles of structuring and coherence to the paragraph by the angry professor, we can probably analyze the faults of his paragraph and revise it to make it more coherent. As the paragraph stands, the class will know that the professor is angry with them. His hostility is clear enough. But they may not be too sure what all the rules are. If they read the paragraph carefully they can probably figure out what the rules are, but the professor certainly didn't make their job easy. In his anger, he got careless or too emotional and wrote a paragraph that's hard to read. Both the content and the structural signals are confusing. For a content signal, he uses *First of all,* but he never uses a *second* or *third.* He does use *finally,* but he uses it incorrectly. What follows *finally* is not a final item in the same series; it's more of a summary, for which *in general* would be more appropriate. As for structural signals, the writer uses them very poorly. In his first sentence he promises a list of rules, but then he fails to state them in a consistent way. He begins by saying *you will.* He shifts to *that's got to,* and follows with the similar *so has,* which ties these rules together. But in discussing late papers, he shifts to *I am not going to.* His final sentence, which should tie the whole paragraph together, seems structured like the rule for late papers—*I won't.*

If we go back and revise this paragraph, putting in the proper content and structural signals, we'll see how much clearer the paragraph will be. We'll see how much easier it will be for the reader to understand something like this:

> From now on you students are going to live by strict rules in my class. First of all, you will attend every class, without exception, unless you have a medical excuse. That means a note from the college doctor or your own doctor. Second, you will get to class on time. Too many of you have been wandering in late every day, which has to stop. Third, you will talk only when I call upon you. There has been too much noise in class. Finally, you will have your papers in on time or receive F's. You have been handing in far too many late papers. In general, I won't be giving you any more breaks: the rules are the rules.

This revision is easier to follow because both its content and its structural signals are clear and consistent. Indeed, they reinforce each other. The content signals are consistent. *First of all, Second, Third,* and *Finally* identify the rules, and *In general* indicates that the information that follows is different from the specific rules. The structural signals are also consistent. Each rule is stated in the form of a duty, in similar words—*you will.* This repetition provides a structural signal that what follows is a rule.

Although this paragraph may seem somewhat rigid, this rigidity has the advantage of clarity. Besides, there is some variety within this paragraph. In between the sentences that state the rules, the sentences are structured differently and perform different functions. The first intervening sentence explains what "a medical excuse" means, while the second, third, and fourth explain the reasons for the rules, though these sentences are structured differently. Of the four, one begins with the pronoun *that,* one with the phrase *too many of you,* another with the expletive *there,* and the last with the pronoun *you.*

Perhaps this clarity of content sacrifices some emotional force. In the clearer, more carefully structured paragraph, the persona does not seem as angry as the original persona. Thus, the writer has a choice to make. If he wants to convey sheer anger, maybe the first version of the paragraph is more effective. If he wants to convey his rules in a clear, orderly way so that his students will know them and be able to follow them, then the second version is more effective. The revising stage is a good time to make this kind of decision. To twist an old saying, "Write in haste, revise at leisure."

As this analysis and revision suggests, revising your paragraphs can be an almost mechanical process. It's a matter of checking both content and structural signals to be sure that the sentences and ideas in the paragraph are properly related to each other and to the pattern of commitments that the paragraph makes. Indeed, in much rhetorical writing, the structure of paragraphs will be and should be very much like argumentative structure. A sentence might be either *coordinate* to another sentence or sentences, or it might be *subordinate* to another sentence. If it's coordinate to other sentences, its structure should be similar, and the content signals should indicate that. If it's subordinate to another sentence, the content signals will often indicate the exact nature of the relationship. A well-written rhetorical paragraph is, in essence, a mini-argument.

Let's look at one more example of a coherent, well-structured paragraph:

As the historical co-founders of English Romanticism, Wordsworth and Coleridge had a lot in common, but they also had some fundamental differences. Both had a tremendous admiration for the imagination and its products, but their attitudes toward their own imaginations differed considerably. Wordsworth trusted his imagination without hesitation, while Coleridge seemed suspicious of his, feeling that it might betray him. Both were poets of nature, but their devotions to nature were unequal, Wordsworth's being deeper and more enduring. Finally, both saw philosophical poetry as the highest goal, but the emphasis of each was far different. Wordsworth cared primarily about poetry. He was happy to have produced a number of great poems. Coleridge, however, cared most deeply about philosophical issues, about creating a system and a method that would intellectually solve the world's problems. Thus, to see only what the two have in common is to miss some underlying differences that set the two apart.

The opening sentence of the paragraph makes a commitment to talk about Wordsworth and Coleridge and the ways in which they are alike and the ways in which they are different. The key content signal in the first sentence is *but,* which balances "a lot in common" against "fundamental differences." The writer uses this signal and its surrounding structure to establish a pattern for the paragraph. He uses three sentences which directly relate to or support the first sentence. Each of the three uses the word *both* at or near its beginning, and each is a two-part sentence with *but* in the middle of contrasting comments. Thus, the sentences are structured alike and use the key words *both* and *but* to signal that they are all related to the first sentence in the same way. The material directly explaining each of these three contrasts is structured a bit differently each time, but there is still a basic pattern of division into two parts, reflecting the central division in the first sentence.

Often the coherence, the clarity, and the persuasiveness of a paragraph will depend on how effectively a writer revises his paragraph after he writes it. For instance, the following paragraph is a good mini-argument in the sense that it contains some solid support for the main assertion:

All public schools should be closed down. In most places, school taxes are the largest single form of local taxes. The education public schools offer is too impractical. Many high school graduates can neither read nor write. Closing these schools will save the taxpayers a lot of money. Besides, most students are bored with what they are supposed to be learning in school. The schools can't even educate people satisfactorily by their own standards. School taxes usually constitute anywhere from forty to eighty percent of local taxes. The schools offer a kind of education that people neither want nor need.

However, the paragraph is not likely to be very persuasive because the reader is overwhelmed by a jumble of ideas that don't seem to be in any very clear order. If the writer can revise his paragraph effectively, he may be able to persuade his reader, or at least get the reader to understand his argument better. Notice the difference in the paragraph after it has been revised to make the content and structural signals clearer:

> All public schools should be closed down. First, closing these schools will save the taxpayers a lot of money. School taxes are the largest single form of local taxes in most places. They constitute anywhere from forty to eighty percent of local taxes. Second, the schools offer a kind of education that people neither want nor need. Most students are bored with what they are supposed to be learning in school. Also, most find that their education is too impractical. This is shown by their inability to get jobs based on what they have learned in school. Finally, the schools can't even educate people satisfactorily by their own standards. This is evident when so many high school graduates can neither read nor write.

The revised paragraph is much clearer, largely because of the content signals (especially the numbers) and the proper grouping of material. The other content and structural signals also help a good deal.

As you should see by now, revising your paragraphs can be as important as discovering what to say and then writing down the material. The paragraph is perhaps the key unit in writing, and if you can produce clear, coherent paragraphs, your reader will understand what you are saying. If he understands you, there's a better chance that he'll be persuaded by your arguments.

Transitional paragraphs

Our discussion of paragraphs has dealt so far with *substantive* paragraphs, those that are the chief structural blocks and the chief carriers of content in our writing. There are, however, other paragraphs, *transitional* paragraphs.

A transitional paragraph is a kind of extended content signal. Rather than carrying information, a transitional paragraph functions to indicate a shift in the material, probably a significant shift between major blocks of material. Because it is more a signal than a carrier of content, the transitional paragraph is usually short, sometimes only a sentence of two. The first paragraph in this section of material is a transitional paragraph. It indicates a shift from the discussion of substantive paragraphs to the discussion of transitional paragraphs.

What a transitional paragraph normally does is to point in two directions. It points backward at the material that has gone before and points ahead to the material that is to follow, perhaps establishing some more precise relation between the two. Here is an example from a professional writer's work:

> Even if new sentencing laws do not deter would-be criminals, they may affect crime rates by taking known repeaters off the streets for extended periods of time, thus sparing society the crimes that might have been committed by them. Criminologists call this the "incapacitation effect" to distinguish it from deterrence.[7]

This transitional paragraph serves as a transition between the subjects of deterrence of crime and incapacitation of criminals. Its first sentence raises a question about whether new laws would deter crime, but then it speaks about another benefit of changing the laws. The second sentence responds to the first by restating the main clause of the first in a definition. The term defined—"incapacitation effect"—becomes the subject of the next section of material.

You might even be thinking of beginning and ending paragraphs as transitional. Like internal transitional paragraphs, they are often short and undeveloped. And they do, in a sense, make transitions. A beginning paragraph provides a transition between the reader's life before he began reading and what you are saying to him. It is an attempt to

7. James Q. Wilson, "Changing Criminal Sentences," *Harper's* (November 1977), p. 19.

pull his attention away from his ordinary concerns and toward your concerns. An ending paragraph is a transition away from the material. It is your last attempt to influence your reader before he returns to other concerns. You want him to leave your writing with some sense of the relevance of this material to his everyday life.

As you'll probably notice in your reading, transitional paragraphs will normally contain a lot of the words that are used as content signals within paragraphs. Words and phrases like *however, nevertheless, on the other hand, as we have seen, as we shall see,* and such abound. And two-part sentences structured around *if . . . then, although . . ., while . . . also,* and such will be common. These signals function in transitional paragraphs much as they do within substantive paragraphs. What they are doing is different only in scope: these signals are giving coherence and direction to the discourse as a whole. They are making sure that larger units—paragraphs, arguments, sections, chapters, and so forth—all fit together and flow as smoothly as individual paragraphs.

Thus many of the devices you have discovered that give coherence to paragraphs are just as useful in giving coherence to the work as a whole. The use of those signals and of transitional paragraphs should give your writing the kind of total coherence that will make it easy for the reader to follow. But the key to the whole, especially in rhetorical writing, is probably the paragraph. If you can produce good paragraphs, you will probably be a good writer.

Paragraphs and the Three Appeals

Although we have in this chapter treated paragraphs mainly as structural units, in reality paragraphs are not only structural units, but they are also elements of our three appeals. The way we write our paragraphs will affect our content, our audience's reaction to the material, and our persona. Loose or tight structuring, implicit or explicit content signals, light or heavy structural signals, and other variations in our methods of putting paragraphs together are bound to affect the elements in our rhetorical situation. We'll look at these effects briefly in the next few sections.

Paragraph and content

In those rhetorical situations where clarity of content is essential, you will want to make both your content and your structural signals as heavy and obvious as possible. For example, if you are writing directions on how to carry out some complex process like putting together a child's toy, assembling a stereo system, baking a prize-winning cake, or performing brain surgery at home on your best friend, you'll want the directions to be absolutely clear and precise. In writing your last will and testament or describing an experiment with dangerous chemicals, you will pay more attention to the content and to your structural and content signals than you would in sending a letter to a friend telling her about your trip to Europe. In situations in which you focus on the content, your persona may seem cold and distant. However, persona is, in some situations, properly secondary to content.

Let's look at how carefully the following paragraph from a recipe separates and describes each step in the mixing of the ingredients:

> After assembling all the ingredients, proceed to mix them, a step at a time, as indicated in the following directions. First, beat the eggs separately with an electric mixer for two minutes. They should be light and frothy. Then, add the milk to them and beat well. At this point, add all the other liquids, beating them quickly, and then mix in your seasonings. Now, using a large spoon, gradually mix the flour in with the liquid, being sure to work out all lumps and inconsistencies. Finally, add the baking powder and mix it in thoroughly.

The preceding paragraph may not be enjoyable reading, but it is precise. It outlines the steps in mixing very carefully. It is, of course, rather stiff and monotonous. Almost every sentence begins with a content signal—*after, then, now, first*—and most of the sentences are structured alike. However, recipes are not designed for pleasant reading; they're designed to tell us how to cook delicious food. Thus, the stiffness of the paragraph is acceptable. The proof of the recipe is in the eating, not the reading.

Paragraph and persona

The persona, or voice, in the paragraph from the recipe was not so much unfriendly as merely impersonal. The writer seemed unconcerned about establishing a warm, friendly persona. He was more concerned about getting the directions on paper in a precise, orderly way. And that's fine and even necessary when precision is important. However, in some cases the persona itself may be as important as the subject matter. Thus, a rural philosopher writing in a small-town newspaper will probably avoid the formal connectives—the structural and content signals—that you'll find in a careful piece of political analysis or in a physics textbook. Let's look at how loosely structured a paragraph can be and what a difference it makes in the persona:

> The price of everything just keeps going up at an alarming rate. A worker has to get a big raise just to keep up with inflation. That forces the price of what he produces up, too. Pretty soon the next worker needs a raise to buy the first worker's goods. He's not going to settle for less than other people. And just when everyone's almost satisfied, someone notices that the price of everything has gone up. The whole thing starts all over again. It doesn't look like it will ever end.

This explanation of what an economist might call "an inflationary spiral of wage increases" is pretty clear, even though the paragraph is rather loosely held together. More important for our present concern, the persona seems casual and reasonably close to us. Part of this closeness is a result of her wording and the way she uses her material, but part of it is a result of the lack of heavy content and structural signals. Let's revise the paragraph by making the signals more prominent. We'll see how that affects the persona:

> Because the price of everything just keeps going up at an alarming rate, a worker has to get a big raise just to keep up with inflation. That, in turn, forces the price of what he produces up, too. As a result, the next worker soon needs a raise to buy the first worker's goods. Since he's not going to settle for less than other people got, he gets a big raise, and so do other people. However, just when everyone's almost satisfied, someone notices that the price of everything has gone up. Consequently, the whole thing starts all over again. Thus, it doesn't look like it will ever end.

Whether you prefer this version of the paragraph, with all its content signals, or the previous one, you can see that the personas in the two paragraphs are different. As a rough rule, it's probably fair to say that a rigidly structured paragraph produces a less personal persona, while a loosely structured paragraph produces a more personal persona.

Paragraph and audience

The audience for whom you write your paragraphs will also affect the way you write those paragraphs. If you have confidence in the abilities and knowledge of your audience, you will probably allow it to draw its own inferences from the material. But if you are unfamiliar with your audience or if you doubt its ability to understand the material, you will probably make both your content and your structural signals clear and explicit. For instance, the following directions are so explicit that they probably insult the intelligence of most Americans, but they might be helpful to someone who is not used to handling electric appliances:

> Before attempting to operate your Deluxe Television, be sure to insert the prongs of the cord into an electrical outlet, being sure that the plug is securely placed in the outlet. After doing this, turn the gold knob at the lower right-hand side to the "On" position. Now wait until the large tube in the center of the television lights up. When this is fully lighted, determine whether there is a recognizable image on the screen. If not, turn the channel indicator (the dial with numbers) until you find a recognizable

image. (Note that local television stations broadcast only from 6 A.M. to 1 A.M. the next morning.)

These directions could go on and on in great detail, but for most audiences they are superfluous. Most audiences that you will write to will not need such explicit details or signals.

If the audience is someone you know well, you are more likely to leave connections and conclusions unstated. The following paragraph from a detective's letter to her assistant is hardly understandable to us, but it should be clear to her colleague:

> Horace Finchley came here from Maine five years ago. He got a job at the bank when he came to town. Collecting old chinaware seems to be his chief hobby. And he regularly receives mail from Ferguson, Iowa.

Now unless you're familiar with this entire mystery, you can't tell the significance of these details. They seem like disconnected facts. However, to the detective and her assistant these clues are extremely significant. They connect Horace Finchley with the crimes that have recently been uncovered.

Although the use of content and structural signals may be a great help to a reader, they can also be a means of deceiving an audience. By using content signals dishonestly (or even carelessly), a writer may lead his audience to conclusions that are unwarranted by the material. Let's take a look at this argumentative paragraph:

> Because they haven't got the ambition to work hard for what they want, a lot of Antarcticans have been going around claiming they're being discriminated against. However, that is not the case at all. As you know, Antarcticans are generally lazy and dirty. As a result, nobody wants to hire them. Thus, it is obvious that the Antarcticans are responsible for their own problems. In fact, their claims of discrimination are absurd.

Notice how carefully the writer attempts to persuade his audience by using content signals. He carefully links sentences together with content signals, even though he provides very little evidence. Notice how powerful and potentially persuasive some of the signals are: *because, as you know, as a result, thus, it is obvious, in fact.* If a reader accepts these connections at face value, he is likely to be deceived.

The number and the strength of the content and structural signals is partly determined by the ability and knowledge of the audience. But by affecting the persona, these signals also affect the audience's reaction to the writer. The fewer signals a writer uses, the closer he is likely to seem to the audience. To create a warmer, friendlier persona that your audience will feel closer to, you can decrease your signals, especially the content signals. To create a less personal relationship with your audience, you can increase your content signals and emphasize your structural signals.

Things to Do

1. Analyze paragraphs from several different sources to see how the writers use content and structural signals. The following sources should be good ones: a letter from a close friend or relative, a textbook on economics or sociology, the text of a formal political speech, and a best-selling work of nonfiction.

2. Analyze some of the paragraphs you have written in your previous assignments. Are the content and structural signals clear and effective?

3. Analyze a magazine advertisement for cosmetics, liquor, beer, clothing, or an automobile. Are the paragraphs well structured? How heavy are the content signals? How precise are they?

Writing Assignments

Be sure you use the standard outline for each assignment.

1. Write a paragraph explaining how to sharpen a pencil. Assume that your audience has only the vaguest familiarity with pencils and pencil sharpeners.

2. Write two paragraphs on the same subject for two different audiences. First, for your history instructor, explain the causes of some major event like the Civil War or the Reformation. Then, for your twelve-year-old sister or brother, explain the same thing.

3. Write a substantial letter to the editor of your local newspaper in which you refute the paragraph on page 191 that advocates the closing of public schools. (As background to the situation, local voters will be deciding whether they are willing to accept a tax increase in order to keep schools open.)

4. For a psychiatrist, psychologist, priest, minister, or other counselor, write a personal report on what you consider the single most important event or influence in its effect on your life and personality. Be sure you develop the subject in detail. Write your paragraphs carefully using content signals that will clearly connect the influence with its effect upon you.

5. Write a substantial letter to the principal of your high school explaining how well or how poorly that high school prepared you for college. Be sure that your paragraphs make clear the connections between high school and college.

6. If you have a textbook, an article in a magazine, or some other piece of writing that you think is confusing because the writing is incoherent, write a letter to the author explaining in detail how he or she could revise the piece in order to make the writing more effective.

7. Revise one of your earlier papers using the knowledge you have gained in this chapter. You may make other improvements as well.

Chapter Eight

THE SENTENCE

Using Sentences

As paragraphs are the building blocks of rhetorical writing, sentences are the building blocks of paragraphs. If sentences fit together in a smooth, orderly, and clear fashion, then they will probably form an effective paragraph. As a corollary, we should judge sentences by how effectively they work in the context of a paragraph. In other words, most sentences are neither good nor bad in themselves; they are good or bad in relation to their verbal contexts, paragraphs. The same sentence that might be excellent in one paragraph might be poor in another paragraph. A sentence has to fulfill the commitments of those sentences preceding it and must prepare for those that follow it. This dual task involves content signals, structural signals, and the content of the paragraph.

While we will judge most sentences by the context in which they occur, we will also judge some sentences as poor in themselves. Sometimes a sentence is poor in itself because its wording, its structure, or its grammar conveys meanings that are unclear, ambiguous, or different from those the writer intended. But most sentences are not that bad; most are simply less effective than they could be in their context. In this chapter we will attempt to discover how to make our sentences more effective in context, more effective rhetorically.

In discussing the effectiveness of sentences, we will talk about their grammar, but the treatment of grammar will be as simple and non-technical as possible. (I am assuming that as native speakers of English, most of you recognize what an English sentence is and how it is used. In effect, you understand the grammar of the sentence because you know how to write sentences, even if you can't discuss them very well in technical grammatical terms.) By examining the grammar of sentences in a conscious way, we will gain a better grasp of some of the rhetorical possibilities that are open to us. Thus, we will merely be refining the abilities that we already have.

The Basic Sentence

The written English sentence can range from two words to hundreds of words. For instance, here are two respectable English sentences:

Dolores screamed.

The worth of a State, in the long run, is the worth of the individuals composing it; and a State which postpones the interests of *their* mental expansion and elevation, to a little more of administrative skill, or of that semblance of it which practice gives, in the details of business; a State which dwarfs its men, in order that they may be more docile instruments in its hands even for beneficial purposes—will find that with small men no great thing can really be accomplished; and that the perfection of machinery to which it has sacrificed everything, will in the end avail it nothing, for want of the vital power which, in order that the machine might work more smoothly, it has preferred to banish.[1]

The first sentence is as short as a standard written sentence can be, while the second, though over a hundred words long, is nowhere near the limits for an English sentence. Some writers have used sentences up to five hundred words

1. John Stuart Mill, *On Liberty* (1859).

long, and their sentences were still clear and readable. Contemporary writers, however, will not often use sentences as long as the second example (written by John Stuart Mill in 1859). Such sentences would be especially rare in rhetorical writing, and they are probably not the kind of sentences that you will want to write. But you may occasionally want to use short sentences like the first.

The first sentence is an example of one kind of *basic* or *minimal* sentence. The basic sentence may consist of as little as a subject and its verb:

Harry slept.

But it usually consists of a subject, a verb, and a *complement* (or completing element) such as a direct object, a predicate adjective or noun, or perhaps an indirect and a direct object. Here are some samples of basic sentences:

The man shot the dog.

The treasurer is honest.

Hortense is the president.

The children were baptized.

Helen had given Bob a watch.

These sentences are as grammatically basic as sentences can be. They consist of a subject, a verb (or verb phrase), and perhaps a complement. The only other words in the sentence are articles like *the* and *a*.

Although the basic sentence is and should be a part of every writer's repertoire, its actual use will probably be rare. At its barest, the basic sentence is infrequent in good prose. Its very bareness makes it striking, something that a writer will want to save for important occasions. It is so rhetorically powerful that a writer will want to use it only when he needs power.

One such use is at the beginning of a paragraph or even at the beginning of a whole work. Because the basic sentence lacks qualifying words or phrases, it has a simplicity that is likely to startle the audience. In an age when every sentence seems as full of qualifying words and phrases as an insurance policy, the basic sentences will seem clear and forceful. Moreover, the persona is likely to seem honest and bold. Consider the effect that some of the following sentences are likely to have at the beginning of a work. Consider the commitments they create for the rest of the paragraph.

The style is the man.

Men are fickle.

Lust begets revulsion.

Experience corrupts.

Harding was a fool.

Such opening sentences attract the reader's attention. The commitments they make are so broad that the sentences that immediately follow them will have to limit the commitment immediately and drastically, but such basic sentences can be effective opening devices to attract and entice readers. They work.

As the preceding sentence illustrates, the basic sentence is also effective at the end of the paragraph. It can dramatically summarize or capture the essence of an entire paragraph. It can create emphasis by simplifying a host of complexities, perhaps in concrete form. It can provide a climax to a sequence of events. Take this passage, for example:

Mr. Herman's system for interlocking directorates, guaranteed incomes, and regional franchises sounds most impressive. However, because I am by nature cautious, I had my lawyer check on Mr. Herman's background. My lawyer hired a detective, who traced Herman's career as far back as he could—back to Chicago, back to Detroit, back to Cleveland. What he discovered, every step of the way, is not at all pleasant, but you ought to know it. Herman is a fraud.

Such a closing sentence is especially effective if the sentences preceding it are long and structurally complex. Then the very brevity of the basic sentence makes it effective both rationally and emotionally. The contrast with other sentences is what makes the basic sentence impressive, whether at the beginning, at the end, or in the middle of a paragraph.

It is extremely difficult for any writer to write more than a couple of basic sentences in a row effectively. If he tries to, the passage will probably seem stiff, awkward, and childish. Let's see what happens if we take one of our examples of a basic sentence and attempt to build a paragraph on it.

Experience corrupts. It is bad. It affects people. They change. The change is detrimental. The person becomes jaded. He cheats. He lies. He cuts corners. He protects himself. He slights others.

This paragraph was as hard to write as it is painful to read. The bareness of the basic sentence is so inflexible that a writer won't be able to convey most messages using only basic sentences. As a matter of fact, even beginning writers, starting as early as elementary school, will use sentences that are more grammatically complex and fuller than basic sentences. One of the chief differences between basic sentences and the more involved ones will be the presence of *modifiers*.

Modifiers

Modifiers are qualifiers—words or phrases that change the meanings of words, phrases, and perhaps whole sentences. A writer can change the meaning of a basic sentence by adding modifiers. Take the following sentences, which are the basic sentences we used earlier, but with modifiers added:

Dolores screamed *hysterically*.

Experience *of the wrong kind* corrupts.

The *unruly* children were baptized *unceremoniously*.

The man *in uniform reluctantly* shot the *rabid* dog.

The *former* treasurer is *reasonably* honest.

The *italicized* words and phrases are modifiers that qualify the meanings of the words to which they refer. For example, the next to last sentence above contains three modifiers. The phrase *in uniform* modifies *man,* identifying him or singling him out from other men. The word *reluctantly* modifies *shot;* it qualifies or adds a new perspective to the word *shot,* suggesting a certain kind of motivation in the subject. The word *rabid* modifies *dog,* explaining the particular quality of this dog. Frequently, as in the third example, modifiers are themselves modified. Thus, the word *experience* is modified by the phrase *of the kind,* with *wrong* modifying *kind.* Such piling up of modifiers can produce sentences like this:

Very large black wolves often cross this barren hill hurriedly at twilight.

A sentence like this last one, despite all its modifiers, is fairly easy to write and to read. One reason that it's easy to write is that most of the modifiers fit into place following the normal grammatical rules for modification. *Very* precedes *large* and that phrase precedes *black wolves,* in which the modifier goes before the word it modifies. *Often* modifies *cross,* and *this* modifies *barren hill,* in which the modifier goes first. Only at the end of the sentence is there a departure from the pattern of modifiers preceding the *heads* (the words or phrases they modify). But even the placement of *hurriedly* and *at twilight* is normal; they are not out of place at the end of the sentence. Thus, the sentence as a whole is still relatively simple, despite the addition of a number of modifiers. It's the kind of sentence that most writers master fairly early, though this one probably has more modifiers in it than most sentences have.

The addition of normal modifiers to basic sentences is one of the easiest and most common ways of expanding sentences and adding new material. The addition of even a word or two can change the broadest and boldest commitment to a limited one. Consider the tremendous changes in content in these pairs of sentences:

Experience corrupts.
Experience of the wrong kind corrupts.

Men are fickle.
Some men are fickle.

Lust begets revulsion.
Lust occasionally begets revulsion.

The man shot the dog.
The man shot the rabid dog.

The addition of the modifier in each of these sentences certainly changes the meaning of the original basic sentence. The change is accomplished simply, directly, and (from the average writer's perspective) quite naturally. Using modifiers in this way allows a writer to make sensible qualifications with a minimum of rhetorical effort. For instance, the addition of the phrase "of the wrong kind" greatly reduces the commitment of the original sentence, "Experience corrupts." As I suggested previously, the effect of putting the original basic sentence at the beginning of a paragraph is to startle the reader and to create a need for qualification in the following sentences. The revision has already greatly reduced the commitment, and we can expect the paragraph to dwell on what constitutes "the wrong kind" of experience.

Such elaborations on the basic sentence are pretty standard. They are what grammarians have traditionally called the *simple* sentence, a sentence that consists of one subject and one verb. The various modifiers packed into a basic sentence do not alter the grammatical structure of the sentence very much. Further on in the chapter we'll contrast the simple sentence to the compound sentence and the complex sentence. For now we'll consider the rhetorical uses and the rhetorical possibilities of modifiers in the simple sentence.

The rhetorical function of modifiers is basically to modify or qualify content. To use one of the previous examples, the word *rabid* clearly changes the meaning of "The man shot the dog." By informing the audience that the dog is rabid, the writer explains what may have seemed a cruel or senseless act. Moreover, by inserting the word *rabid,* the writer probably has saved himself the trouble of writing another basic sentence, "The dog was rabid." That was his other rhetorical choice. But once he had decided to use a modifier, the writer had no choice on the position of that modifier: he had to put it between *the* and *dog*. *Rabid*, then, is a *fixed* modifier, a modifier with a fixed position in the sentence. A writer can choose to use it or not to use it, but he hasn't any choice about the position of the word. He can't write the following sentences without either changing the meaning or lapsing into nonsense:

The rabid man shot the dog.
The man shot rabid the dog.
The man rabid shot the dog.

In sum, meaning and grammar do not allow for choice, for flexibility. There is, in effect, no rhetorical choice possible.

Free modifiers

However, many modifiers are not fixed modifiers; they can take different positions in the sentence. Such modifiers can be called *free* modifiers. The most common of these modifiers are the *adverbial* (or *sentence*) modifiers, modifiers that qualify either the verb or the sentence as a whole. Here are some examples of free modifiers and the various positions they can take in sentences:

The woman *rapidly* fired six shots.
Rapidly the woman fired six shots.
The woman fired six shots *rapidly*.

The earth seems reborn *after a heavy rain*.
After a heavy rain the earth seems reborn.
The earth *after a heavy rain* seems reborn.
The earth seems, *after a heavy rain*, reborn.

Just as the rhetorical effect of a whole work varies with the order of its parts, so too will the effect of a sentence vary with the order of its parts. Every change in the position of a modifier will produce a slightly different effect, even though the wording or semantic content of the sentence may be the same. The first of the examples using "after a heavy rain" tacks the modifier onto the end of what might be a complete basic sentence. Such a sentence is quite normal in the sense that we often complete an idea or predication and then qualify it. The sentence is functional: it's clear and unobtrusive. The second example creates some suspense by beginning with a modifier but not introducing the heart of the sentence right away. But that sentence is not really so unusual since adverbial modifiers are, next to subjects, the most common way of opening sentences. The third and fourth examples, however, are more unusual and startling. They interrupt the flow of the sentences, separating the elements that make up the basic sentence—the subject, the verb, and the complement. In breaking up the normal flow that the reader expects, the sentences cause the reader a slight pause, an intellectual tension. The reader must incorporate this modifier into his thoughts while preserving the connection between the subject and the rest of the core sentence. Because modifiers in unusual positions cause readers tension, readers pay more attention to such sentences. They work harder reading such sentences.

Should a writer make his readers work harder? Should he put his modifiers in unusual positions? Should he break up the normal connections among subject, verb, and complement?

The answers to these questions are complex. But if we apply the theory of commitment and response to individual sentences in a paragraph we have a starting place. First, the reader expects sentences to be structured like others that contain similar content. For instance, if the topic sentence has three main supporting sentences, the reader will comprehend them better if the writer structures the supporting sentences similarly. Second, any native user of the language expects, through long experience, a certain pattern in prose (usually subject, verb, and complement, with free modifiers at the end or beginning of the sentence). Since the reader will be upset or overtaxed by too many exceptions to this pattern, the writer will generally try to write most of his sentences fairly close to it. In this way the writer will be fulfilling his implicit commitment to the reader to explain things as simply as possible.

However, there may be good reasons for deviating from the normal pattern of commitment and response. A reader may be bored by too monotonous a flow of normal sentence patterns. In order to avoid too much regularity of the subject-verb-complement pattern, the writer will want to vary the pattern occasionally. (The real trick is to be able to vary the pattern at the right time—when the paragraph shifts direction and when the variation won't confuse the reader.) Or the reader may need a little nudge, a signal that the writer is saying something important. In order to emphasize or give a special twist to what he has to say, the writer will often vary his sentence pattern. One possible way of accomplishing this is to place a modifier in an unusual position in the sentence, perhaps between the subject and the verb. Such a sentence often makes the difference between a merely adequate sentence and a good sentence.

In general, then, a writer will normally form his sentences in order to fulfill his reader's expectations. But he may vary the expected pattern if he has a good reason for doing so. This seemingly confusing answer will be clearer if we look at some sentence patterns in context.

The paragraph in chapter seven about closing all public schools offers a good example of how some variations in the positions of modifiers can improve a paragraph. The paragraph (page 191) is a revision of an earlier paragraph, one that was a jumble of disorganized sentences. The revision is much clearer, but it is also rather rigid. However, a few changes in the positions of modifiers can make another version of the paragraph even more effective.

All public schools should be closed down. First, closing these schools will save the taxpayers a lot of money. *In most places* school taxes are the largest single form of local taxes. Second, the schools offer a kind of education that people neither want nor need. Most students are bored with what they are supposed to be learning in school. Also, most find that their education is too impractical. This is shown by their inability to get jobs based on what they have learned in school. Finally, the schools can't, *even by their own standards*, educate people satisfactorily. This is evident when so many high school graduates can neither read nor write.

This paragraph contains only two changes from the earlier revision. In the third sentence, the modifying phrase appears at the beginning of the sentence rather than at the end. This change is a minor one, mostly to avoid stiff repetition, and the third sentence is a good place for it because that sentence's link to surrounding sentences is clear. It explains the preceding sentence and is explained by the following one. Thus the variation in pattern is acceptable, especially since the beginning of the sentence is a common place for such a modifier. In the next-to-last sentence, the modifying phrase is much more prominent, breaking up the flow of the verb phrase *can't educate*. The modifier creates a kind of suspense as the reader has to pause to consider it before he can find out just what *can't* be done. Moreover, the very meaning of the modifier takes on more emphasis, giving it a cutting or even sarcastic edge. To emphasize "even by their own standards" is severe criticism, and the unusual placement of the modifier gives that simple sentence a lot of force. It's a strong, effective sentence.

Content signals

Another way of getting variety into sentences is to vary the positions of content signals and other devices of coherence. A writer may, for instance, put his content signals well into the sentence, as in this sentence. The phrase *for instance* could have been placed at the beginning of the sentence, but it can also be moved about. Consider some of these possible shifts in arrangement:

On the other hand, Austen is a master at creating ridiculous or inept males.
Austen, on the other hand, is a master at creating ridiculous or inept males.

However, this new program will require a tremendous commitment from all of us.
This new program, however, will require a tremendous commitment from all of us.
This new program will, however, require a tremendous commitment from all of us.

There is, of course, a limit to the movement of content signals. You would hardly want to write a sentence like this:

The schools offer a kind of education that people neither want nor need, secondly.

The placing of the content signal at the end of the sentence weakens its value as a content signal and seems very awkward. But appropriate changes in the position of content signals can offer some of the same advantages as changes in the position of modifiers, for content signals are a kind of modifier, and moving their positions can add emphasis and variety.

Before going on to look at more sentences in context and at other kinds of sentences, you should probably work with some of the possibilities of building upon basic sentences, moving various parts of them around. As you do so, try to imagine the different effects that each will have. Reading sentences aloud can help you hear whether they are smooth, rough, or awkward, and may indicate to you just how well a particular sentence works.

Exercises

1. Insert modifiers for the italicized words into the following basic sentences.
   a. The *woman* drank the scotch.
   b. The *book* violates the *law*.
   c. The brook *overflows* the banks.
   d. Harriet is a *scientist*.
   e. Tigers *feed*.
   f. Vanessa *is virtuous*.

2. Insert a free modifier into each of the following sentences. Write as many different versions of the sentence as you can by changing the position of the modifier.
   a. The angry woman kicked her husband.
   b. The senator visited her state.
   c. The usually narrow brook overflows its banks.
   d. Charles is a good father.

3. Insert a content signal into each of the following sentences. Write as many different versions of the sentences as you can by changing the position of the content signal.
   a. The book is the best one on the market.
   b. The zoo has tigers, wallabies, and ostriches.
   c. King George was good to his wife.

4. Read the following paragraph, in which all free modifiers occur at the ends of sentences and all content signals occur at the beginnings of sentences. Then make the sentences more effective by moving some of the modifiers and content signals to different positions. Although you may want to test a lot of possible revisions and orders, your final version need not involve a lot of changes.

> Baseball is a slow game in contrast to basketball. However, it has an excitement of its own. The excitement is dramatic in form. It builds up to key situations gradually. A pitcher faces a hitter in a tight spot. The count runs to three-and-two eventually. The rivals are both under intense pressure until the pitch. Nevertheless, it will build into another dramatic peak again in all likelihood

Combined Sentences

The examples of whole paragraphs in the previous sections of this chapter all seem somewhat strained and unnatural. The paragraph in exercise 4 contains especially good examples of some rather awkward sentences. They are awkward because they are all simple sentences—sentences with only one predication in them (one subject and one verb). They were written under the kind of constraint or limitation that no writer would abide by in the normal process of writing. A normal paragraph is likely to look more like this:

> Thus I suspect (though confessedly without knowing) that the vast majority of the honest folk of Westmoreland county, and especially the 100% Americans among them, actually admire the houses they live in, and are proud of them. For the same money they could get vastly better ones,

but they prefer what they have got. Certainly there was no pressure upon the Veterans of Foreign Wars to choose the dreadful edifice that bears their banner, for there are plenty of vacant buildings along the track-side, and some of them are appreciably better. They might, indeed, have built a better one of their own. But they chose that clapboard horror with their eyes open, and having chosen it, they let it mellow into its present shocking depravity. They like it as it is: beside it, the Parthenon would no doubt offend them. In precisely the same way the authors of the rat-trap stadium that I have mentioned made a deliberate choice. After painfully designing and erecting it, they made it perfect in their own sight by putting a completely impossible pent-house, painted a staring yellow, on top of it. The effect is that of a fat woman with a black eye. It is that of a Presbyterian grinning. But they like it.[2]

Of the eleven sentences in this paragraph, five are simple, two compound, two complex, and two compound-complex. Moreover, many of the sentences contain verbal phrases (e.g., "having chosen it") that increase their intricacy, even though the phrases do not technically make a sentence compound or complex grammatically. Thus most of the sentences that the author, H.L. Mencken, uses in this paragraph are *combined* sentences, sentences that result from combining simple sentences into one sentence. Whether or not the percentage of each kind of sentence that he uses is typical of most writers, the truth is that most writers will probably use a combination of all grammatical types in their writing. Since that is the case, we will want to see how good writers use the various types of sentences so that we can apply the same principles in our own writing.

Compound sentences

Compound sentences are sentences in which two or more simple sentences are combined in equivalent main clauses. The clauses are joined by *and, but, or nor, for, so yet,* or a semicolon (or, though rarely, a colon). For example, the

2. H. L. Mencken, "The Libido for the Ugly," *A Mencken Chrestomathy* (New York: Alfred A. Knopf, 1949), p. 576. Copyright 1927 by Alfred A. Knopf, Inc. Reprinted by permission of Alfred A. Knopf, Inc.

following sentence from Mencken's paragraph (with some elements left out for clarity of illustration) is a compound sentence:

But they chose that clapboard horror . . . and . . . they let it mellow. . . .

What precedes *and* could be a sentence in itself, and what follows could be a sentence in itself. When two such main or *independent* clauses are combined, we have a compound sentence. That is the basic principle of compounding: one sentence is added to another. Thus, the following two sentences can combine to form one compound sentence:

Ervin lives in Omaha. His wife lives in Des Moines.
Ervin lives in Omaha, but his wife lives in Des Moines.

The combining of two simple sentences into a compound sentence is more than a mechanical process. It is a rhetorical one as well, for the combining of such sentences suggests that the two belong together. There is something significant or unusual about Ervin living in one city and his wife living in another. The closer linking of the separate sentences adds emphasis to the linkage. This is the virtue of the compound sentence.

One danger that a writer has to avoid when he starts combining sentences is using too many compounds or using simple-minded compounds that don't really belong together. You may remember writing a sentence like this in the fifth grade when your teacher asked you to tell about what you did during the summer:

Last summer I went to see a double-header in Cleveland, and the Indians lost both games, and I had five hot dogs, and I also went fishing with my grandfather, and I caught eight perch, and on my birthday I got a new bike, and I did lots of other stuff.

While such a sentence is grammatically a compound sentence, it's rhetorically a monstrosity, acceptable for a fifth grader but not for a college student. The trouble with the sentence is that it indiscriminately links information with *and,* whether the information belongs together or not. At least three of the *and*s don't belong, and more could probably be eliminated or changed to some other word.

In the process of combining sentences, you may also end up with something other than a compound sentence. Notice what happens as this sequence progresses:

Horace ate seven hot dogs. Horace drank five bottles of beer.
Horace ate seven hot dogs and he drank five bottles of beer.
Horace ate seven hot dogs and drank five bottles of beer.

The last sentence is not technically a compound sentence because it has only one subject. Rather, it is technically a simple sentence with a compound predicate (the verb *ate* and its complement and the verb *drank* and its complement). But the technicalities are less important than the effect. By compounding simple sentences and eliminating grammatically similar elements, we can get a variety of compound structures, whatever the exact grammatical status of the sentence. Consider some of the following examples:

Claudine was born in California, grew up in Kansas, went to college in Michigan, and got her first professional job in Delaware.

Kansas, Nebraska, and Iowa are agricultural cornucopias.

This is a government of, by, and for the people.

Geraldine loves meat and potatoes.

The general effect of such compounding is to tie material closer together while saving words. When you combine two or more sentences in a compound structure, you are saying that the ideas belong together. Moreover, when you reduce compound sentences to compound subjects, predicates, or some other parts, you are using fewer words. You are making your writing more economical, and that means that your reader doesn't have to work as hard to grasp the material.

One special form of compound structure is the *balanced* structure. The balanced sentence is one in which the two combined structures are balanced against each other to create a strong contrast. Take this sentence, for instance:

Lyle spent his life working for peace, but he ended it making war.

Both halves of the sentence are structured similarly in order to increase the contrast between the phrases *working for peace* and *making war*. Notice how the contrast is diminished by less careful combining:

Lyle spent his life working for peace, but he was making war at the end of his life.

Sometimes the contrast can be so carefully balanced that even the number of syllables and the sounds of words are almost identical:

Joan was faithful to her man; John was faithless to his mate.

Such carefully balanced sentences can be very powerful if you use them sparingly. Because they are unusual, they can have both a strong emotional effect and a precise rational effect. They highlight contrasts and inconsistencies very well. They are likely to be easy to remember, which is why companies try to write advertising slogans that contain balanced sentences:

It costs less, and it lasts longer.

If you like cream, you'll love Cre-ate.

Even if you don't use a fully balanced sentence, you can use balanced structures that result from combining sentences and subtracting duplicate elements. These sentences create the same sharp contrast as fully balanced sentences:

John was rich but happy.

Joanne bought beautiful clothes but wore them sloppily.

Bears love honey but hate bees.

Maxiplast is tomorrow's product for today's world: it's light but strong, easy to apply but impossible to damage, inexpensive to use and thrifty to maintain.

Helen is a fine scholar and a finer teacher.

In general, then, balanced structures clarify, contrast, and make sentences emphatic. They are strong sentences for strong rhetorical effects.

Complex sentences

Complex sentences are sentences in which two or more simple sentences combine into one that contains a main clause and one or more subordinate clauses. The subordinate clauses are linked to the main clause by a *subordinator*—a subordinating conjunction (such as *if, after, when, although, since*), a relative pronoun (*who, whom, whose, which,* or *that*), or *what* (in some uses). This sentence from Mencken (with some elements left out) is a complex one:

. . . the authors of the rat-trap stadium that I have mentioned made a deliberate choice.

The main clause of the sentence is basically "the authors made a deliberate choice"; the subordinate or *dependent* clause is "that I have mentioned," with *that* referring to the stadium. With minor adjustments in grammar the subordinate or dependent clause might be a sentence, but as it stands it is subordinate in that it qualifies or identifies the stadium.

Combining simple sentences into complex ones isn't very different from combining them into compound sentences. Consider the choices for combining in this example:

It rained Sunday. The picnic was cancelled.
It rained Sunday, and the picnic was cancelled.
Because it rained Sunday, the picnic was cancelled.

The first combination is a compound sentence. It links the two clauses with *and,* thus showing some connection, though a rather loose one. The second combination is a complex sentence. It uses *because* as a link between the two clauses, thus expressing a more precise causal relationship. Here are some other examples of how complex sentences are formed by combining simple sentences with subordinators:

I read the book. The book is on the table.
I read the book that is on the table.

The Americans dropped atomic bombs on Japan. The Japanese quickly surrendered.
After the Americans dropped atomic bombs on Japan, the Japanese quickly surrendered.

I don't drink. I don't object to (some) people. (Some) people drink.
Although I don't drink, I don't object to people who do.

I know something. You dislike me.
I know (that) you dislike me.

Among the chief advantages of complex sentences are that they group material more conveniently and they express relationships more precisely. By using subordinate clauses as modifiers (as in the second sentence above), we get the modifiers much closer to the words they modify. By using precise subordinators, we are able to express complex relationships much more precisely and accurately. Such *coordinators* as *and, but, or,* and *nor* do little more than link; however, subordinators such as *unless, even though, if, as soon as,* and others are capable of expressing exact relationships very efficiently. Again, though, the context in the paragraph and the meaning we wish to convey will determine whether we should leave sentences separate, put them into compounds, or make them into complex sentences.

Compound-complex
sentences

As the name indicates, *compound-complex* sentences are combinations of compound and complex sentences. They contain at least two main clauses and one subordinate clause, though they may well contain several more subordinate clauses. Mencken's second sentence is a compound-complex sentence:

For the same money they could get vastly better ones, but they prefer what they have got.

The main clauses are "they could get vastly better ones" and "they prefer"; the subordinate clause is "what they have got." This is a very uncomplicated compound-complex sentence. Some of them run to enormous length and complexity, as does this example:

The notion of mere trustees influencing the choice of textbooks was—and is—thought scandalous; but the same people who called such interference fascism backed, or were indifferent to, legislation which twenty-five years later would permit the Attorney General of the United States (ironically, a former college president) in a Republican administration executing laws passed by a Democratic Congress, to pry out of a thoroughly private association—the American Institute of Real Estate Appraisers—the promise to destroy a textbook called *The Appraisal of Real Estate* in which appraisers are advised that the ethnic composition of a neighborhood in fact influences the value of real estate.[3]

Whether a compound-complex sentence is as short as Mencken's or as long as William F. Buckley's, it does much the same thing. It combines potentially independent sentences, and it groups them in specific kinds of relationships to each other. As such, the compound-complex sentence is excellent for tracing a complex argument or series of ideas in a way that reveals the relationships among ideas. It is especially useful for showing subtle relationships and fine qualifications in argumentative and expository prose. Buckley's sentence is a good example of both the strengths and dangers of the compound-complex sentence. Its complexities, its shifts from idea to idea, invite us to meditate along with him on the relationships he points out, almost tracing the movements of his mind. To break that sentence

3. William F. Buckley, Jr., "Giving Yale To Connecticut," *Harper's* (November 1977), p. 45.

into several short ones would interrupt the flow of ideas. However, the sentence, though it's a good one, really takes effort and concentration from the reader. That concentration may be justified by the insights that Buckley offers his readers. But not all ideas or subjects benefit from such complexities, and not all readers can follow such involved structures. Some readers may get lost in compound-complex sentences, especially if the writer uses too many of them one right after another. We'll say more about such complexity in relation to the elements in the rhetorical situation later in this chapter.

Verbal phrases

Besides combining sentences into compound and complex structures, a writer may also use verbal phrases to combine sentences in a slightly different fashion (as I have done in this sentence). Mencken, for example, uses several verbal phrases in this sentence:

> After painfully *designing* and *erecting* it, they made it perfect in their own sight by *putting* a completely impossible pent-house, *painted* a staring yellow, on top of it.

The italicized words are *verbals,* verb forms that cannot serve as the main verbs in independent clauses and that function as modifiers or nouns in sentences. Besides the present participle forms *(designing, erecting, putting)* and past participle forms *(painted)*, verbals can also occur as infinitive forms *(to hear, to be seen)*. *Verbal phrases*—verbals and their complements and modifiers—are shortened forms of clauses. Thus, instead of using verbal phrases, Mencken might have written his sentence with full clauses:

> After they had painfully designed and erected it, they made it perfect in their own sight, for they put a completely impossible pent-house, which they painted a staring yellow, on top of it.

However, the paragraph as Mencken originally wrote it seems shorter and smoother. Verbal phrases often seem smoother and less choppy than full clauses.

Here are some other examples of verbal phrases, with the verbals underlined. The sentences with verbals are followed by sentences that contain much the same material in full clauses.

Having been to Las Vegas once, he had no desire *to gamble.*
Because he had been to Las Vegas once, he had no desire that he should gamble.

To know her is *to love* her.
If one knows her, he will love her.

Running errands is not a glamorous job.
A job on which one runs errands is not glamorous.

Backed into a corner, Joan tried *to lie* her way out, *having succeeded* at it once before.
When she was backed into a corner, Joan tried a way out by which she lied, because she had succeeded at it once before.

They tried *to think* of any excuse possible *to avoid attending* the party.
They tried any excuse which they thought was possible by which they might avoid the party that they were attending.

As the last two sample sentences show, trying to avoid verbals can result in wordy, garbled, tortuous sentences. The last sentence descends into imprecision and even nonsense. It seems to say that they, the subjects, will somehow avoid attending a party which they are already attending. Writing without using verbals is like trying to type using only one hand.

Another feature of verbals is that their position is often moveable. Consider the following sentence:

Struck by the shock of a divorce, Harry crumbled, unable to pull his life together.

This sentence might be written this way:

Harry, struck by the shock of a divorce, crumbled, unable to pull his life together.

Or it might be written this way:

Struck by the shock of a divorce, Harry, unable to pull his life together, crumbled.

Each version of the sentence creates a slightly different effect, thus giving the writer some rhetorical options.

Sentences in Context

Since I have been saying throughout the chapter that we have to judge sentences in the context of paragraphs, it is time that we looked at some variations in sentences to see how well they work in context. We will be looking at a number of variations of a single paragraph. This paragraph was written by a noted philosopher in a business magazine, *Fortune*. The other versions are variations of the same paragraph with as few changes in wording and content as possible. Some grammatical forms have been changed, and some words and phrases have been added, left out, or rearranged to make good idiomatic English, but the main differences among the paragraphs are in the way sentences are combined or broken down. Here is the first, but not the original, version of the paragraph:

Man might have kept to the straight and narrow path of using signs. He would be like the other animals. Perhaps he would be a little brighter. He would not talk. He would grunt. He would gesticulate. He would point. He would make his wishes known. He would give warnings. Perhaps he would develop a social system like that of bees and ants. The system would have a wonderful efficiency of communal enterprise. All men would have plenty to eat. They would have warm apartments to live in. The apartments would be exactly alike. The apartments would be perfectly convenient. Everybody could and would sit in the sun or by the fire. They would use whichever one the climate demanded. No one would talk. Man would just bask most of his life. His every want would be satisfied. The young would romp. The young would make love. The old would sleep. The middle-aged would do the routine work almost unconsciously. They would eat a great deal. But that would be the life of a social, superintelligent, purely sign-using animal.

This version of the paragraph is made up exclusively of simple sentences, many of them basic sentences. There are few compoundings, and even those are almost unavoidable, as in the first sentence where the phrase "straight and narrow path" is an idiomatic compound phrase that would be awkward to break up. The result is that the passage seems wordy, repetitious, and choppy. The content seems too sophisticated for the sentences. But here is another version of the paragraph, a version that will build directly on the first version:

> Man might have kept to the straight and narrow path of using signs, and he would be like the other animals, but perhaps he would be a little brighter. He would not talk, but he would grunt and gesticulate and point. He would make his wishes known, and he would give warnings. Perhaps he would develop a social system like that of bees and ants, and the system would have a wonderful efficiency of communal enterprise. All men would have plenty to eat, and they would have warm apartments to live in. The apartments would be exactly alike, and they would be perfectly convenient. Everybody could and would sit in the sun or by the fire, for this would be demanded by the climate. No one would talk, but all would just bask most of their lives, and everyone's every want would be satisfied. The young would romp and make love, and the old would sleep. The middle-aged would do the work almost unconsciously and would eat a great deal, but that would be the life of a social, superintelligent, purely sign-using animal.

This second version of the paragraph consists exclusively of compound sentences, some of which have other compound elements within the main clauses. For example, the last main clause in the first sentence has a compound predicate consisting of three verbs. Like the first version, this paragraph also seems wordy and repetitious, but it is not as choppy. If anything, it has too much flow. The problem here results from excessive compounding: ideas that don't belong together get tied together in one sentence. This is especially evident in the last two sentences, where the material about "the middle-aged" should probably go with the preceding rather than with the following sentence. Moreover, ideas that probably should be grouped together

are separated. The two sentences about apartments probably should be combined into one sentence, yet the flow of
the compound sentences seems to work against that combination.

The passage can be improved by eliminating some of
the full clauses and by using, instead, compound elements
within clauses. Here is that version, based directly on the
second version:

Man might have kept to the straight and narrow path of using signs,
and he would be like the other animals, but perhaps a little brighter. He
would not talk, but would grunt, gesticulate, and point. He would make his
wishes known and give warnings. Perhaps he would develop a social system
like that of bees and ants, and the system would have a wonderful
efficiency of communal enterprise. All men would have plenty to eat and
warm apartments to live in. The apartments would be exactly alike and
perfectly convenient. Everybody could and would sit in the sun or by the
fire, for this would be demanded by the climate. No one would talk, but all
would just bask most of their lives and have their every want satisfied. The
young would romp and make love; the old would sleep; the middle-aged
would do the work almost unconsciously and eat a great deal. But that
would be the life of a social, superintelligent, purely sign-using animal.

This third version, which is made up of compound
structures (though not necessarily compound sentences in a
grammatical sense), is much better than the second version.
It is less wordy and repetitious, but there are still problems
with the grouping of ideas. The sentence in the middle of
the paragraph about the social system doesn't seem a good
compound sentence. The second main clause doesn't seem
to be equivalent in content to the first; it seems to explain
the first in a kind of subordinate relationship. Moreover,
there still seems to be too much flow in the paragraph, too
much easy compounding of ideas that are not equivalent
and that should be grouped differently. The passage can
still be improved. Here is yet another version, based on the
third version:

Had man kept to the straight and narrow path of using signs, he would
be like the other animals, though perhaps he would be a little brighter. He

would not talk, but would grunt, gesticulate, and point. Since he could make his wishes known and give warnings, perhaps he would develop a social system like that of bees and ants that would have a wonderful efficiency of communal enterprise in which all men would have plenty to eat and warm apartments, which would be exactly alike and perfectly convenient, to live in. Everybody could and would sit in the sun or by the fire, as the climate demanded. No one would talk, but all would just bask most of their lives and have their every want satisfied. The young would romp and make love; the old would sleep; the middle-aged would do the work almost unconsciously, and would eat a great deal. But that would be the life of an animal that was social, superintelligent, and purely sign-using.

The fourth version uses subordinating along with coordinating devices to link material within and among sentences. These sentences contain full subordinate clauses sometimes expanded from phrases that are not full clauses. Some of the sentences also have subordinate clauses replacing coordinate clauses. Thus, this version does make some of the relationships among ideas clearer than they were in the coordinate structures. For example, the use of two subordinate clauses in the first sentence is a decided improvement. But the third sentence is a problem. Certainly the relationships among the parts of the sentence are clearer; but the sentence becomes so long and complicated that it is hard to read. Excessive length and excessive complexity are the great dangers of complex sentences. Even the last sentence seems unduly complicated when it has a full clause rather than just a series of modifiers. In short, using subordinate clauses won't solve all the problems, but it will help, especially if some of the subordinate clauses are converted to phrases. This next version is based on the fourth version:

Had man kept to the straight and narrow path of using signs, he would be like the other animals, though perhaps a little brighter. He would not talk, but would grunt, gesticulate, and point. Since he could make his wishes known and give warnings, perhaps he would develop a social system, like that of bees and ants, having a wonderful efficiency of communal enterprise. In that system, man would have plenty to eat and warm apartments, exactly alike and perfectly convenient, to live in. Everybody could and would sit in the sun or by the fire, as the climate demanded. No one would talk, but all would just bask most of their lives and have their every want satisfied. The young would romp and make love; the old would sleep; the middle-aged would do the work almost unconsciously, eating a great deal. But that would be the life of an animal that was social, superintelligent, and purely sign-using.

This fifth version also uses subordinating along with coordinating devices to link material within and among sentences. But because this version uses phrases in place of some full clauses (especially participles, *having* and *eating*), the sentences are better in that they contain fewer unnecessary words. Moreover, some of the longer sentences are divided so that they are easier to read. All in all, this version of the paragraph avoids excessive dividing, excessive compounding, and complicated subordinating. However, whether it expresses the content, the emphasis, and the intentions of the writer is difficult to say. Perhaps we should look at the original version of the paragraph just as the author wrote it:

If man had kept to the straight and narrow path of sign using, he would be like the other animals, though perhaps a little brighter. He would not talk, but grunt and gesticulate and point. He would make his wishes known, give warnings, perhaps develop a social system like that of bees and ants, with such a wonderful efficiency of communal enterprise that all men would have plenty to eat, warm apartments—all exactly alike and perfectly convenient—to live in, and everybody could and would sit in the sun or by the fire, as the climate demanded, not talking but just basking, with every want satisfied, most of his life. The young would romp and make love, the old would sleep, the middle-aged would do the routine work almost unconsciously and eat a great deal. But that would be the life of a social, superintelligent, purely sign-using animal.[4]

In the original, Susanne Langer certainly uses a good deal of compounding, and her sentences seem quite long.

4. Susanne K. Langer, "The Lord of Creation," *Fortune* 29 (January 1944), pp. 139–40.

Nevertheless, the sentences are clear enough to read, easy enough to follow. Let's try to understand her strategy in using sentences as she does. We'll use the last version preceding the original for comparison.

The first sentence is about the same in each of the versions, with the subordinate clause as an essential qualifier and modifier and the main clause focusing on man as an animal. In each version, the final modifier is added as an afterthought, a mild qualifier that leaves man still "like the other animals." The second sentences are also about the same in each version.

In the third sentence, however, we see how Langer's version differs from the other version. Langer's third sentence includes the material of the next four sentences in the revised version. Perhaps more significantly, she treats the words "develop a social system" as coordinate to "make his wishes known" and "give warnings," while in the other version these two structures are subordinate to "develop a social system." At this juncture sentence structure becomes crucial to meaning and actually determines meaning. To Langer, developing a social system with all the refinements which she then describes is still unimportant, roughly equivalent to giving warnings. For man is still an animal, and all the refinements of this comfortable social life won't make him any different from other animals. Thus, she uses compounding here and throughout this sentence as a means of showing her intention. She is emphasizing—both by the compounds and by the length of the sentence—that all these differences are relatively trivial. The writer of the other version sees developing a social system as more important, and he thus puts it in a main clause. Moreover, to that writer, the separate ideas are important enough to put in separate sentences, a point on which Langer disagrees.

The next-to-last sentence in Langer's version is roughly equivalent to the other version. The only meaningful difference is that the phrase "eat a great deal" is a compound or coordinate in Langer's version (thus following her general pattern), while it becomes a subordinate in the other version.

The last sentences in the two paragraphs also differ. Langer chooses to end her sentence on the substantive word *animal*, with the modifiers preceding that word. In effect she ends her paragraph by emphasizing what man might have been—merely another animal. In contrast, the other writer ends with a series of modifiers, thus giving more emphasis to the modifiers than Langer does. In effect, here is another sentence in which differences in structure indicate differences in meaning.

Which version of this material is better? Is Langer's better than the revision to which we compared it? Is one of the other versions even better than either of these? The questions are difficult to answer in an absolute sense, but a few points should be clear. First, differences in sentence structure produce differences in meaning and different effects on the audience's interpretation of the material. Second, while we cannot know absolutely what Langer intended (what her external purpose was), we can see a clear pattern (an internal purpose) in the paragraph—an emphasis on man as animal—that she conveys better than the other writer. While we cannot say with complete assurance that Langer's version is *better* than the other writer's version, we can say that she seems successful in achieving her own purposes. Perhaps the other writer was achieving a different purpose by simplifying the sentences for a different audience than Langer's.

Sentences and intentions

Some of you may object that this analysis of Langer's sentences is unduly complicated, and such an objection is understandable. We seem to be giving her credit for almost superhuman intelligence in planning each sentence and relating it to her meaning, suggesting that Langer pondered this paragraph for hours, weighing the values of compounding and subordinating. It seems that if she actually had done so with each sentence, it would have taken her years and years to complete the essay.

Perhaps Langer wrote this paragraph in a few minutes—perhaps five, perhaps fifteen—and never gave a conscious thought to compounding, subordinating, or other grammatical concepts. She may have sat down and written the paragraph without too many revisions. Perhaps she was able to write so easily because she was already a skilled writer who had years of practice behind her. On the other hand, she may have made extensive revisions as she prepared this piece for press. It is even possible that she did in fact spend hours and hours working on this paragraph. Even the best writers occasionally get bogged down. Because they are so concerned about style and meaning, they do spend hours perfecting what seems adequate to less sensitive or less experienced writers.

Without actually checking on Professor Langer's habits of composing her work, it is impossible to tell how she wrote this or any other paragraph. Actual methods of composing vary from writer to writer. Some writers compose rapidly and produce polished sentences and paragraphs that require almost no revising. Others compose slowly and hesitantly, revising as they go, word by word and sentence by sentence. Still others compose rapidly and then go back and revise extensively, sometimes making changes two or three times successively. There is no single ideal method for writing well.

Unless you are a confident and experienced writer who can revise as you write, you should probably start by getting your ideas down on paper. Write while the ideas are clear in your mind. Then go back and revise your sentences. At this stage of the writing process, you may want to divide, unite, or otherwise restructure your sentences. You'll be working consciously and slowly. But as you progress as a writer, these decisions will become less conscious and more natural. Eventually you may do most of your revising in your mind, before you get a single word down on paper; you may become that fluent and skillful. However, no matter how skillful a writer you may become, there will be times when you will have to revise and revise and revise again, tinkering with individual sentences until they satisfy you.

Many of the exercises and assignments in this chapter are designed to help you think carefully about your sentences. While you complete the exercises, think about the principles we have just discussed, and consider how different versions of a sentence convey your meaning or sound in your ear or feel on your tongue.

Exercises

1. Revise the following brief paragraphs by combining the simple sentences into the most effective patterns. You may add connectives or change function words, but you should keep the same basic content.
   a. His message is this. Life is good. Life is rich. Life is meaningful. Life is not for the timid people. Timid people often want no risks. Timid people often want no danger.
   b. I walked to town. I saw a man. He wore a black hat. He laughed at me.
   c. Literature is like life. It doesn't fit rigid patterns. It doesn't follow strict rules. Each literary work is individual. A snowflake is individual. No snowflake is exactly like another snowflake. No literary work is exactly like another literary work.

2. Select from one of your earlier assignments one that would benefit from changes in the way sentences are combined. Revise your sentences to improve the sentences and the paragraph as a whole.

3. Using a classmate as a partner, select a common topic on which to write paragraphs. Then, after each of you has written a paragraph, exchange paragraphs and revise the sentences in your partner's paragraph as you see fit. Be sure not to discuss your intentions or your partner's intentions when you exchange. However, after you have done your revising, you and

your partner may want to discuss your different versions as they relate to intentions. (You might want to put the two versions on the blackboard or on a sheet that could be duplicated. Then you and your partner could discuss your versions for the benefit of the whole class.)

4. Improve the following paragraph (written by a student) by revising the ways in which sentences in it are combined:

I suppose you could avoid your family to some degree. You cannot avoid the problems that you yourself will face. Living together, first of all, will bring about economic problems. The two of you have probably decided to make all the financial payments together. This may at first seem like a good deal. What will happen if she wants to buy something and you don't feel it is necessary? Arguing may result, which will get the two of you nowhere. Giving in is no good either. You may begin to feel that you can't spend money on yourself any more and that she is in control. Even if the two of you can reach agreement on financial matters, you will find that you will be spending a lot more money than before, and just think how hard it is to make ends meet for yourself right now as an out-of-town college student. And of course we cannot neglect the possibility of her getting pregnant. That will only add to the financial burdens.

Sentences in Themselves

At the beginning of this chapter I said that most sentences are neither good nor bad in themselves, but rather only in relation to their contexts. They are good or bad depending upon how they fit into paragraphs and into rhetorical situations. Consider the following sentence:

A problem I have sometimes a great deal of difficulty with which is sentence structure.

In one sense this is a terrible sentence. It is awkward and poorly structured. However, in another sense it is excellent, for it illustrates perfectly what the writer is saying. The sentence itself, by its poor structure, illustrates the kinds of difficulties the writer is having. Thus, in its rhetorical context, the sentence is excellent.

Although that awkward sentence may be useful in some contexts, it is not a very good one in most contexts. The misplacing of parts in the sentence makes it awkward, unusual, and difficult to read. It is a sentence that most native speakers of English, most readers, and most editors would say is bad in itself. And there *are* sentences that we would generally describe as bad or weak in themselves. This section of the chapter will deal with some of the faults that make sentences weak in themselves.

Sentences are weak usually because they distort the content and confuse the reader, while perhaps weakening the persona. And weak sentences usually stand out—they are noticeably bad to the reader, while good sentences often go unnoticed. When every sentence is working properly, the reader probably won't notice the individual sentences. He'll read along without trouble. The same is true of the human body. I don't notice that my heart, my lungs, my liver, and my stomach are working well. I notice these organs only if something starts to malfunction. In pointing out the faults that make sentences malfunction, I will try to prescribe remedies that will help you correct the faults, just as a doctor prescribes medicine for bodily disorders.

Disunity

Disunity in a sentence may take several forms. Sometimes, if the writer links ideas that don't really belong together, there is a simple lack of unity in the content. Here is a blatant example of simple-minded compounding:

The stock market fell sharply today and Harriet agreed to marry me.

The linking of material about the stock market with the material about the agreement to marry seems both illogical and emotionally insensitive. If there is a connection between the marriage and the stock market, the writer ought to make that connection clearer; if there isn't, the writer ought to separate the material. As the sentence stands, it lacks unity of content.

Most disunity of content, however, is not as obvious as the example. It is subtler, harder to detect and deal with. Consider this example:

Erie, Pennsylvania, which is located on the shores of Lake Erie, the shallowest and most southerly of the Great Lakes, is a manufacturing center for heavy industry but also the site for some important events in American history, most notably the building of Oliver Hazard Perry's ships in the War of 1812, when Perry defeated the British fleet in western Lake Erie, close to the present city of Sandusky, Ohio.

This sentence is disunified in that its idea and focus are scattered. Its grammatical subject is Erie, Pennsylvania, but its focus shifts from the city to Lake Erie, back to Erie's industry, then to Erie's history, then to Perry's battle, then to the location of the battle. Thus, it is hard for a reader to tell what the sentence is really about. Is the sentence about Erie, Pennsylvania, about the lake, or about Perry? The writer needs to revise the sentence, tossing out some material and giving focus and emphasis to the material he considers important:

Erie, Pennsylvania, a manufacturing center on Lake Erie, is important historically as the site at which Oliver Hazard Perry built his ships in the War of 1812.

If the writer wishes to add other details he should probably use more than one sentence.

Other kinds of disunity in sentences result from improper shifts of subject and focus. These shifts make reading more difficult, and they may even obscure the meaning. Let's look at some examples. Consider these sentences as examples:

Our society values marriage highly, but divorce is rapidly increasing among us.

The value our society places on marriage is high, but we increasingly resort to divorce.

Marriage is highly valued in our society, but we increasingly resort to divorce.

All three of the sentences say about the same thing, despite some shifts in wording and emphasis. And all three sentences are understandable. However, all three sentences are weaker than they should be because of shifts in ideas, focus, or grammatical form. In the first sentence, the subject of the first clause is *society*, but the subject of the second clause is *divorce*—a shift of focus that makes the information harder to read. In the second sentence, the subject of the first clause is *value*, but the subject of the second clause is *we*—another shift in focus. In the third sentence, there is not only a shift in subject but an unnecessary shift in *voice* (a grammatical form) from the *passive* voice *(is valued)* to the *active* voice *(resort)*. These shifts complicate the sentence. To avoid these complications and to make things easier for the reader, the writer should unify the sentence by choosing a consistent pattern. Here are some possible revisions:

Our society values marriage highly, but we increasingly resort to divorce.

The value our society places on marriage is high, but the value we place on divorce is rapidly increasing.

Marriage is highly valued in our society, but divorce is increasingly valued.

The first two of these revisions are vast improvements, because they have a consistency of focus provided by related subjects in both clauses. The third is a bit awkward, but it is still an improvement, even though the main clauses have different subjects—*marriage* and *divorce*. These subjects are compatible in that they are related concepts in the same grammatical form—nouns. The two opposites provide a clear focus for the sentence.

Sometimes lack of focus is a subtler thing. Here's a sentence about the World War III survival problem in the early chapters of this book:

The man's skill was of no practical use to us, and without it he would be lost.

Although the shift in subject from *man's skill* to *he* is not so great as to be disturbing or hard to follow, this sentence lacks unity. The focus of the first clause in on his value *to us*, but the focus of the second clause is on his value *to himself*.

Not all shifts of focus are wrong or disturbing. Sometimes the very point of the sentence is the contrast that such a shift emphasizes. For instance, consider this sentence:

John loved Mary deeply, but Mary loved John very little.

The contrast of content in the balanced structure is itself the focus of the sentence. And such sentences as the following one shift subjects naturally and gracefully:

He worked hard for peace, but his efforts were futile.

Nevertheless, a careless shift of subject or focus can cause disunity in a sentence.

Improper coordination

As you've seen in this chapter and the previous one, *coordination* is a process by which related ideas are placed in grammatically equivalent structures and positions: main clauses are coordinated with main clauses, adverbials with adverbials, nouns with nouns, and so forth. At times, however, writers may create confusing, awkward sentences because they fail to put coordinate constructions into parallel slots. Consider the following sentence:

John got into trouble shooting pool, smoking cigarettes, and talked dirty.

This sentence suffers from improper coordination. *Talked* is not similar in grammatical structure to those terms with which it is supposed to coordinate, *shooting* and *smoking*. The terms would be properly coordinate if the sentence were like this:

John got into trouble shooting pool, smoking cigarettes, and talking dirty.

Here are some other examples of faulty coordination or *faulty parallelism,* as it is also called:

Monica is beautiful, intelligent, and has earned a letter in baseball.
Utopia College's academic reputation is high, but don't go there.
Jack was lucky in love, but in cards he was unlucky.

In the first example, the writer has tried to put a structure and an idea into a coordinate structure, but the structure and idea don't belong in a coordinate series. The writer should probably say this:

Monica is beautiful and intelligent, and she has earned a letter in baseball.

Or the writer might revise the content to preserve the parallelism:

Monica is beautiful, intelligent, and athletic.

In the second example, the first clause is a declarative sentence, while the second is imperative (giving directions). A good way to gain coordination is to shift the wording of the second clause into declarative form:

Utopia College's academic reputation is high, but you shouldn't go there.

In the third example, the writer has parallel or coordinate ideas, but he doesn't express them in parallel forms. He should write this:

Jack was lucky in love, but [he was] unlucky in cards.

When a writer uses parallel forms well, he is grouping the material in more logical patterns and is also making things a lot easier for his readers. Parallel structures make the content more readable. However, sometimes parallelism itself can be a fault, as the following material will illustrate.

Sometimes improper parallelism occurs for reasons of content rather than form. For example, notice this sentence, in which the coordination is strictly grammatical:

When the flood came, I lost my house, my wife, my car, and my shoe.

The trouble with this last sentence is not in the structure. Rather the writer's thinking is all wrong if he places his shoe in the same category as his house, his wife, and his car. A shoe is of so little value compared to a wife or even a car that it doesn't belong in the same series. There is semantic incompatibility of coordinate elements. And although this example may seem extremely ludicrous, I have seen similar things in print. I once read a newspaper story that opened with this sentence:

An Erie man was charged with aggravated assault and cruelty to animals late Tuesday after he allegedly shot his wife through the cheek and killed a German shepherd dog.[5]

For this typical newspaper opening, the writer tries to cram in all the essential information. However, he badly misuses parallel structures by making *cruelty to animals* coordinate with *aggravated assault* and by making *killed a German shepherd dog* coordinate with *shot his wife*. In effect, the writer seems to say that shooting a dog and a person are of equal importance, for he gives the two equal emphasis grammatically and structurally. What he should have done was to use two separate sentences, with the information about the wife in the first. Thus, he might have said:

An Erie man was charged with aggravated assault late Tuesday after he allegedly shot his wife through the cheek. He was also charged with cruelty to animals for allegedly killing a German shepherd dog.

You probably won't ever make a slip like that one, nor should you be afraid to use coordinate structures. However, you need to be alert for possible flaws in coordination. Even when material is grammatically coordinate, it should also be semantically suitable. That means that the ideas must be of

5. Erie *Morning News*, March 1, 1978, sec. B, p. 1.

approximately equal value. Though slips may occur, the advantages of good coordinations far outweigh the occasional slips.

Improper subordination

Flaws in subordination are like flaws in coordination: they usually involve faulty relations between the content and the grammatical form of a sentence. The most blatant form of improper subordination occurs in the following sentence:

The President, who just announced the beginning of a nuclear war with the Soviets, took office last month.

The trouble with this sentence is that what seems to be the important idea (the nuclear war) is put in the subordinate clause, while less important information (when the President took office) is placed in the main clause. The error is magnified because the chief idea is buried in the middle of the sentence and the less important idea is placed where it gets a lot of emphasis—at the end of the sentence. Such a sentence would be better if the main idea were in the main clause and the subordinate idea were in the subordinate clause:

The President, who took office last month, announced the beginning of a nuclear war with the Soviets.

Other examples of similar improper subordination are the following:

Harry, who lost his wife and family in the flood, broke several fingers.
The English teacher, who is admired by all his students, is thirty years old.

Students often write sentences that are bad because of improper subordinations. They bury main ideas in subordinate structures or put unimportant ideas in main clauses. Perhaps the most common form of this error is the overuse of dummy subjects, the indeterminate *it* and the expletive *there*. They create sentences in which the main clauses do not carry the real substance of the sentence. Here are some examples:

It is a fact that Erie is the third largest city in Pennsylvania.

There are many careers that English majors can pursue after college.

There is no shortage of physicians in New Jersey.

It can be said that truth is the highest virtue for a scholar.

The writers of these sentences could have improved these sentences by using substantive subjects. This means that they should have put their *conceptual subjects* (or main ideas) in the subject positions of their main clauses. Indeed, if you make your conceptual subjects your grammatical subjects, your sentences are likely to be clearer and more forceful than if you bury your conceptual subjects somewhere in the middle of subordinate clauses. The rule is not absolute, but it can help clarify a great many sentences. Consider how these revisions are better than the examples above:

Erie is the third largest city in Pennsylvania.

English majors can pursue many careers after college.

New Jersey has no shortage of physicians.

Truth is the highest virtue for a scholar.

Although you may think that some of these revisions lose some content, you can see that the revisions are generally clearer and less wordy.

As James Sledd and other grammarians have pointed out, the rule about putting main ideas in main clauses and subordinate ideas in subordinate clauses is not an absolute one. Nor is it even an easy rule to apply. Many common and quite acceptable sentences seem to violate this rule. Consider this example:

The newscaster announced that President Kennedy had been shot and killed.

The main clause, at least grammatically, is "The newscaster announced," but the main idea is clearly "President Kennedy had been shot and killed." But even the pickiest critic would probably not find fault with the sentence. Moreover, it is sometimes difficult to judge which idea is the main idea, the most important content. Consider the following series of sentences:

She said that the world will end tomorrow.

Some religious nut said that the world will end tomorrow.

Billy Graham said that the world will end tomorrow.

The Pope said that the world will end tomorrow.

The Secretary of Defense said that the world will end tomorrow.

Walter Cronkite said that the world will end tomorrow.

Clearly the ending of the world would be a momentous event, yet in each of the examples the idea of such imminent doom is modified by a reader's judgement of the source of the information. Thus, the most important idea in each sentence is probably the source of the statement. Which source strikes you as authoritative—"some religious nut," "Billy Graham," or "the Secretary of Defense"?

Similarly, many perfectly fine English sentences begin with the expletive *there* or the pronoun *it* without an antecedent. For instance, Jane Austen's *Pride and Prejudice* begins with this sentence:

It is a truth universally acknowledged, that a single man in possession of a good fortune, must be in want of a wife.[6]

Austen's sentence is an excellent one, as are many other sentences beginning with an indeterminate *it* or *there*.

Another problem in subordination is excessive subordination. Sometimes sentences have so many subordinate

6. Jane Austen, *Pride and Prejudice*, Norton Critical Edition, ed. Donald J. Gray (New York: W.W. Norton & Company, 1966), p. 1.

elements, one piled on another, that the reader loses the thread of meaning in the sentence:

Rudolf Messier, a well-known adventurer and political intriguer, who once worked for the CIA when they were attempting to establish contact with political insurgents who were attempting to overthrow the government of the Philippines, which was then becoming increasingly tyrannical, managed to get himself declared Emperor of Boronesia, a tiny island that had remained democratic until 1958, when Itu Somaliari overthrew the government.

Among a number of faults, this sentence suffers from excessive subordination. One subordinate structure is followed by another and that in turn by another until the reader loses track of which ideas are the important ones. This kind of sentence occurs in the children's story, "The House that Jack Built":

This is the dog that chased the cat that worried the rat that ate the malt that lay in the house that Jack built.

While such a sentence may be fun in a children's story, it's a bad sentence in rhetorical writing. What the writer needs to do with sentences that contain excessive subordination is to break them into several shorter ones or even to eliminate subordinate material that is not directly related to the central content.

While formulating any absolute rules for subordination is probably impossible, you can generally improve your sentences by putting main ideas in main clauses (especially as grammatical subjects) and subordinate ideas in subordinate clauses, by avoiding dummy subjects when possible, and by reducing excessive subordination.

Excessive complications

Sometimes sentences are bad in themselves because they are excessively complicated or unnatural in their structures. For instance, the sentence about Rudolf Messier in the previous section is bad for more reasons than mere excessive subordination. Along with excessive subordination is a related problem—the subject of the main verb, *managed,* and the rest of the main clause are separated by far too many words. When a reader loses track of the relation among the subject, the verb, and the complement in a sentence, he is likely to get confused. Too many modifiers or clauses between the basic elements of a sentence will make reading difficult for the reader. Consider a sentence like this:

That evening, Rita, having fully thought over the results that her act would produce, results that were not likely to be pleasant for either her or her family, decided, without malice or petty personal motives, to kill, as painlessly and as humanely as possible, her husband, who had gotten even more boring as the years went on.

While the writer apparently has a good deal of sympathy for poor, bored Rita, she doesn't seem to have much sympathy for her reader. If she had had more sympathy, she never would have separated the elements of the main clause so widely. Her reader must struggle to learn that "Rita . . . decided . . . to kill . . . her husband . . . ." Most of the qualifying material is helpful or necessary, but the writer should have reorganized and rewritten this material so that the structure of the main clause was clearer. This doesn't mean that a writer should never separate main elements. Sometimes such qualifying words and phrases are the very point of the sentence. Usually, however, such qualifiers merely confuse the reader.

Besides excessive distance between the core elements in a sentence, another fault that makes sentences weak is unnatural sentence structure. Occasionally every good writer will use a sentence that doesn't follow normal or even near-normal order. Good writers will take liberties to write sentences like these:

Him I detest.

With speed came he to the rescue.

To Rome lead all roads.

However, such sentences are unusual ones, and you should recognize them as unusual. In each of them, one or more elements is taken out of its natural order and moved forward in the sentence. For instance, the natural order for the third sentence is "All roads lead to Rome." Thus, the whole sentence is *inverted*. In the first sentence, only *him* is out of place; it would normally be the last element in the sentence.

Inverted sentences are quite unusual. Because of this, you probably should use them only for very special effects. You might use them to imitate a special tone of the ordinary speaking voice in a sentence like this:

Handsome am I.

Or, because inverted sentences are more common in poetry than in ordinary prose, you might use them to create an effect of solemnity or some other mood that you would find in "poetic" passages. Notice how the inverted sentences work in the following passage:

Faithful to the end was Orin. Others had followed him early in the movement, when their hopes were undiminished by defeat or failure. Still others joined him as the movement grew to power. Eventually, as he gained control of the government, even his enemies flocked to his feet. But when his reforms floundered, failed, and then recoiled upon him, even his first followers urged him to abandon his ideals. They begged him to give up his revolutionary goals, at least for the time being, and to consolidate his power so that he could save himself and them. That he would not do.

The first sentence and the last are inverted. The first one catches our attention because of its unusual structure. Its solemnity prepares us for the tragic narration that follows. Then the final sentence with its inversion calls attention to the strength of Orin's convictions. In this context, both of these sentences are rhetorically appropriate; they contrast so strikingly with the more commonplace and longer sentences around them.

Such sentences should be rare. You will want to use them only in the most dramatic contexts; your persona should be serious, even somber. Otherwise an inverted sentence is out of place. Overdone they easily can be. Them should you use sparingly. Monotonous if overused are they. Notice how the italicized phrases in the following passage seem out of order and therefore distracting:

We gave Mrs. Smith's "independent study program" a chance to prove itself, but it never did. We weren't learning anything new, while the rest of Mrs. Smith's students excelled in the French they were learning. *Very nicely* we talked to Mrs. Smith and asked her to accept us back into the regular French class. *To do it* she refused because she said we were troublemakers.

The first inversion is only slightly awkward, but the second seems extremely awkward. There don't seem to be good reasons for the inversions. The sentences are merely peculiar rather than forceful.

Another common problem that makes sentences bad in themselves is the *dangling* or misplaced modifier, often a participle. Dangling modifiers are modifiers, usually phrases, that don't clearly modify a specific word or phrase. The basic rule for modifiers in English is that they should be as close to their heads as possible. For instance, here is a dangling modifier at the beginning of this sentence:

Having studied only two hours, the exam was very difficult.

Grammatically this sentence seems to be saying that the exam studied for only two hours. Clearly that isn't what the writer meant. He probably should have said:

Having studied only two hours, I found the exam very difficult.

This revision adds the word to which the modifier refers.

A sentence with a misplaced modifier has all the words it needs, but the modifier is placed in the wrong position and seems to modify the wrong term.

Lying in a broad meadow overlooking the Susquehanna Valley, I consider my house beautifully situated.

This sentence says, grammatically, that the writer is "lying in a broad meadow," but what he probably wants to say is this:

Lying in a broad meadow overlooking the Susquehanna Valley, my house is beautifully situated.

Such misplaced and dangling modifiers are forms of structural complication that may confuse readers.

In rhetorical writing, your first goal is usually to inform your readers in a clear, accurate way. You must avoid too many complicated structures that will produce weak sentences and confuse your readers.

Excessive length

Some sentences are too long because they contain too many words for a reader to comprehend easily. While some literary masters may use sentences of several hundred words for special effects, and while some philosophical writers may feel that they need sentences that long to qualify complex ideas, such sentences are probably out of place in rhetorical writing. They demand too much attention on the part of readers. Longer sentences are harder to read than shorter ones. That's why many texts in business communications suggest that the average sentence in a business letter should be around fifteen words long. Such sentences are an aid to clarity. The following sentence, written by a young woman in her biographical sketch as part of her medical school application, is probably too long for her rhetorical purpose:

I have purposely decided to graduate from college in three years because I am married, with one small child, and I felt a rigorous schedule would be the best for me because it would better prepare me for the rigors of medical school and make those to whom I am applying aware that a family need not be a handicap in medical school if that family is stable, as is mine, and the person applying to school is strong, dedicated, mature, and responsible.

In many ways this is an admirable sentence. The writer keeps her structures relatively clear. However, at eighty-three words, it is apt to leave a reader intellectually breathless. Had the writer broken this one long sentence into two or three shorter sentences, she probably would have been more effective. She simply makes her reader work too hard without an intellectual pause.

Although some sentences are far too long in the actual number of words they contain, many are far too long in relation to their content. Consider the following sentence from a student paper on the World War III problem:

Even though the prostitute was not at a very old age, her career or field could not enlighten our minds to a very profitable aspect of life.

Even though this sentence is only twenty-seven words long, it is, in a sense, far wordier than the previous example, for the eighty-three words in the other sentence were all conveying important information. The second example can easily be cut to something like this without a serious loss in content:

Even though the prostitute was young, her career would not teach us anything profitable about life.

This revised version contains only sixteen words, which indicates that eleven words, or over one-third of the words in the sentence, weren't doing anything. Or worse, they were taking up space and making the reader work harder, but they were not conveying any meaning.

Wordiness produces bad sentences that are hard to read even when the ideas are simple. Part of the reason for this problem is that you've probably been taught that big words and long sentences are better than little words and short sentences, and that writing is supposed to be impressive to the reader. Thus you write something like this:

Now whatever our destiny, we must obtain an optimistic attitude.

What you should say is this:

Now whatever our destiny, we must be optimistic.

This second sentence is simpler and shorter—two words shorter out of a total of ten. And it leaves out such impressive filler words as *obtain* and *attitude*. Such important-sounding but empty filler words increase the length of the sentence without adding to the content. Among the most popular filler words, which we'll discuss at length in the next chapter, are *aspect, factor, element, relationship,* and *background.* (Of course, I am overlooking the chief advantage of such filler words: they allow you to write five-hundred-word papers when you have only three hundred words' worth of material. Such padding results in many dull and lifeless papers.)

Whatever the practicalities of academic survival, wordy sentences are bad sentences. They make readers work too hard for too little. They are worse than long sentences that contain a lot of material but are worth the words. Wordy sentences need careful editing and careful thinking, which are always hard work.

Exercises

1. Some of the following sentences suffer from disunity. Revise them to make them more unified. Your revision for each should consist of one sentence.
   a. Texas, which is known as the Lone Star state because it was previously an independent country whose flag had a single star, is one of the chief sources of petroleum in this country, which now imports a large percentage of its petroleum.
   b. Without petroleum, our society would come to a halt, but many Arab countries are modernizing with money they have earned from petroleum exports.

    c. Although Jack was determined to make a lot of money, service to society was an important goal to him.

    d. He sat sullenly at his table, and good service from the waiter was demanded by him.

    e. Life may seem meaningless to you, but enjoyment from life is what a lot of people get from it.

    f. While America's power has grown in this century, the decline of power by Britain has been taking place.

2. Some of the following sentences suffer from improper coordination or improper subordination. Revise them to overcome the faults.

    a. George is stupid, clumsy, tactless, but has lots of money.

    b. Harriet Peters, who is the mother of sextuplets, is quite short.

    c. There are many landmarks that are of historical importance in Philadelphia.

    d. It is a true fact that Washington is the capital of the United States.

    e. There is a book which is on the table which is in the house which is on First Avenue and the book, which was signed by George Washington, is called *Elements of Surveying*.

    f. Susan is sweet, soft-spoken, tells raunchy jokes, and is intelligent.

    g. Eunice Marois, whose work as a spy for France during World War II saved many thousands of Allied lives, was born in Mexico.

    h. With this poison, death will be swift, sure, and painless.

    i. There is a very important hospital for the treatment of cancer in Buffalo.

    j. The earthquake toppled many buildings, killed two people, injured hundreds, and forced the postponement of the senior prom.

3. Some of the following sentences are excessively com-

plicated, long, or wordy. Revise them in any way you see fit to improve them.

   a. At her age, the doctor has very little to offer in the reproductive aspects.

   b. Unity has been an important factor in every enduring society since the beginning of time.

   c. Because Willard, who was only eighteen at the time, had very little experience with city women, who generally didn't share his enthusiasm for square dancing and fishing, which were his favorite forms of recreation back in Beaver Crossing, he got very depressed, which affected his grades, on which his scholarship depended, in Chicago, the only big city he was ever in.

   d. In Cambridge is located Harvard University.

   e. This early rejection had the effect of affecting his interpersonal relationships with other people.

   f. In the beginning God created the heaven and the earth.

   g. Being in a large hotel for the first time, room service seemed elegant and exciting.

   h. His dog, because it was suffering from rabies, Jack had to put to sleep.

   i. In the area of the arts, there are many fine schools on the college level of education.

   j. To whom was the letter addressed?

   k. Having done very well in mathematics, the college presented Eleanor with a certificate of merit.

Sentences and the Three Appeals

As we have seen, sentences are building blocks of paragraphs. We normally judge sentences by how well they fit into paragraphs, how well they work in relation to the other sentences in the paragraph. We also recognize that some sentences are weak in themselves. Some are too complicated, awkwardly structured, too wordy, or too long. Some use coordination or subordination improperly. An awareness of such structural weaknesses helps us evaluate sentences, but other factors are equally important. Sentences are also elements in the rhetorical context. They affect our content, our audience's reaction to the message, and our persona. As we know from earlier chapters, the kinds of sentences we use will affect and be affected by content, audience, and persona.

Sentences and content

The kinds of sentences that you write on any particular occasion probably depend a good deal on the content and your purpose. Some subjects are inherently more complex than others, and will probably demand more complicated sentences than simpler subjects will. A letter to a friend about last weekend's fraternity party will probably use sentences that are less complicated than those in your research paper in educational psychology on the relation between social class and educational achievement. When a writer is explaining a complicated idea that requires a great number of fine distinctions, he will probably use some complicated, involved sentences. Cardinal Newman's sentence explaining how the human mind comes to be aware of the existence of God is about a complex subject, as his sentence indicates both in its structure and length:

As from a multitude of instinctive perceptions, acting in particular instances, of something beyond the senses, we generalize the notion of an external world, and then picture that world in and according to those particular phenomena from which we started, so from the perceptive power which identifies the intimations of conscience with the reverberations or echoes (so to say) of an external admonition, we proceed on to the notion of a Supreme Ruler and Judge, and then again we image Him and His attributes in those recurring intimations, out of which, as mental phenomena, our recognition of His existence was originally gained.[7]

7. John Henry Newman, *The Grammar of Assent* (Garden City, N.Y.: Doubleday & Co., 1955), p. 97.

If Newman's sentence seems long and complicated, such length and complication is surely a result of the complexity of the subject. Because the content is complex and difficult, Newman probably could not have used short, simple sentences. His long, complicated sentence is justified by the profundity of his material.

Many writers, however, especially college students, thinking that complicated sentences are themselves a sign of profundity, use complicated sentences even with relatively simple subjects. They complicate the material more than is justified by the material itself. If you are giving directions on how to get to your apartment or on how to build something simple like a birdhouse, your sentences should be simpler than if you were explaining the concept of socioeconomic class or how the safety controls work in a nuclear reactor.

In rhetorical writing, you should remember that your goal is usually to clarify your content, not to impress your reader with your sentences. Sentences are a means to your end. You should not be afraid to use complicated sentences if your content demands it, for not all subjects can be treated well in short, uncomplicated sentences. Some subjects will require all your skills as a writer and a sentence-builder. But you should not look at every writing situation as an opportunity to exercise your ingenuity in writing complicated sentences. Try to use sentences that fit your content and purpose. As you've seen earlier and as I'll point out again, your sentences will also affect your audience and your persona.

Sentences and audience

The chief principle to remember in relating sentences to audience is that, as a general rule, the longer and more complicated sentences are, the harder they are to read. Of course this general principle has its limits, for if a writer reduced every sentence to a series of short, simple sentences he would defeat himself by impeding the flow of the material, the connections between sentences. A good example of this shortcoming is the first version of Langer's paragraph earlier in the chapter, in which most of the sentences are simple sentences.

Your job as a writer is to judge how much sentence complexity your content justifies for your audience. If you are writing about a complex subject, you may have to decide that only a well educated audience will understand or be interested in your subject. On the other hand, you may decide that in the interest of reaching a wider audience you want to simplify your content and your sentences. You may rightly judge that only a well educated and philosophically oriented audience will be interested in the concept of reason in Kant's philosophy, yet you should also recognize that the Bible was written for people who never attended college.

If your first goal is to be understood, you will keep your sentences as simple as possible. Often you can divide long sentences in two at some convenient place. As I mentioned before, many experts in business communication suggest that the average sentence should be about fifteen words and that none should be longer than twenty-five words. Such a rule is too rigid, but it is a reminder that you can usually simplify your sentences without any loss of meaning. An audience of sophisticated readers will be able to understand less complicated sentences, but an unsophisticated audience will get befuddled if sentences get too complex. Even a sophisticated audience shouldn't have to work unnecessarily hard to understand relatively simple material. In sum, give your reader a break by making your sentences easy to read.

Sentences and persona

In the passages by Jim Bouton and Henry James in chapter four, you will remember that the different kinds of sentences that each used helped to define their personas. So too the length and complexity of your sentences will help to determine your persona. The more complicated your sentences are, the more qualifying phrases and clauses they contain, the more complex your persona is likely to appear. But complexity, in itself, is not always desirable. Sometimes

directness, openness, and casualness may be more important than obliqueness, complexity, and thoughtfulness. Consider the following passages:

> I believe in capital punishment, most of the time. It won't deter crime.
> But it will prevent a person from killing again. It will prevent the killing of
> prison guards and other inmates. It will protect society at large from the
> killer. Society protects itself from vicious dogs that bite people. It ought to
> do the same with vicious humans.

> I believe in capital punishment even though it won't, most of the time,
> deter crime, for it will prevent a person from killing again, killing prison
> guards and other inmates, and will protect society at large, which, just as it
> protects itself from vicious dogs that bite people, ought to do the same with
> vicious humans.

Except for some changes in connective words and
phrases, the content of these passages is the same. Yet the
personas are quite different. Because he uses short, choppy
sentences, the first persona seems direct, sure of himself,
and perhaps even a bit opinionated. The fellow knows what
he believes in, and he's not afraid to speak his mind rather
bluntly. Because the second persona uses a single long
sentence with numerous pauses, qualifiers, and interrup-
tions, he seems much more hesitant, thoughtful, and perhaps even unsure of himself. Because the whole sentence
flows together more smoothly, the persona may even seem
to be arriving at his opinions in the course of the sentence.
He doesn't seem as blunt as the first persona.

Which kind of sentence and which kind of persona are
better are questions of rhetorical situation. It depends on
such things as the attitudes of the readers, the writer's
purpose, and so forth. Some of you may prefer the first
persona; others may prefer the second. But it should be
clear that different kinds of sentences produce different
personas. Indeed, sentences will affect all the elements in
the rhetorical situation and will affect how well the rational,
emotional, and personal appeals work.

Things to Do

1. Start collecting striking sentences. Every time you read an unusual and effective sentence, jot it down on a special page in your notebook. Then refer back to that material from time to time. It may give you models for effective sentences of your own.

2. Find some unusual sentences and examine their contexts to see if you can determine why they are effective or ineffective. You might examine some professional writing that you find in magazines, books, or elsewhere and compare it with your own or with a classmate's writing. Can you see similarities and differences in the way that unusual sentences occur?

3. Find a short piece of writing that has a distinctive style to it (for examples, an article in *Time,* a column by William Buckley, the editor's column from *Cosmopolitan,* or even a magazine ad) and change the rhetoric of the piece by altering the sentences. Change the words and content as little as possible.

Writing Assignments

1. Suppose that your closest friend, who's at another college, writes a letter to you asking whether you think he or she is doing the right thing in planning to live with a person of the opposite sex without being married. Send a letter to him or her stating your views and attempting to persuade him or her that your advice is correct. Try to use your sentence structure persuasively.

2. Write the first few pages of your autobiography or the biography of a friend or relative so that a reader browsing through a library would want to read on. Try to use your sentences to help create a strong impression of the person about whom you are writing.

3. Write two different versions of a few pages about some significant and difficult decision you have had to make. Try to use your sentences to make one version sound calm and objective and the other emotional and personal.

4. Write a single long sentence (between fifty and a hundred words) on a subject about which people are likely to have strong feelings (abortion, marriages between the races, outlawing of firearms for private citizens, mercy killing, or some other topic that is controversial now). Then revise your sentence, dividing it into shorter sentences. Finally, revise the structures of the individual sentences to make them more effective, if possible. Your audience should be the readers of your local or college newspaper. Be sure to indicate which.

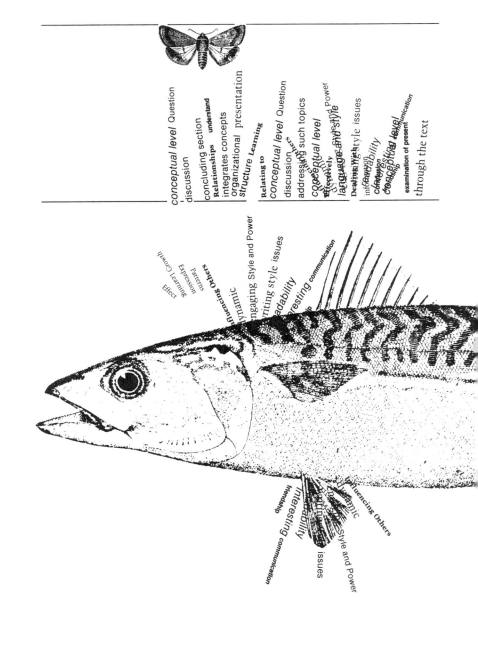

Chapter Nine

THE WORD

Words in Context

If sentences have to be judged in context, the same is true of words. While sentences may be good or bad according to context, words actually change their meanings in context. The same words may mean one thing in one context and something very different in another context. Consider, for example, these two sentences:

Lassie is *some bitch.*

Pamela is *some bitch.*

The phrase *some bitch* is probably complimentary if you apply it to a dog, Lassie, but it's quite uncomplimentary if you apply it to a woman, Pamela. In the first sentence, the phrase probably means "a fine female dog" or even "a fine breeder." In the second sentence, it means something like "a complaining, domineering woman." Thus, the meanings of a word or phrase can and do change from context to context.

This elementary principle is one with which all users of English and any other language are familiar. You might consider which of the following things you like and which you dislike: a cold beer, a cold man, a cold woman, a cold supper, cold cash, cold facts, a cold spring, the cold war, a cold baseball team, a cold freezer, cold molasses, or cold pizza. You recognize, without even stopping to think, that a *cold* beer might be fine, but a *cold* man or a *cold* woman can be quite unpleasant.

Even a function word can change the meaning of another word. For instance, if you are a male and you hear that someone wants to meet you *in* the alley, it probably means that the person wants to fight you. But if you hear that someone wants to meet you *at* the alley, it probably means that the person wants to bowl with you. These common little words that change the meanings of other words so radically make up *idioms,* or *idiomatic expressions.* Idioms are basic ways of saying things in English (or any language), and they do not necessarily follow any logical pattern. Thus, we go *down*town, but criminals are sent *up* the river, though they never fall *in* the drink, where they might cool *off* instead of heating *up.*

Other seemingly simple words have a host of meanings which don't quite seem to have any logical consistency. Think of what it means to get a car, get a job, get ready, get lost, get with it, get going, and get pushed. All these idioms use the word *get* in different ways. Moreover, some idioms vary among different groups who use English. For instance, an American would take someone *to the hospital,* but a Canadian or Englishman would take him *to hospital.* Likewise, an older, more conservative user of English would probably *depart from* Boston, but a younger speaker—who was used to the language of airlines—would probably *depart* Boston.

All these differences seem terribly complex, and they are. However, if you are a native speaker of English who has made it to college, you have been able to make yourself understood pretty well until now. You can get something to eat in a restaurant, buy your textbooks, ask a girl or guy for a date, and do hundreds of other things that depend on the use of words. You already have a good deal of skill in manipulating words to achieve your goals.

However, spoken English is easier to communicate with than written English is, for in spoken English you get immediate response from your audience. If your audience doesn't understand you, it can ask a question, demand clarification, and so forth. Because written English implies a separation in space and time between the writer and his audience, it requires greater care and effort if communication is to be successful. Thus, even though you have been communicating orally for many years, you will have to pay greater attention to words and their meanings in order to communicate effectively in writing. To write well you may need a larger vocabulary than you do to speak, and you will certainly have to use words more precisely.

How are you to learn to use words more effectively? There is no simple answer to this question. You learn to use words with precision through experience (just as you learned to talk, though quite a bit more consciously). You learn by increasing your vocabulary, as you have probably done in this course and other courses. In this course, you have learned new terms like *persona* and *rhetoric,* and you've learned to use words like *audience, attitude,* and *rational* in new ways. In other courses, you may have learned such new terms as *dissonance, historiography, acculturation,* and *alienation.* You also learn by listening to and reading more educated and sophisticated users of the language. You hear your professors and other students, and you read everything from textbooks to scholarly journals to popular magazines (especially the more sophisticated magazines that you may be reading for the first time—*The Atlantic Monthly, Harper's, Esquire, Forbes,* and so forth).

To help the process along, you can try to be sensitive to new words and their meanings. When you hear or read a new word, pay special attention to how it's used. The context will usually tell you its meaning. If you are puzzled by a word, look it up in a dictionary or, if it's a technical term, in the glossary or index of your textbook. Then, try to use the word as soon as you possibly can. Use it in speech or writing until you fell comfortable with it. There is no sure-fire easy way to become a skillful user of words. You must be sensitive to words, read and listen to sophisticated users of the language, and use words as carefully as you can.

In the rest of the chapter I will be making suggestions for using words carefully and precisely. I will suggest criteria for judging effective and ineffective uses of words.

Some of the distinctions may seem terribly obvious to you, while other distinctions may come as revelations to you—or may escape you entirely. These differences in response are normal. The important thing is not to worry too much about the technical categories of words. Don't worry about whether a word is abstract, colloquial, or referential. Rather judge it by how well it fits the context, your meaning and intention, the audience, and your persona. The distinctions in categories are meant to help you understand words better so that you may eventually use them better, especially in writing.

Words and Content

Our first perspective on words will be in relation to content. A writer's first goal with words is to express his content as accurately, as precisely, and as fully as possible. He wants to use those words that best express his intentions and reflect his content. At least that is how we will be looking at words for now.

Accurate words

When we speak of a word having a meaning, we should recognize that the meaning lies in the way that people use the word, not in the word itself or in a dictionary. For instance, consider the following sentence:

My heart tells me that I should marry her.

It seems perfectly clear, but Peter Pedant might respond to it by saying something like this: "My dear young man, your heart is merely a muscle for pumping blood throughout the body. You, as a biology major, ought to know that the heart is incapable of influencing one's judgement about the choice of a spouse. What you should say is that your emotions, not your heart, tell you that you should marry her. *Heart* is simply not the right word."

With whom do you side—the speaker or Peter Pedant? Which one is correct in his choice of words? If you side with the speaker, you are correct, for the word *heart* is commonly used by speakers of English to refer to the source or place of affection, even though those same speakers know perfectly well that the heart, as an organ, has nothing to do with emotions. Because the word *heart* is used by speakers of English in a certain way, that usage has become a meaning of the word. To believe that a word has a fixed, eternal meaning, even though nobody regularly uses the word that way, is to misunderstand words and meaning. Thus, to say that although everyone calls these things *doughnuts* they are really *frycakes* is to misunderstand language. If everyone except the speaker calls something doughnuts, they are doughnuts.

While Peter Pedant and other such purists are often wrong about the meanings of words, they are trying to be careful users of the language. And using words carefully is something that every writer should do. Consider another of Peter Pedant's distinctions: "What people call a buffalo is not really a buffalo: it's really a bison. Buffaloes are not native to North America. They come from Asia and Africa." Although Peter is still being too fussy, he may be on firmer ground here. He should not go around saying that Americans are using the word *buffalo* wrongly. What Americans call buffaloes are buffaloes. But perhaps he could point out that what Americans call buffaloes are in a different biological classification than other buffaloes. In other words, in a biological context, the word *bison* is probably preferable to and more accurate than the word *buffalo*.

One way in which we can use words carefully is to make fine or precise distinctions between words with similar meanings. For example, we might want to distinguish between the word *hero* (or *heroine*) and the word *protagonist*. In ordinary conversation about a movie or television show, we might simply call the chief character the *hero,* but in a literature class we would want to use words more carefully and precisely. In such a class we might say, "Although Willy Loman is the *protagonist* in *Death of a Salesman,* he is hardly the *hero;* for there is nothing heroic, noble, or inspiring about him." Similarly, if another student asked you where you *lived*, you might say, "Lyons Hall." But if she asked again, this time indicating that she meant your home town, you might say, "Trout Falls." If you had been especially precise and especially alert, you might first have said, "I *live* in Lyons Hall, but I *reside* in Trout Falls." Such a distinction between *living* and *residing* is perhaps too fine for ordinary conversation, but since the term *reside* may have important legal meanings—affecting such things as driver's licenses, state scholarships, taxes, and so forth—you may have to say things like, "Although I live in Pennsylvania all year, I am still a resident of Ohio."

Quite often, you as a writer will have to choose from among a great number of words having similar meanings but fine distinctions. You may have to choose from among *disgrace, dishonor, ignominy,* and *infamy.* You may have to discriminate among *differentiate, distinguish,* and *discriminate.* You may have to use *disinterested* rather than *uninterested.* Such careful selections of words are the mark of a good writer. However, even better than being a good writer is being a good rhetorician, one who recognizes when such distinctions are important and when they are not. You need to be able to convey information precisely and accurately. Such ability can be tremendously important to you. But you needn't be so fastidious about words that you end up making trivial distinctions in inappropriate social situations.

General and specific words

Among the word choices that will affect your content is the choice you have between general and specific words. Consider these assertions about the same subject:

Hank Aaron is a great athlete.
Hank Aaron is a great baseball player.
Hank Aaron is a great hitter.
Hank Aaron is a great home run hitter.

The word *athlete* is the most general of these words; that is, it applies accurately to the largest number of people. For the name Hank Aaron you could substitute the names of people from any number of sports: Muhammed Ali, Guy LaFleur, Bill Walton, Franco Harris, and so forth. At the other end of the scale, the phrase *home run hitter* is the most specific term. Your choice of names to substitute for Hank Aaron would be limited only to baseball players who were especially good at hitting home runs. You couldn't properly call Bruce Jenner or Bill Walton great home run hitters.

As these examples illustrate, *general* and *specific* are relative terms, except at their extremes. For instance, *baseball player* is more specific than *athlete* but more general than *hitter; hitter,* in turn, is more general than *home run hitter.* But the word *being* is probably the most general term in our language, while the names or designations of singular things are absolutely specific. Farrah Fawcett-Majors, the Empire State Building, the North Star, my copy of Milton's *Paradise Lost,* and our cat Snowball—these items are absolutely specific. However, the choices you will make between words and phrases will not generally be from the extremes. You are unlikely to say that Hank Aaron is a great *being,* though you might call him a great *person* or a great *American.* Rhetorically speaking, your choices for expressing your content will generally be from terms that are relatively close in meaning.

If you wanted to write about Hank Aaron's achievements you might start with a couple of choices. You might call him either a great baseball player or a great hitter. If you decide to use the more general term, *baseball player,* you are making an implicit commitment to compare him with other great players—Ty Cobb, Larry Bowa, Babe Ruth, Pete Rose, and perhaps even pitchers like Tom Seaver and Sandy Koufax. Because the term *baseball player* is general, you have to write about skills like fielding, running, and throwing, as well as hitting. But if you decide to use the more specific term *hitter,* you can narrow the range of your subject and evidence. Neither word is inherently better. Your choice depends on your intentions and content.

Most students err on the side of generality rather than specificity. They write too many generalizations without ever using specific words. They are content to leave their material general and therefore vague. They make a few generalizations which they leave unsupported. Here are two paragraphs from a student paper comparing the ease with which old and young people adjust to poverty:

> Older people are more set on their values and priorities. They are used to some luxuries in life and would find it hard to make a change from these. Young people have not lived with these luxuries as long, and it would be easier for them to make adjustments.
> Usually an older person has poorer health than a young person. If he lived in poverty it could cause his health to get worse. The same conditions would not affect a young person as much because he would be stronger. This would make it easier for him to live in poverty.

In these two paragraphs the writer uses a lot of general terms which leave his meaning vague, rather blurry. However, by substituting more specific words and phrases, we can make the meaning more precise:

> People over sixty have inflexible values and priorities. They are used to numerous luxuries in life and would find it painful to relinquish these. People under thirty have not become accustomed to these luxuries, and it would be less traumatic for them to deny themselves.
> Usually a person over sixty has more frequent and serious illnesses than one under thirty. If he lived in poverty, his illnesses might be aggravated. The same conditions would not bother someone under thirty as much because he would have greater resistance to illness. This would allow him to survive in poverty.

By changing some of the general words to more specific ones, we have made the passage more vivid and precise. Substituting *painful* for *hard* and *relinquish* for *make a change* are the kind of revisions that improve the passage. But there is still another way to improve the passage: we could add specific details to support some of the general terms. Let's see how the paragraphs would look:

> People over sixty have inflexible values and priorities. They are used to numerous luxuries in life such as dining out, drinking expensive liquor, taking frequent trips and vacations, and entertaining guests; and they would find it painful to relinquish these. People under thirty have not become

accustomed to these luxuries, and it would be less traumatic for them to deny themselves.

Usually a person over sixty has more frequent and serious illnesses than one under thirty, especially such incapacitating illnesses as heart disease, cancer, and respiratory ailments. If he lived with inadequate food and infrequent medical attention in rundown draughty housing, his illnesses might be aggravated, weakening and eventually killing him. The same conditions would not bother someone under thirty as much because he would have greater resistance to illness. This would allow him to survive in poverty.

This version of the material is even better than the second version, largely because of the addition of specific details such as *heart disease, cancer, inadequate food,* and *draughty housing.* Such details add force and life to the passage. Their addition illustrates a timeworn bit of advice from teachers to students: when you make general statements, you should support the generalizations with specific details. If you can do that in your writing, you probably have a good command of your content.

Although most students use writing that is too general, there is nothing wrong with making generalizations. Generalizing, the ability to unify a great many details in one statement, is the heart of any systematic study. Thus, you should not be afraid to make generalizations like this:

The wealthier a person is, the more likely he is to be a Republican.

Despite their proclamations of liberality, most English professors cannot stand grammatical and mechanical errors.

Photosynthesis is the basis for all life on earth.

Such generalizations are necessary and interesting, but you should use them only if you can then support them with more specific wording and with specific details. If you can't find specific support for your generalizations, especially examples, you are probably guilty of bad thinking as well as bad writing.

Although most student writing is too general, some

writing may be too specific. Consider the following two sentences:

When I went to Europe last summer, I grew up both intellectually and emotionally.

When I flew to Europe last summer, I grew up both intellectually and emotionally.

The sentence that uses the general word *went* rather than the specific word *flew* is better because the focus of the sentence, the commitment it makes, is the writer's growth in Europe, not his means of transportation. *Flew* puts undue emphasis on a detail that's probably irrelevant to the writer's main intention.

Similarly, too many specific details in a sentence may draw attention away from the writer's chief intention. Consider the result if a witness in a courtroom offers this testimony:

The robin's-egg blue Ford LTD with plush velour seats, retractable head-lights, and the attractive European-style grill was going quite fast.

All the details about the car distract attention from the speaker's point. Unless the purpose of the testimony is to identify the car, the details distract the audience.

Such overuse of details explains why many television commercials sound phoney. Characters say things that no one would say in ordinary conversation. For instance, Mrs. Meddle might say this to Mrs. Bride:

Don't fret, dear. You can get his dull, grimy shirts as shiny white as the snows of the Swiss Alps if you'll switch to new improved hard-water Phizz, with the miracle water-softening ingredients that work five ways to make your whole wash, from delicate nighties to sweaty work shirts, come out so white and bright you'll think they were washed in clear, fresh mountain streams.

Such overuse of specific details would never occur in ordinary conversation. The only justification for them is that advertisers are trying to drum slogans into consumers' heads. Unless you go into advertising, you will probably never write sentences like that. You should avoid too many specific words on unimportant details.

Much of what we have learned about general and specific words in relation to content will also be true of concrete and abstract words.

Concrete and abstract words

Concrete words refer to realities—things, actions, qualities—that we perceive through our senses. Such nouns as *rose, scream, book, salt,* and *hyena* are concrete because we can perceive them through sight, sound, taste, smell, or touch. Verbs like *run, punch, scream, scratch, file,* and *drink* are concrete verbs because we can perceive them happening. Similarly, such adjectives as *fat, heavy, green, speedy, sweet, acrid,* and *smooth* and such adverbs as *slowly, smoothly, sporadically,* and *bullishly* are concrete.

Abstract words refer to realities that cannot be directly perceived, realities that are a result of human thinking. For example, such nouns as *love, friendship, religion, philosophy, organization, system,* and *anger* cannot be directly perceived. You may see that Stephen gave you ten dollars when you were broke, let you stay at his apartment, and let you use his car, but you can never directly perceive his friendship for you. All that you can experience are concrete acts that lead you to conclude, intellectually, that he is your friend. Verbs like *abstract, organize, believe, comprehend,* and *forgive* are abstract because you cannot directly perceive them. You arrive at these notions, these abstractions, by perceiving concrete acts and by then abstracting, or drawing out, unified concepts from them. Similarly, adjectives like *just, fair, honorable, faithful,* and *spiteful,* and such adverbs as *justly, nobly, honestly, truthfully,* and *charitably* are abstract. The meanings of these words result from the human mind's sense of connection between specific concrete actions.

You should not think of *concreteness* and *abstractness* as discrete and wholly separate categories. Rather, there is a kind of scale from concrete to abstract. For example, Fang is a concrete living, breathing, biting creature. He is a collie (relatively concrete), a dog (less concrete), a mammal (less concrete), a pet (fairly abstract), my friend (even more abstract), and the preserver of my sanity (quite abstract). Similarly, I am a human being, a male, an adult, a professor, an intellectual, a liberal, a rhetorician, and an Anglophile—among many other fine things. Which of these terms are concrete and which are abstract may cause some difficulties occasionally, but the broad differences should be clear.

Although there are differences between general words and abstract words and between specific words and concrete words, in actual writing there is a great deal of overlap. Abstract words tend to be general; concrete words are often specific. So we might refine our rules from the previous section and say that we should support our generalizations and abstractions with specific and concrete words.

Figurative language

One way of combining the concrete and the abstract without wasting words is to use *figurative language,* words that mean more than the literal or surface meaning would seem to indicate. For instance, most of our common proverbs and sayings have survived—perhaps far too long—because of their concise combination of the abstract and concrete. "A bird in the hand is worth two in the bush" is, we recognize, not about birds alone. It is a statement about the relative value of a good already achieved or possessed in relation to goods that could possibly be achieved. (Notice how wordy I got explaining that brief proverb.) Or, for another instance, when we call Andrea "a diamond in the rough," we clearly mean that she has great potential that has to be developed, or "polished."

These examples are a bit shopworn, but they do illustrate the power of figurative language, of using concrete terms to stand for abstractions. Figurative language—metaphor, simile, and so forth—is especially effective when it is new, fresh, and based on material familiar to the audience. Thus, to say that Ralph is as interesting as a commercial in the program of life might be an effective metaphor for a modern American audience, but it may not mean much to Tibetans, nor would it have meant much to Shakespeare's audience (who loved metaphors from the theater). As we've seen before, metaphors have the advantage of often carrying strong emotional overtones, which can be a powerful means of persuasion. To call a policeman a *pig* almost magically makes him less than human in the eyes of the speaker, and perhaps the audience. Moreover, metaphors needn't always be fully and explicitly developed. Sometimes they can be suggested in a single word, usually a verb. You've probably all heard about the man who *golfed* and *cocktailed* himself into a vice-presidency with the corporation and who then *bought* the silence of the chief accountant. You've also probably heard of the actress who *slept* her way into many fine movie roles.

In sum, figurative language is one means of combining the solidity and vividness of concrete words with the generalizations of abstract words.

Exercises

1. Evaluate each of the following assertions about words. Which distinctions show an understanding of how words work, and which are pedantic or trivial? Explain your answer.
   a. A *mongoose* isn't really a *goose;* it's really a mammal.
   b. Only fussy people get upset over the interchanging of similar words like *imply* and *infer* or *affect* and *effect.*
   c. Although people in New England call it *soda,* it's really *pop.*
   d. The *Jerusalem artichoke* isn't really an *artichoke;* it's a species of sunflower.
   e. The ad says that there will be a *minimal* charge, but it probably should say *small,* since minimal means *lowest possible.*
   f. I can't *drop over to* Harry's house because I don't have a way to fly; he should have asked me to *come* to his house.

g. When I kept honking my horn, Linda told me to *cut it out,* but I said that I didn't have a knife.

h. You Englishmen have got it all wrong: the word *corn* means the stuff that grows on ears, not just any grain.

2. Start with some specific thing or action and refer to it in a series of five increasingly general terms.

3. Start with the same thing or action and refer to it in a series of five increasingly abstract terms.

4. Take a well-known proverb, saying, or expression and state its meaning in abstract, general terms in a single sentence. Then, for an audience of junior high school students, explain the proverb using mostly concrete terms.

5. Which, if any, of the following sentences are too specific in the wrong places for a normal rhetorical context? Explain your answer by discussing your assumptions about context.

a. As I was sitting at the bar drinking a sixteen-ounce bottle of New Improved Bores Beer, two masked men came in the door.

b. After the fight, Paul was rushed to the hospital suffering from a fractured skull, two broken ribs, and a deep gash in his left arm.

c. William Smith, 33, of 9803 Seventh Street, was arrested for allegedly buying a stolen twenty-four-inch Zenith television set.

d. The scholarship winner was Joyce Schaum, daughter of Dr. Wolfgang Schaum, the noted heart surgeon who was recently sued for malpractice by Senator Crowley's wife.

e. Be sure to stop at Brown's Superior Drug Store, conveniently located at Eighth and Cherry Streets, with all-night prescription service, and get me some rubbing alcohol.

6. Create three figures of speech based on your life at school, your hobbies, your special interests, or various jobs you've held. For instance, you might say,

"He changes his mind as often as a stereo changes forty-fives." Or you might say, "Taking the final exam in anatomy is as much fun as being dissected alive."

Words and Audience

In earlier sections of this chapter, we considered how words work in context and how they work in relation to the content. Now we will consider words in relation to the audience. We will consider how words affect our audience's emotions and comprehension. We will see how the rules for context and precision will help us decide which specific choices to make among words of similar meaning in order to most effectively deal with our audience. Some synonyms will be more effective emotionally; some will be more effective intellectually. Let's look at the basic principles.

Referential and
non-referential meaning

Almost all words (except perhaps function words— prepositions, conjunctions, articles, and a few auxiliary verbs) have two kinds of meaning: *referential* or *denotative* meaning, and *non-referential* or *connotative* meaning. The referential meaning of a word is what it refers to, what it points to in reality. For instance, the word *fox* refers to a certain dog-like wild animal, generally of the genus *Vulpes*, to be biologically accurate. That is the referential or denotative meaning of the term. However, the word *fox* also has non-referential or connotative meanings. These are associations in the minds of users of English that are not strictly referred to by the word but are nevertheless present. When speakers of English hear the word *fox*, they are likely to think of stolen chickens, sinister cleverness, and general deceitfulness. These qualities are part of the meaning of the word, yet they are hard to pin down.

If we consider matters objectively, the fox and the lion are both animals that live by killing other animals, but the word *lion* has largely favorable non-referential meanings (kingliness, nobility, power), while the word *fox* has largely unfavorable non-referential meanings (deceitfulness, sneakiness, thievery). In reality, of course, both creatures are animals, neither more nor less moral than the other.

Sometimes words have the same referential meanings, but they differ markedly in their non-referential meanings. Consider the following series of judgements: "I am *firm;* you are *stubborn;* he is *pig-headed.*" All three terms refer to a refusal to change, but their non-referential meanings suggest a virtuous refusal, a mildly unfavorable refusal, and a terribly unfavorable refusal, respectively. Similarly, I furnished my house *inexpensively,* but my neighbor furnished his *cheaply.*

Some words are largely referential in meaning, while others are largely non-referential. We might think of the range as a continuum or scale from almost pure denotation at one end to almost pure connotation at the other end. Words like *hypotenuse, carbon dioxide, twelve, iamb,* and a great many technical terms are almost purely referential in meaning. The word *hypotenuse* refers to the side opposite the right angle in a triangle. It is unlikely to arouse any great emotional response among most people; thus, it has little non-referential meaning. Some words like *nice, terrific, beautiful, pretty, ugly,* and *icky* are almost wholly non-referential in their meanings. Their meanings are the emotional force they carry, the favorable or unfavorable attitudes they express, rather than any specific realities they point to. What you consider a *beautiful* lamp, I may consider *ugly* or *gaudy.* What I consider a *terrific* novel may be a book that you found *terrible.* These possible differences in judgement, which can't be effectively resolved, indicate that the meanings are largely non-referential or connotative.

Most words are neither purely referential nor purely non-referential. Most have both kinds of meaning. Indeed, some terms that seem to be at either end of the continuum do have both kinds of meaning. For instance, some people consider the number *seven* lucky and the number *thirteen* unlucky, even though *five* or *fourteen* don't have strong non-referential meanings. Similarly, some words that seem purely non-referential like *creep* (as a noun) or *square* (referring to a person) do have precise referential meanings for some users.

Knowing about referential and non-referential meaning is only a first step. We will have to learn how to control these meanings, especially the non-referential meanings, which are much more elusive.

Insuring proper referential meanings is basically a matter of using words accurately. When in doubt, you can consult a dictionary and then relate the word to the reality to which you are referring. In using the word *seven* to count trees, cars, books, or rabbits, seven is either the right or the wrong number. Of course, you'll have to be aware of fine distinctions among referential meanings. You'll have to be aware of subtle differences among words like *live, reside,* and *inhabit.*

But controlling non-referential meanings will be much more difficult. It will probably take some of you a good deal of time to really become skillful in handling the emotional force of words. Your skill will probably advance in three stages, each stage roughly equivalent to each of the following rules.

Your first goal as a writer is to avoid inappropriate connotations—non-referential meanings that clash with your referential meaning or your other non-referential meanings. Consider the following passage, for example:

> She's the kind of broad I want to take home to my mother. She has a certain mouthiness that makes her fun to be with. I look forward to living with her in the boonies and raising our progeny. She'll make a wonderful female parent, and I'm sure that our life together will maximize my satisfaction in my familial roles.

This passage is ludicrous because so many of the non-referential meanings clash with the referential meanings and with what seems to be the writer's intention. The writer obviously thinks very highly of the woman he plans to marry, but his use of the term *broad,* with its suggestions of cheapness or sexual looseness, clashes with the idea of taking her home to *mother,* a word that has such respectable connotations. Similarly, the words *mouthiness* and *boonies* have unfavorable connotations when they should have favorable ones. The latter half of the passage is full of neutral or scientific-sounding words when it should have strongly favorable non-referential meanings. Words like *female parent, maximize,* and *familial roles* sound too cold and impersonal to describe the feelings we expect in a situation like this.

Although this passage illustrates how non-referential meanings can clash, it contains mistakes so obvious that most students would never make them. The next passage, however, suffers from some subtler slips in non-referential meaning. It is from the opening of a memoir that a male student wrote about a teacher whom he admired greatly. Can you find some of the slips in connotative meaning?

> She was always honest, but sharp, and it was a cruel ordeal for the student under fire. I felt sorry for those she criticized, including myself, but it never affected my passion and admiration for her. Our friendship was odd and amazing and I can see now that it was because she was so odd and amazing. I came to know her like a grandmother, like a best friend, like a lover. I often flatter myself by thinking I am the only one who really knows Margaret Turner, the English teacher. Surely, others close to her were in on the secrets; she had to leave some of them with the many people she shared her strange life with. I am firmly convinced, however, that I am the only one with the pep to recount that life.

There are two main problems in the passage. First, the words *passion* and *lover* have sexual overtones or connotations that the writer did not wish to suggest. *Affection* or *fondness* would be much better than *passion,* and *sweetheart* or *girlfriend* would sound less sexual than *lover.* Second, the words *odd* and *strange* carry unfavorable connotations, overtones of the bizarre or unhealthy. The word *unusual* might serve better than *odd,* and *singular* or *unique* might be better than *strange.* One other minor problem is the word *pep,* which sounds too light for the context. Perhaps *enthusiasm* or *energy* would be much better. These conflicts of non-referential meaning did not make the passage ridiculous, but they prevent a good passage from becoming an excellent one.

You might consider the inappropriate connotations or inconsistent connotations in these sentences:

Your perfume has a pleasing odor, dear.

The bride looked so lovely swaggering down the aisle.

John is so powerfully muscular and squat.

This whiskey has a rare flavor, something like kerosene mixed with dog urine.

Each of the sentences above contains one word with a non-referential meaning that clashes with its context. The word *odor* should be replaced with a term that has more elegant connotations, such as *fragrance.* John should probably be described as *compact* rather than *squat,* because the connotations of *compact* are more consistent with the favorable connotations of *powerfully muscular.* In the fourth sentence, *rare,* with its positive connotations, needs to be replaced with the neutral *unusual,* or the slightly unfavorable *strange,* or the unfavorable *odd.* Which do you think is best? The word *swaggering* describing the bride probably needs a neutral connotative term like *walking* or a favorable connotative one like *gliding.*

There is one exception to the rule about using connotations that are appropriate to the denotations of words. If someone wishes to ridicule some person, institution, or idea, he might deliberately use sarcasm. For instance, in order to criticize the power that Franklin Roosevelt achieved as President and the way in which he wielded that power, a historian might say, "Franklin Roosevelt ascended the throne in 1933 and ruled until 1945, the longest reign of any monarch in American history." By using words that have the connotations of kingship, which are inappropriate for the President of the United States, the writer would be suggesting that Roosevelt acted like a king, a ruler who felt he was above the law. Normally, however, you will want to avoid connotations that clash with your denotations.

Your second goal as a writer is to use non-referential meanings that actually strengthen your referential meanings. This means that your words should not only refer accurately to what you mean but also that they should reinforce the attitudes that you wish to convey toward this material. For example, if a professor at your college were under pressure because his political, social, or moral views were unpopular, you might defend him in a letter to the college newspaper by saying:

Professor Jones is the incarnation of the highest ideals of the teaching profession. If his quest for truth carries him beyond the narrow confines of conventional opinions and bigotry, we should applaud his moral and intellectual courage. We should support his sacred right to seek the truth and to proclaim it openly without fear of retaliation from the totalitarian minds who seek to make everyone goose-step to their tune.

In this paragraph, the non-referential meanings consistently support the referential meanings and the writer's intention. Professor Jones and his actions are described in religious and moral terms that are highly favorable: *incarnation, ideals, quest, moral, sacred, proclaim,* and so forth. His opponents are described in terms that have highly unfavorable connotations: *narrow, conventional, bigotry, retaliation, totalitarian,* and *goose-step.*

Using connotations that support your denotations does not prove your case, make you right, or necessarily convince anyone else, but it is a step in the right direction. It indicates that your meanings are all pulling together, like teammates should in a tug of war. (As we'll see, however, overuse of connotative or non-referential meanings may be ineffective in some rhetorical situations.)

Your third goal as a writer is to use non-referential meanings that are appropriate for your audience, situation, and purpose. Consider the following description of a tax bill being considered by Congress:

This bill is designed to make the corporate fat cats pay their fair share of the tax burden instead of hiding under cozy tax shelters that are supported by fancy-talking lawyers and Wall Street banking interests.

Is the writer using his non-referential meanings well? He is certainly following the first two principles for using connotations. But that doesn't fully answer the question, for the writer's success will depend on his audience. If his audience is made up of some group that supports this kind of reform, say Americans for Democratic Action or a labor union, this sentence is likely to be effective. It will gain both the intellectual and the emotional support of the audience. If, however, the writer's audience consists of corporate executives or some other group favorable to business interests, say the Chamber of Commerce, this sentence is likely to be ineffective. Its non-referential meanings attack business people so viciously that they are likely to become enraged. After hearing themselves described in this way, they are unlikely to consider the bill with open minds, even if its provisions really won't change things for them very much.

But what about a neutral or undecided audience? How are they likely to respond? A neutral audience might consider this sentence overdone, too emotional. The attack on business interests seems one-sided and unfair, substituting loaded language for facts. To persuade an uncommitted audience, you needn't avoid all use of non-referential meanings, but you should rely on referential words to carry most of the meaning. Here, for instance, is how that sample sentence might be revised if you wanted this uncommitted audience to consider the bill more carefully:

> This bill is designed to make corporations pay percentages on their earnings that are closer to the percentages that individuals pay on their income taxes, which only seems fair. Further, the bill will eliminate many of the exemptions that corporation lawyers and big banks have sought to perpetuate.

Is this revision free from the bias of non-referential meanings? Hardly. Such words as *corporations, individuals, fair, big, banks,* and *perpetuate* all indicate your support for the bill. However, the wording doesn't immediately arouse the suspicion of those you are most likely to persuade—an uncommitted audience. It may even get a fair hearing from those who oppose the bill.

In some situations, strong emotional appeals using heavily connotative words and phrases are quite acceptable and normal. For example, when a conservative politician speaks to the main supporters in his constituency, he's liable to pepper his speech with phrases like "federal giveaways," "bleeding-heart liberals," "free enterprise system," and "criminal-coddling judges." A liberal politician, however, would probably use such phrases as "big business interests," "tax loopholes for the rich," "unequal justice," and "Pentagon cost overruns." These emotional phrases, so full of connotations, are what a partisan audience wants to hear. A political rally, like a pep rally, is meant to be ego-boosting and unifying to the group. However, if these two politicians, the liberal and the conservative, were to meet in a televised debate during a close election campaign, they would probably be much more moderate in their use of language. Their words would probably be more denotative and less connotative, and their arguments more rational and substantive.

In other situations, a writer may wish to avoid non-referential meanings as much as possible. In scientific or technical reports or in any other kind of writing in which emotional judgements are to be excluded in favor of reason, strict avoidance of non-referential meanings is an ideal goal. Thus, a sociologist will probably use a neutral term like *upward mobility* rather than a term like *social climbing*, which has unfavorable connotations. Similarly, your biology instructor would not refer to the animal you are dissecting as a *bunny*, a *kitty*, or a *pooch*. He may simply refer to it as a *specimen* so that your emotions won't interfere with your thinking.

Range of usage

The non-referential meanings of words affect the audience's feelings and emotions. When we discuss levels of usage, we will be dealing mostly with the intellectual abilities of our audience, though matters of appropriate context and proper tone are also important. In judging how words are appropriate or inappropriate to our audience, we must consider the range of usage. We can divide words into three broad categories: *written* words, *spoken* words, and *common* words. We'll also add a few special categories for certain special kinds of words.

Written words are those words which appear in the writing of educated users of English (or in prepared speeches, which are really a special form of writing). Written words rarely appear in the casual conversation of speakers of the language. Such words as *ameliorate, pedagogue, vacuous,* and *lucidity* are words that we are more likely to read than to hear.

Spoken words are at the other end of the continuum from written words. Spoken (or *colloquial)* words appear almost exclusively in the speech of a wide variety of native speakers of the language. They will generally not appear in writing unless the writer is deliberately trying to imitate habits of speech, as in some forms of fiction. Such words or phrases as *gonna* (which would be written as *going to), yak* (meaning to talk or chatter), *clam up* (meaning to keep quiet), *screw you* (and almost all obscenities), *shoot the bull, OK,* and *nut* (meaning a mentally unstable person) are words that we are more likely to hear than to read.

Common words are common to both spoken and written English. They are the everyday words of both speakers and writers of the language, the core of the language, the words that have often been part of the language for centuries. They are the words that English speakers and writers have in common whether they live in Boston, Atlanta, Omaha, Dallas, Toronto, London, Dublin, Glasgow, Auckland, Melbourne, or Honolulu. Common words are used by the most and least educated users of the language. Such words as *fish, house, love, man, burn, bury, cut, eat, food,* and *small* are common words. They refer to the most basic things, actions, functions, and emotions in our lives. If someone didn't know what *man, eat, food,* or *small* meant, we would say that he didn't understand English.

These three classes are general classes, and the borders between them may blur a bit. Some words that I might consider spoken or written, you might consider common. No two persons' perceptions of the English language are likely to be identical. Nevertheless, these three categories give us a tool for talking and thinking about our words.

Besides these three classes of general usage, we should be aware of some special classes or subclasses. *Slang* words and phrases are very popular for a short time but then quickly fade from the language. In the 1920s *to put the mash on* meant to make physical advances toward a woman. In the 1950s, when I was a teenager, *necking* was considered a *cool* thing to do, but *petting* was considered *going too far.* (*Necking* meant kissing and hugging, but *petting* included touching various parts of another's body.) What words are in use now, I don't really know, and even if I did those words might be out of use by the time you read this book. You might consider how many of the following slang phrases from the past several decades are still a part of the language: *play it cool, be with it, DA* (a haircut), *my bag, square, A-OK, my thing, hanging loose, sit-in, teach-in, let it all hang out, come on board, acid,* and *hippies.* Most of these words and phrases will have brief fads and then will drop from the language, never to be used again. But some slang words like *carpetbagger, sucker* (an easily deceived person), and *dumbbell* have become permanent parts of our language.

Jargon is the special language of some particular group, trade, business, or interest group. For example, college students talk about *dorms* (instead of dormitories), *cuts* (of classes), *psych, bio,* and *T.A.S.* College students as a group understand these terms, but people who are unfamiliar with college life may not understand them at all. Baseball fans and players refer to *Texas leaguers, swinging bunts,* and *Baltimore chops,* and football fans know about *blitzes, coffin corners,* and *two-minute drills.* These technical terms are familiar to insiders but almost incomprehensible to outsiders. Every group or business is likely to have its own jargon, which facilitates communication within the group but is hard for outsiders to understand.

A *regional* usage is a word or phrase that is familiar only in one geographic area or region. Such usage is often known as *dialectal* usage. Some words or phrases may be familiar to people in a small area only, while others may be part of the dialect of a whole country. In Rhode Island, where I grew up, the words *cabinet* and *frappe* were used to refer to what most Americans would call *milkshakes.* In various parts of the United States, the words *soda, pop, soda pop,* and *tonic* are used to refer to carbonated beverages, and their uses in any given region may confuse people from outside that region. Similarly, in other parts of the world, people use words that may be unfamiliar to Americans. Canadians say *hydro* for *electric* in such phrases as *hydro lines* and *the hydro* (for the electric company), and Englishmen use *lorries* instead of *trucks* and *lifts* instead of *elevators.* Of course, since most people grow up in one country and one region of that country, they may not be aware that they are using a regional usage until they come in contact with speakers or writers from other regions.

In sum, English words fall into three main classes of usage: written (educated), spoken (colloquial), and common. Besides these main classes, slang, jargon, and regional words may be important subclasses.

How do these classes relate to rhetoric? Since your first goal as a writer is usually to make sure that your audience can understand you, you will want to use words that will be familiar to your audience. Thus, if your audience is uneducated or not highly educated, you may want to avoid using too many written words. For instance, if you were trying to explain to a group of seventh graders what the term *philosophy* means, you wouldn't give them a definition like this:

> Philosophy is a systematic inquiry into the ultimate, most universal, or most comprehensive principles underlying the origin, nature, and degree of certitude attainable about reality through human intellection rather than supernatural revelation.

Such a definition would completely confuse a group of seventh graders. Words like *universal, comprehensive, certitude, intellection,* and probably others would be simply beyond their range. Members of that audience would not understand what you were telling them because they wouldn't understand what the words meant. The vocabulary would be too sophisticated for the audience.

Similarly, if I were to tell a group of auto mechanics that a *phoneme* is "the basic unit in the phonological system and may be represented by many different allophones," I probably would not get them to understand me. The problem here is similar to the problem with seventh graders, but in this case I am guilty of using the jargon of linguistics rather than ordinary English. (Of course, the auto mechanics have a jargon of their own which linguists may not understand.) Likewise, you should be cautious about using slang and regional usages unless you are sure that your audience will understand you.

These warnings do not mean that you shouldn't use written, jargon, slang, or regional words in your writing. Rather the warnings should make you aware of your audience. In writing for your sociology, biology, and English professors you will often have to show a command of the basic jargon of each subject. Nor should you hesitate to use more sophisticated words, which your teachers will expect you to understand and use. But keep in mind that you needn't *always* use educated words. Most of what you have to say can probably be said in common words. And remember, an educated audience will always be able to understand common words, but an uneducated audience may not understand written or educated words. Thus, if you are in doubt about the education and sophistication of your audience, you'll be safer using mostly common rather than written words.

Other considerations in deciding which words you want to use are the social context and the kind of relationship you have with your audience. For instance, as a native speaker of English, you recognize that spoken English, especially slang or regional usage, is not appropriate in many writing or even speaking situations. Thus, you probably wouldn't have wedding invitations printed like this:

> Mary Wilson and Jim Reel will be getting hitched the day after Christmas. You all come to see them kick off their new life. There'll be eats and drinks in the basement of the church afterward. Be sure to give Mary's mom a call if you'll be showing up.

Although you may use all sorts of spoken words, including slang and regionalisms, in writing to close friends and relatives, you probably won't want to use them in applying for jobs, writing class assignments or reports for employers, or writing for publication. Of course, an occasional slang phrase or colloquial expression may get the attention and perhaps the respect of an audience. In the last twenty years, the use of colloquial English has become more common in written English, and many of this country's best written and most sophisticated magazines allow for more casual uses of language. Former Governor George Wallace of Alabama was very successful in using southern regionalisms like *nitty gritty* in his speeches, but he was also careful to avoid too many regionalisms in speaking before a national audience. Then he used a vocabulary that was understandable to almost all Americans.

Trite and fresh words

Words can affect an audience in other ways too. If the words are trite, they may bore the audience; if they are fresh, they may surprise and delight the audience. The following paragraph is from a paper that a student wrote in response to an article called "Rip-Off at the Supermarket."

> Supermarket people are human, too. They are in business to make money like anyone else, and few are any more dishonest than we ourselves. Supermarket rip-off is a two-way street. How many times have we been aware of someone else's mistake in our favor and kept it to ourselves?

The writer may have a good point, but he weakens his case by the words he uses. Too many of his words are trite. They have been used so many times in similar contexts that the reader is likely to lose interest because he's heard the message before. Thus, just as we head for the bathroom or the refrigerator when a television announcer says, "And now, an important message," so we let our minds drift off when we read words and phrases like *human, to make money, two-way street,* and *how many times.* Just as we know that "an important message" isn't really important, so, too, we sense that a writer who uses such hackneyed words and phrases can't have very much worth saying.

The overuse of clichés is one of the chief faults of this kind of writing. It's sad but true that from dawn to dusk students work like beavers grinding out papers that are as old as yesterday's news and so dull that they couldn't cut butter. (After reading the preceding sentence, can you understand why the brains of so many English professors turn to oatmeal?)

The opposite of trite wording is fresh wording. This means using an unusual or unexpected word, a word that will surprise the reader but that accurately conveys what the writer wants to say. Such a word need not be so unusual or complex that the reader won't understand it. Rather, a simple, ordinary word in a new context will often be more effective than a word that has to be hunted down in a thesaurus or dictionary. For example in his "Ode to a Nightingale," John Keats uses the line "Now more than ever seems it rich to die." The word *rich* is simple enough, yet it makes the line much more powerful than would the word that most writers would choose, *right*. By using the unexpected word, Keats enriches his meaning and keeps his reader interested and alert.

Very few writers will ever come near the brilliance of Keats, but they—and you—can capture and hold a reader's attention by choosing the fresh word or phrase. The following paragraph, the opening one in a regular column from a magazine, uses fresh words to captivate the reader:

> Can it be that regionalism in America is declining in the same way that patriotism has—that it is more noisily insisted upon, but by fewer and fewer people? It used to be a peculiarly American trait to brag on where you lived. The most aggressive of these geographical chauvinists would extol their climate and belittle everyone else's, would rhapsodize over the outdoor beauty to be found close at hand, and would solemnly assert that their region molded people of superior character.[1]

The writer certainly has command of a fine vocabulary, using written, educated words precisely and carefully: *aggressive, extol, rhapsodize,* among others. However, the most surprising and yet appropriate phrase amid all that edu-

---

1. Thomas Griffith, "Party of One: Show Me the Way to Go Home," *The Atlantic Monthly* (December 1974), p. 29.

cated usage is *brag on,* a colloquial and probably regional usage that seldom appears in print. Most writers would say *brag about,* but *brag on* seems so much better here because it captures the flavor of times past and of rural, unsophisticated people who were proud of their regions. It is far better than some more educated words like *vaunt* or *expatiate upon* would be.

Clearly, fresh wording can be overdone. Occasionally an inexperienced writer will try to impress his teacher with big words and fancy synonyms. Such writing quickly becomes tiresome and sometimes ludicrous. But that problem is easy enough to correct. The more common problem with most students is that their writing is full of clichés, trite words, and overused phrases. I'll say more about such faults in the section on gobbledygook. For now, I'll offer this advice: as you write, try to avoid clichés and try to find an occasional fresh word to enliven your writing. Your reader will be appreciative.

Concrete and abstract words

Choosing between abstract and concrete words may also have a considerable effect on the way your audience will react. In general, concrete, specific words that create a picture in the reader's mind can excite the audience's emotions. The rule that writers of novels and short stories advocate—*show* your reader instead of *telling* him—is good for rhetorical writing as well. If you want to arouse your audience's feelings, present it with a vivid picture. In his famous essay, "The Fight," William Hazlitt captures the harshness, the brutality of bare-knuckle boxing and the courage of the boxers:

Hickman generally stood with his back to me; but in the scuffle, he had changed positions, and Neate just then made a tremendous lunge at him, and hit him full in the face. It was doubtful whether he would fall backwards or forwards; he hung suspended for a second or two, and then fell back, throwing his hands in the air, and with his face lifted up to the sky. I never saw any thing more terrific than his aspect just before he fell. All traces of life, of natural expression, were gone from him. His face was like a human skull, a death's head, spouting blood. The eyes were filled with blood, the nose streamed with blood, the mouth gaped blood. He was not like an actual man, but like a preternatural, spectral appearance, or like one of the figures in Dante's *Inferno*. Yet he fought on after this for several rounds, still striking the first desperate blow, and Neate standing on the defensive, and using the same cautious guard to the last, as if he had still all his work to do; and it was not till the Gas-man was so stunned in the seventeenth or eighteenth round, that his senses forsook him, and he could not come to time, that the battle was declared over. Ye who despise the FANCY, do something to shew as much *pluck*, or as much self-possession as this, before you assume a superiority which you have never given a single proof of by any one action in the whole course of your lives![2]

The description of Hickman's bleeding is sufficient to capture the spirit and nature of the boxing. Hazlitt doesn't have to tell us in abstract or general terms that the fight was brutal or that Hickman was courageous. Hickman *was* courageous. The description allows us to participate in the scene and to draw our own conclusions.

Most rhetorical writing will rely on abstractions and generalizations, but they need to be supported by concrete details that create a picture and convince the reader that the intellectual claim has some emotional force behind it. Here is another selection from the student's essay on his favorite teacher. Notice how the concrete details reinforce the initial generalization and place the teacher right before our eyes:

Without that spark, she would have been like every other teacher she resembled. I often wondered if teachers were prefabricated people being popped out of colleges and into high schools. And were they ever young? At first glance, she was one of the typical antiques: a little too much powdered rouge, prim clothes of brown or gray, clunky "sensible" shoes, and old-fashioned brooches of rhinestone and pearl.

If you recognize the teacher or her type, the student has done his job.

2. William Hazlitt, "The Fight," *Selected Writings* (Baltimore: Penguin Books, 1970), p. 93.

As we have seen in this part of the chapter, the choice of words will affect the way a reader responds both emotionally and intellectually to our writing. If we choose individual words and phrases carefully, we will not only convey our content to our reader accurately, but we will try to help him understand the material and feel toward the material as we want him to.

Exercises

1. Improve the following sentences by replacing the italicized words with words that have more appropriate non-referential meanings.
   a. Helen is gorgeous—tall and *skinny* like a model.
   b. When Lucille discovered the backed-up sewage in her basement she *dove into* the clean-up immediately.
   c. In the lurid coverage of the trial, one reporter described her as "a leggy blonde with a *toothy grin*."
   d. When Harry stood before the "Mona Lisa," he gasped, "It's a *corker*. It's absolutely *pretty*."
   e. Monsieur Raphael's offers that special atmosphere of elegance and *glitter* when you want to *grab a bite*.
   f. According to the Bible, King Solomon was one of the *smartest guys* who ever lived.
   g. General Lee finally *quit fighting* at Appomattox Courthouse.

2. Arrange the following groups of words in an order from least favorable to most favorable in the context indicated. Be prepared to explain your answers.
   a. Harry says he's proud of being _____ .
      (flexible, wishy-washy, spineless)
   b. I can hardly stand Georgette; she's so _____ .
      (proud, snotty, arrogant)
   c. Having a woman like Margot for my _____ is all that I ever hoped for.
      (spouse, old lady, wife)

3. Revise the passage on page 275 in order to make the connotations more appropriate.

4. Is the level of usage in the following paragraph from a student paper appropriate for an audience of eighth graders? Be prepared to explain your answers.

> Thanks for your letter asking me to explain Marxism. I realize that it is a controversial subject and that you have probably heard both favorable and unfavorable opinions of it. Rest assured I will give you as factual and unbiased a report as I can. Please allow me to give you first a basic explantation of Marxism and then some of my own insights.

5. Can the passage in exercise 4 be improved merely by changing the level of usage of certain words, or must the content and material as well as the wording be changed?

6. Fill in the blanks in the following passage with the trite words that seem to fit: When I got the news, it knocked me down quicker than a _____ . I lay flatter than a _____ . I couldn't _____ it. I kept asking myself, "_____ ? _____ did it have to happen to Ed?" He was such a _____ . He didn't have an _____ in the _____ . He never _____ a _____ . I'm sure that he'll be _____ by _____ . Well, I guess only the _____ die _____ .

7. Rewrite the paragraph in exercise 6, but change the wording and content to avoid triteness. Try to keep the writer's reaction intact as much as possible.

Words and Persona

As we've seen before, especially in the chapter on persona, your persona will be affected by the words you use. If you generally use one kind of word to the exclusion of other kinds, your persona is likely to be influenced by this tendency.

Probably the decisions that will affect your persona most will be those you make about levels of usage. If you predominantly choose spoken words (with some common words), your persona will be far different from the persona you would get using written words. Spoken words are one of the chief devices advertisers use to create friendly personas, personas that we'll listen to and buy products from. Notice the differences in the personas created by the next two passages, which are mainly different in wording only (though most advertising has, if you remember, special sentence structuring):

How'd you like a great car? A car to wow guys and gals alike? Novella has four on the floor, a 370 V-8, and the now look. Your NM dealer's is where it's at.

Would you enjoy a powerful automobile? An automobile to impress both ladies and gentlemen? Novella has a four-speed manual shift located on the floor, a 370-cubic-inch V-8 engine, and a contemporary appearance. A National Motors dealer's is where you will find the Novella.

The two personas are quite different, even from the first sentence. A speaker who says *how'd you* is different from the speaker who says *would you,* and the speaker who says *great car* is unlikely to associate with one who says *powerful automobile.*

A writer who uses predominantly technical or predominantly dialectal words is also likely to create a distinct persona. In fiction we recognize seamen, cowboys, southerners, blacks, hillbillies, Englishmen, policemen, private eyes, ministers, Irishmen, and many other groups by regional dialects, technical terms, or other peculiarities of wording. Consider who the personas behind these openings are:

Ahoy, mate.

Howdy, pardner.

Hey, man.

These opening words go a long way toward establishing each persona.

Another feature of wording that may create a distinct persona is the use of heavily emotive words that have very strong non-referential meanings. When a writer uses words that clearly show his attitude toward the subject in strongly connotative terms, we may consider the persona as biased, overly emotional, or even as irrational—especially if we happen to disagree with the speaker. For instance, here are the first two paragraphs from a letter to a newspaper urging that the United States withdraw from the United Nations:

> October 24th should be proclaimed a *Day of Shame*.
> In October 1971—on the 26th anniversary of the founding of the United Nations—the UN voted to expel the Republic of China and to seat instead the regime of Mao Tse-tung and Chou En-lai. Thus, the greatest mass-murderers in human history were welcomed to this world body. For long minutes the packed hall rang with applause and cheers for the winners. There was rhythmic clapping. The word "gleeful" was generally used to describe those who had voted to oust the peaceful government of America's staunchest ally, Chiang Kai-shek, and seat in his place the world's premier warmongers. Symbolically and appropriately the delegate from Communist Tanzania danced the Watusi when the results of the vote were announced.[3]

Such words and phrases as *shame, mass-murderers, peaceful, staunchest,* and *warmongers* indicate the writer's attitude quite clearly, but may also weaken her persona. For unless we share the writer's views completely, we are not likely to be persuaded by her. We may judge her as a crank or fanatic, someone who is more interested in advocating her own views than in persuading others rationally.

This section has reviewed briefly the most prominent ways in which wording affects persona. Certainly, as the chapter on persona indicates and as this chapter on words reaffirms, the words you choose will be an important element of your persona.

3. Letter, Erie *Times*, October 28, 1974, sec. A, p. 4.

Gobbledygook

In this section we will deal with a misuse of words that has become very common in our society and in most other modern societies. This misuse is referred to as *jargon, doublespeak, gobbledygook,* and other terms. We will use the term gobbledygook to talk about this prevalent and perhaps dangerous misuse of words. Gobbledygook is inflated, pretentious language with which a writer seeks to impress his audience. Instead, he merely confuses the audience. Gobbledygook is sometimes called jargon, but that word is better used to describe technical words and phrases that are proper in special trades, businesses, and professions. Gobbledygook describes the kind of elaborate, pretentious, vague, meaningless, abstract, and wordy prose that we too often hear or read from politicians, businessmen, military men, scientists, social scientists, and teachers. Here's a sample of a memo from a college dean to a professor:

Professor Humble:

In reference to the interpersonal student consultative conference in which the role of an academic program advisor was performed by you, it has been brought to my attention that the advisee, Carolyn E. Hurst, has certain insufficiencies in her performance record which indicate that the request for approval of the recommendation for graduation would be inappropriate. Should it be the desire of the student to evaluate the criteria for the decision communicated to you, it would be appropriate to indicate that the most expeditious means available have been sought to help insure that the disruption of the time frame for graduation can be minimized. Should further clarification of the situation be sought, my office will be only too happy to assist with the implementation of such information.

Sincerely,

Harold H. Hughes, Dean

Let's revise the paragraph and see what it looks like in plain English:

Professor Humble:

Carolyn E. Hurst, the student who consulted you, cannot graduate because she has not passed two courses in American history. If she thinks there is an error, tell her to see me. I'll do my best to help her graduate as soon as possible.

Sincerely,

Harold H. Hughes, Dean

This letter is shorter, more specific, easier to read, and more meaningful than the other letter. It does what it should do—it conveys information.

Origins
of gobbledygook

If plain English is so much better than gobbledygook, why do so many people write and speak so much gobbledygook? Why don't they write and speak simply and directly, saying what they mean and meaning what they say?

One reason for gobbledygook is that people are often more concerned about their personas, how they look, than about what they say. People in positions of authority are often defensive about their power, so they attempt to justify it by appearing to know more than they actually do. One means to this end is using elaborate words and phrases to explain simple things. For instance, a principal of an elementary school, when asked how children in his school are punished, might tell parents that they are punished by non-corporal means, such as visual and social exclusion from the peer group. In other words, kids often have to stand in the corners facing the walls, but that sounds so simple. Do we pay a man a big salary to say simple things? Similarly, if you rush to the doctor with a growth on your chest and he tells you that it's a *sebaceous protrusion,* aren't you more impressed than if he tells you it's just a pimple? Every now and then, we all succumb to the desire to impress others by using fancy words or elaborate phrases that make us look smart.

Another reason for gobbledygook is that people often want to deceive people by using language that either hides or distorts meaning. For instance, if a school administrator is under pressure because the students in his school are doing poorly on standard achievement tests, he probably seeks to avoid blame by saying something like this:

> The ultimate validity of such testing instruments must be evaluated in relation to the total learning experience of the whole student. Without such an evaluation, the long-range goals of the educational process could be sacrificed to limited test-oriented skills.

In other words, maybe the student is learning something that can't be measured by any tests. Maybe.

Unfortunately, military leaders have used gobbledy-gook to deceive both their superiors and the public. For example, an illegal attack into enemy territory is called "a pre-emptive defensive strike," which basically means, "We attacked them in order to prevent them from attacking us." The deceit lies in the word *defensive,* which implies response to an attack. Or leaders in police states refer to their forms of government as "controlled freedom"—which means no freedom. Or consider what you sometimes write on an exam when you haven't read your assignment:

> It is not untrue to say that while certain similarities may exist between the tribal structures of the Yubetans and the Angesians, such cultural analogues are not invariably indicative of fundamental structural similarities. Such similarities may be attributed to various cultural, social, moral, and technological causes.

That's the old B.S. It's better than telling the professor that you don't know what you're talking about. Besides, on an essay test you have to say something.

In general, then, people write gobbledygook either to try to impress us or deceive us. They are not really interested in communicating the truth to us; rather, they are trying to dazzle us with the surface of their writing. The motive may be relatively harmless and the deception unintentional, or the motive may be sinister and the deception intentional. However, the result is the same: confusion for the audience. And gobbledygook has become so prevalent that at this point it's probably easier to write it than plain

English. Plain English is hard to write because it requires careful thinking and careful use of words.

Writing gobbledygook

In this section we are going to do something that I normally tell students not to do—we are going to write gobbledygook. We are going to take some simple English and turn it into gobbledygook so that we can understand how gobbledygook comes about. What follows are the rules for gobbledygook, first outlined by George Orwell in his essay, "Politics and the English Language."

First, never use a short, simple, or concrete word when you can use a long, elaborate, or abstract word. For example, use the word *employment* instead of *work, communication* instead of *letter,* and *finalize* instead of *finish.* Better still, find a whole phrase to replace a single word. Instead of having a *talk* with someone, have an *interpersonal oral communicative session.* If you want people to work more efficiently, talk about *maximizing personnel productivity outputs.* This last example also suggests that in our scientific age we should try to use scientific or mathematical sounding words like *maximization, variable, ratio, algorithm, system,* and *correlation.*

Second, find ways to get rid of precise, concrete verbs and nouns and replace them with dummy subjects, filler nouns, and weak, empty verbs. For example, don't be content with a basic sentence like, "I hope the weather clears by tomorrow." Convert the verb *hope* to a noun, replace *I* with a dummy subject, and begin with "It is my hope that . . ." Now make *weather* a modifier of a general-purpose noun and replace *clears* with similar changes and you have a wonderfully elaborate sentence like this: "It is my hope that the condition of the weather will be clear by tomorrow." And use the passive voice whenever possible. If the college catalog says, "The student will be informed of the requirements," nobody can blame me if he isn't.

Third, rely heavily on elaborate introductory phrases, overused and outdated metaphors, and popular catchphrases, the meanings of which are impossible to determine. A good way to begin any sentence is with a powerful and empty phrase like "it is a not unjustified assumption that," "with respect to the variables existing in the external situation," or "taking into consideration all the factors involved in the decision-making process." These openings and many similar ones can be tacked on at the beginning of any sentence. They will save you the embarrassment of having to commit yourself to a decision by saying "I think" or "I believe."

Also, be sure to fill your writing with worn-out and inaccurate metaphors, the finest clichés available. Such phrases as "an axe to grind," "grist to the mill," "pouring oil on troubled waters," and "biting the bullet" are especially good since very few people in our urban society know much about grinding axes or biting bullets or what grist is. The vagueness of such phrases is an advantage because you won't get pinned down to any precise meaning.

Finally, always use the faddish word, even if you don't know what it means. If you don't know, neither will your audience, but they will be impressed by your knowledge of current affairs. In the *time frame* since I've *come on board*, I've witnessed the rise and demise of *cool, charisma, participatory democracy, bra-burning, pacification,* and *open classrooms.* As I write this, I know that there's strong pressure for *accountability* in schools and that many colleges are now giving official course credits for such *educational experiences* as being in the military, holding a job, or travelling to Europe. By the time you read this, there'll be new terms to toss around.

These rules are very helpful, but the underlying rule is is to dress up any material as much as possible. Don't ever say anything simply, or people might think you are simple-minded.

The trouble
with gobbledygook

Now that we've seen why and how gobbledygook occurs, let's discuss the rhetoric of gobbledygook. First of all, if so many people use it, why shouldn't we? The answer is that gobbledygook deceives and hides meaning, whether intentionally or not. It is a form of dishonesty. There may be times when, out of good motives, we find it hard to tell the blunt truth, but these times should be rare. I can't tell you what your morals should be, nor can I give you the courage to act decently when it would be easier to act otherwise; but I can tell you that using gobbledygook is a moral issue. Great political, social, and moral wrongs have been disguised by gobbledygook.

Second, is there really anything so wrong with using unnecessarily elaborate language? Does it really do any harm? The answer, I think, is yes, for when we dress up simple ideas in elaborate language, we often think we've done something important. We hypnotize ourselves by our fancy words into believing that we're doing great stuff. If I talk about "the process of evaluating a student's academic progress profile," I almost believe I've done something more profound than averaging the student's grades.

Third, don't we all know what clichés and catch phrases mean? Aren't they so familiar that we all understand them? The answer, I'm afraid, is that clichés and catch phrases are deceptive because we all *assume* that we mean the same thing by them—an assumption that doesn't always hold up under careful scrutiny. For instance, if you've listened to disc jockeys, you've probably heard one say something like this: "Big Al here, pinch-hitting for Big Ed on tonight's record review of the top forty." What does *pinch-hitting* mean? In baseball, the source of the word, a *pinch-hitter* bats for another player because the man being batted for is not a very good hitter. Is that what Big Al means—that he's better than Big Ed? Or is he merely substituting for Big Ed? The meaning gets a bit blurred. Similarly, when someone asks what your *point of view* is, do you give them your opinion, or do you tell them the particular *perspective* from which you see things? When the distinctions become blurred, language loses some of its precision. If *point of view* means opinon, we can't always tell when it might mean *perspective.*

In general, then, gobbledygook is bad rhetoric because it fails to communicate material effectively. For a reader or listener, gobbledygook is difficult to understand. Even worse, because of its seeming profundity and its familiarity in our culture, gobbledygook often deceives the reader or listener into believing that he understands what the speaker is saying. That's worse than most bad writing, for with most bad writing, the reader knows that he's confused or that he has incomplete information.

There may be times, of course, when you may want to use gobbledygook to impress or confuse people. That's certainly a rhetorical choice that's open to you, but the danger is that such language will become a habit. Moreover, those whom you impress or deceive are probably not worth very much of your time and effort. Anybody who can be easily fooled by empty wording isn't worth fooling, and those who are worth fooling won't be fooled so easily.

Avoiding gobbledygook

The rules for avoiding gobbledygook are basically the converse of those for writing gobbledygook. Use the shortest, simplest words that will convey your meaning adequately. Try to use as few words as possible. This means using specific, definite nouns and verbs, not dummy subjects and general verbs. A good rough guideline is to avoid *it* or *there* as the subject of a sentence; instead, make the actual subject of your thought the grammatical subject of your sentence. Eliminate any needless wording, any phrases that don't contribute directly to your meaning. To test whether a phrase contributes anything, leave it out and decide whether your audience is likely to understand you. Finally, avoid clichés and catch phrases as you would a snarling police dog. If you can't express something in plain English, you probably don't really understand what you're talking about, and your audience won't understand either.

This last rule is a way of saying that *you* should control words, and not let them control you. In order to write clearly, you must first think clearly. You must be sure that the words are behaving as you wish them to. If they're not, they will, like spoiled children, bring grief upon their parents.

Things to Do

1. Using a magazine as your source, analyze the headlines in some of the ads and articles. What kinds of words are used? Are they primarily referential or non-referential, concrete or abstract, spoken or written? You might compare the headlines in a general circulation magazine like *People* with those in a limited circulation magazine like *The Atlantic Monthly* or a specialized magazine like *Cosmopolitan, Playboy, Ebony, Sport,* or *Modern Romance.*

2. Take a short passage of your own writing and count the number of words and the number of syllables you use. Now revise the passage, using more educated and abstract words. Count again. Finally, simplify the original passage, using more common and concrete words. Count again. Does this count tell you much about your prose style? (The number of syllables divided by the number of words should give you some useful information.)

3. Examine some of your textbooks (especially those in the social sciences) for gobbledygook. Are you able to find some? If so, "translate" some of it into plain English. How does the change affect the meaning?

4. Start a collection of gobbledygook. Keep a collection of words, phrases, and sentences that are especially prominent uses of elaborate or meaningless phrases designed to impress, confuse, or deceive readers.

Writing Assignments

1. Using largely referential diction, narrate an event or simple incident factually, as it might appear in a news story in a newspaper. Then, using heavily connotative diction, rewrite the narrative so that it will arouse the emotions of your audience. (Indicate who your audience is and how you expect it to react.)

2. Explain some technical or abstruse subject with which you are familiar to an audience of junior high school students. Choose a subject that you can treat in one or two paragraphs. Then, changing your choice of words but keeping the same basic content, revise the passage so that your persona appears pompous, over-educated, and superior to the audience.

3. Take some fairly obvious comment or generalization about human nature and by following the rules for gobbledygook, expand it to a whole paragraph. For example, you might use a statement like "Women like men."

4. Write a letter to a newspaper on a subject that requires scientific, technical, or other specialized knowledge, but be sure to explain your views so that most newspaper readers will be able to understand you (which means using simple words). Good subjects are the environment, the educational system, or local government policies.

5. Write an autobiographical essay in which you make several generalizations about yourself, and then support those generalizations with plenty of details, using concrete wording. Be sure to have a good balance of abstract and concrete, educated and common words. You should use connotations so that your audience will sympathize with you.

6. As an exercise in wording (and sentence structure), write a letter to a magazine in response to an article or to a newspaper about some current issue or editorial, but limit your response to a maximum of fifty words. To do this, you will have to choose words that will capture your audience's attention. You will also have to be concise and precise.

INDEX